Life
In-Between

Julia F Richardson

Copyright © 2021 Julia Fiona Richardson

ISBN: 9798583320578

DEDICATION

For my four beautiful boys: Toby, Jon, Ben and Joe,
I love you to the moon and back, always and for ever.
And for Teresa. Where you are is home.

CONTENTS

THANK YOU

Thank you to my mothers and fathers, known and unknown. Mary and David, Margaret and Stephen. My three sisters Kate, Jane and Sarah, we didn't grow up together but we knew each other when we met. My family of birth and of nurture and all the other families I have become part of. You all have given me gifts I treasure.

Monday writers, Janet, Ali, Francesca, Emily for support and encouragement and being my readers.

Diane Shifflett Editor extraordinaire, friend and fellow traveller.

Anne Heffron, author and the best writing Coach, Mentor and Friend. Pam Cordano, Anne and Sunday 'Adoptee Church' of Flourish 2020-2021. Adult Adoptees of Twitter and Instagram and the world, I love you, I see you and you are enough.

My friends online and face to face who get me and see me and cheer me on, recovery people everywhere you rock.

'You've got to search for the hero inside yourself,

Search for the secrets you hide.

Search for the hero inside yourself

Until you find the key to your life.'

— Pickering and Heard 1995 M People, Bizarre Fruit

PROLOGUE

Julia Anne — birth name
Fiona Margaret — adopted name
Julia Fiona — reclaimed name

Mary, Mum Mary — birth mother
David — birth father

Margaret, Mum, Mummy —- adoptive Mum
Stephen, Dad, — adoptive Dad

Teresa —my wife

Toby — oldest son
Jon — second son
Ben— third son
Joe — fourth son

Jane — oldest maternal half sister
Kate — second maternal half sister
Sarah — third maternal half sister

Gather round and let me tell you a story. The fire is burning brightly and we can take some time together. I recommend a giant mug of tea and a comfy seat. Bring a blanket and your best friend or a teddy bear. Snuggle up.

This is my story of hope and faith and love. It is also a story of trauma and loss and grief and abandonment. It is a true fairy tale with the grim darkness running through it alongside the brightness.

This is not a children's story, although millions of children are involved. So many people are affected. In the end we only have our stories to connect us. Stories are magic. We can look at the stars in the flames and drink our tea and we can listen to each other. When I hear the truth my body resonates. True stories are a gift for all of us. This is a true story. It is my story.

When I start writing about adoption I'm opening the airing cupboard and standing back. It is all falling out onto the floor and I am trying to sort it out. But there will be mix ups and confusion along with the organising. There is the phrase, 'don't wash your dirty linen in public'. My mum and my birth Mum would have both felt this was dirty linen. But this is my airing cupboard and I want the fresh air to blow right through and the sweet scent of lavender reminding me that we are all doing our best.

The way I have written the book illustrates the way in which my brain has processed and lived with trauma. Writing this book was something I just had to do. Trauma triggers flashbacks and so the stories here can flip backwards and forwards in time. Sometimes I am the adult looking back, sometimes I am the child experiencing and reacting. I have left this alone because it is a true reflection of adoptee reality.

I have added photographs to the book because they represent so much of the joy of connection. This was so important to me. Seeing who I looked like was probably the most important part of my longing to connect with my birth family. Having no genetic mirror until I had my own children was an enormous loss. The power of connection through our eye, brain, body is instinctive. As babies we search for our mothers with mouths, hands and eyes. The people in the pictures are all important to me. Sometimes the camera lies and sometimes it tells a story we can only see in hindsight. If you are here, thank you for being part of the gallery.

CHAPTER 1 BIRTHING AND BREATHING

The Church of England Children's Society 21 April 1958

Julia is quite a nice little baby. She has brown hair and blue eyes which will probably change. Mrs L (foster mother) said she is a very good baby

The baby is of placid disposition, has normal intelligence for age, has good health. She has dark hair and dark eyes — considered suitable for a professional home, mother is well educated.

B Toye Moral Welfare Officer.

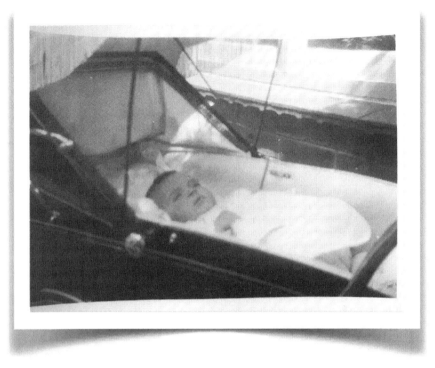

Baby Julia Anne 1958

Dear Baby Julia

I see you in your pram there. You are going to be safe. Your life will be beautiful. It all works out. Hold on.

Love, Big Julia (Me) xxxx

My Mother and Other Mums

We had a family secret but secrets always come out. To most people who know me, my adoptive mum, Margaret, is my only Mum.

But that is not the whole story. I had another mother first. She pushed me out of her body one afternoon in March in 1958 in a nursing home in Kent. She had no-one with her except the medical staff. I don't know much about my early days. My first mother and I had just two weeks of living in the same place but we were mostly in separate rooms. She didn't hold me often or talk to me or sing to me. She didn't give me my first feed. My birth mother told me later when we reunited that she held back from becoming attached to me because she always knew that she wasn't going to keep me. We had no opportunity to bond. I have seen the damage it did to both of us. My body remembers what my mind has forgotten. The trauma of our separation marked us both.

Through my life my birth mum was a longed-for stranger. For many years I told anyone who asked that I had had a happy childhood and that I was close to my parents. That was the truth as I understood it then. I laughed and joked and performed and I only saw what I was expected to see. But underneath I had a feeling of not quite belonging, of something that just didn't quite fit and of not having the connection that I saw in other people's families.

My birth mother handed me over to a 'moral welfare officer', the precursor to social workers, in March 1958. I was taken to a foster-home at two weeks old and I stayed there until three months later I was sent 'on trial for adoption' to the people who would become my parents a year later. The language is significant. 'On trial' meant they could change their minds. I could be sent back. It takes a long time for the adoption process to go through.

I have had other mothers too. The foster mother who took me in and was fond of me, who held me and fed me and cared for me for three months. I didn't look for her when I was pursuing the search for my birth family. I knew where she was and didn't contact her. I think I was too afraid of rejection and only had enough energy for one reunion. I have had friends too who taught me to be a mother and friends who have mothered me.

Whilst I was at that foster-home I was visited and inspected by another family who decided not to adopt me. What would have happened if I had gone to them instead?

9/5/58
Re: Julia Anne Newman

Dear Mrs Biggs,
As this baby did not appeal to the Taylors, we are now writing to send her particulars to Dr. and Mrs. Zachariah of Hertfordshire. We enclose their Notes for you to see, also the usual forms in case you have not those sent the other day to hand.

We are also enclosing the Pink Medical in this case for you to give to the Foster Mother.

Yours Sincerely
A.J.
For Secretary

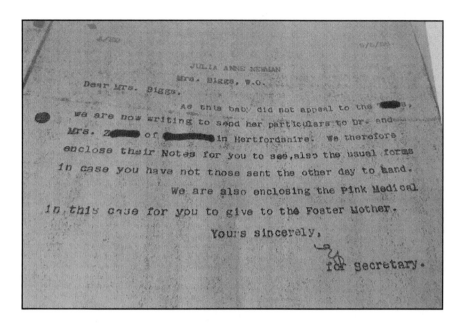

The adoption lucky-dip

Reading my adoption file notes I feel like I am watching a film where every new image could be a different life. My life was chance. I was the next baby on the conveyor belt for the lucky winners.

CONFIDENTIAL.   13th May 1958
Dear Miss Toye (Moral Welfare Officer)
Re: Julia Anne Newman

Unfortunately the Zachariah's are unable to accept a baby just at present as they are moving. We are therefore sending Julia's particulars to some other adopters - Mr. and Mrs. Richardson who live in Yorkshire

I was given to adoptive parents, a Mum and Dad, who were kind and loving. But luck didn't have anything to do with it. The decisions were made by a woman who couldn't bring up a baby on her own and a bureaucratic system. My mother wasn't a teenager. She wasn't forced to give me up by her parents. I have never found it easy to accept that she had no choice. I second guess myself all the time when I write down how I really feel. I say it and then I panic. *Is that really true? Is it unfair? Will it upset people? What would my mothers say? What about my sisters, my children?* There are multiple versions of what happened back then. This is mine.

Mostly my story is about feelings, beliefs and understanding. The understanding I have of myself and other people, my relationship with both my Mothers. And my journey of the search to connect and unite with my birth family.

I am a retired social worker and counsellor in child and family services and young people's mental health. I was also a teacher. My understanding of adoption is from my own experience. I am not an innocent bystander. I have struggled with the concept of adoption even as I have been a part of the system that perpetuates it. I am biased.

Author Anne Lamott writes: 'Remember that you own what happened to you'. I have to weave this story through the lives of others. My birth parents, my adoptive parents and family, my relationships and marriages and children and friendships. The people who appear here are important to me. I don't want to upset them. I am offering you a pair of cutting scissors as you read. You can take them and cut out the parts you don't like. For me they will stay in, even the parts that make me squirm. I can't make this a tidy story. It just won't be told that way. Sometimes this tale will skip from time to time, from one mother to another. My brain needed to write this down in chunks that made sense to me. Sometimes that may seem distracted or unfocused. Sometimes it may seem contradictory. Adoptees are often labelled with conditions like Attention Deficit Disorder (ADD). I think a more accurate response is to recognise the trauma that comes from separation at birth for adoptees and for birth mothers. We are two sides of a coin that were melded together then broken apart.

I often wish that I could cry like I want to. I think I used up all my tears. Maybe they will come back to me one day when I am filled up again. Feelings sit inside my body aching to be released. Other people cry for me. I am touched by everything, I feel everything. I feel so much of what everyone around me feels that sometimes it feels like my skin is just a permeable membrane for emotion to flood through and swamp me.

Some days writing this has felt like the bravest thing I have ever done and I know I have done some brave things. I am a trier. It used to be one of the few things I could say about myself when every day felt like a battle I had to get through. In the midst of depression and addiction and life just feeling too hard I knew that if there was one thing about me that was true it was that I kept going. I kept trying. I have always been trying to find my way back to somewhere called home. I didn't know where it was or what it looked like. I didn't know who would be there until I had kids and then I knew I had found a place I could be.

I didn't know who I was — and then I was a mother. If I had five minutes left to live I would want to see my boys' faces just one more time. The silver thread of the real me ran though my life and I played a game of hide and seek to find her. I want to tell you what I had to do to get home. Sometimes it feels like I have too much to say, but not enough words to say it. Then I realise that in a way it is because there aren't the words. Some of what I want you to know comes from a pre-verbal place. When there is too much to say I start to feel terror and get overwhelmed. That is part of my story too. It is my search, and a pilgrimage to find moments of truth and connection. I am going home. I am an observer.

Lives don't fit into boxes until they are over. All my parents are dead now. I have only just found out that my birth father is dead. It wasn't unexpected but it was still a shock. I never met him and that makes me sad. But the fact that they are all gone makes a difference. I feel free to say what I want. I am conscious of time passing and my own life span. I wouldn't have written this book the way it is if they were still alive. I would be too scared of hurting them even though everything I say is true. My own children are grown and independent and I have time and space that I have never had before. It is psychic space — not just the physical sense of being in the house with just me and my wife.

Two days after I was born my maternal Grandmother came to visit. I learnt later that my mother's younger sister, Margaret, came too. From the stories I have been told by my birth family, I have the impression that my grandmother was a force of nature, not someone to be argued with. When I met her, my birth mother Mary said that her mother, Hilda, swept into the room at the nursing home and demanded "'Where is she, where is the baby? Have you seen her, why isn't she here with you?''

Mary told me, 'Mum sent me to get you. I hadn't seen you since you were born but Mum said I had to. She told me off for leaving you in the nursery. She held you and rocked you and then she said, "What are you going to call her?"

Mary said "I don't know, I haven't thought about it".

I heard that my grandmother looked at me, she drank me in with her eyes and I hope she was imprinting me on her memory, "You must call her Julia. She looks like a Julia. Julia Anne".

And so I was named. Julia Anne. I am grateful for the 'e' on the Anne. It makes me feel like I was special enough to get that extra letter. Not just common or garden Ann but Anne with an E. My grandmother gave me my name. And it fitted me. I don't know why she chose that name. I asked my birth mother Mary why. I hoped there would be a family connection but there wasn't. Much later my birth mother said, "I'm glad you aren't still called Julia because that was the name of the woman my husband cheated on me with". It felt like a slap in the face. But Julia is my name.

When I was relinquished by my birth mother it wasn't my choice and I didn't have a say. On 25 March 1958 Mary signed the legal papers handing her first baby girl over to an adoption agency. It was the same day she registered my birth. I became Julia Anne Newman, but not for very long. I never liked 'goodbyes'. I stayed with the foster carers for three months. All that time I was called Julia.

Language

Words are not our only language. Our bodies tell stories too. My body speaks to me when words fail. My body says she is hungry or cold or in pain and needs looking after. Sometimes my body trips me up and I fall down, I have accidents and bumps and find it hard to keep my feet under me. When I am sad or tired or traumatised my body reacts. Sometimes I don't know what words to use. I don't have the vocabulary for the embodied memories. Words have always mattered to me. I have always told stories. I have written myself into other worlds for as long as I can remember. I told myself stories of other families, of searching and finding my birth family, of having children and rescuing them from some terrible danger. I wrote and imagined myself into being the hero of my own life even whilst I wondered who I was. I had two mothers and two fathers but I didn't meet them all. I'm sure I have relatives I have never met and who don't know I exist. I have a 'family of origin' and an 'adopted family'. I have four, now adult, children who came out of my body.

Named and Reclaimed.

My first given name was changed. That act, through adoption, took away any legal connection to my past and my identity. I lost my ancestors and my parents, grandparents, cousins and aunties and uncles. My first name and the names of my ancestors, including my mother and my father, were sealed in a record that was intended to be forever hidden. No-one knew then that the laws would change giving adoptees back their right to know about themselves. In infancy my baby brain heard my first name for a few months and I also heard the voice of my birth mother throughout those months I grew inside her womb until I was taken away and transplanted. Like a seedling I was uprooted and re-planted in new soil. My roots had been cut off and making new ones was hard.

Here is your new home our baby girl. Your new name, for you are ours now and will always be. Fiona Margaret. Fiona is Scottish and means 'the fair or white one' which I am not. I never liked it. The Margaret was for my new Mum and her Mum, my Nana. But my roots carried genetic material, neural pathways deep in my brain, those forgotten remembered memories of familiar unfamiliar voices. The visceral instinctive knowledge of a name that resonates through the years. Much later I changed my name back to my first precious name as I rediscovered my identity. 'Home is where the heart is' they say. My home is where I make it. As Shakin' Stevens says 'It's where I hang my hat', or where I am called by my name.

Poem for my Grandmother
Named as you held me
The day we met
Two days old and
Waiting for
The scent, the touch
The feel of
familiarity.
Not quite known
But nine months
Of swimming
Inside her womb.
This daughter
This granddaughter

'Julia Anne'
You said
'That is her name
Because
She looks like a Julia

Naming and Reclaiming
You call me by my name
Two months of voices
This is who I am
But then new strange hands
I am arching and crying
At the unfamiliar sounds
Different scent and touch
Milk from a bottle
More please.
Who am I now?
A new name is chosen
For me

'It means a pearl' you said
Chosen and precious

But I can't forget who I am
Something inside whispers
To remind me
I recognise my name
It resonates and trembles
In recognition
As I reclaim myself
Julia Anne
Fiona Margaret
Julia Fiona

CHAPTER 2 SECRETS

I didn't always know that the story I grew up with was a secret. My origins were hidden and my acquisition was disguised. My adoptive parents brought me up with the knowledge that I was adopted. They told me when I was so little that I don't remember them telling me the first time. The story was repeated to me sometimes and it went like this:

When you were a baby we came to see you in a room full of other babies. The sunlight was coming in through the window and we looked at all the babies but when we came to you, you just smiled at us with this big smile and we knew you had chosen us. So we took you home with us and you were our baby.

Every word of that is a lie.

Apart from this story that was given to me as if it were a fact, talking about my adoption was taboo. At home. I don't remember asking many questions although I know I had them inside. I never knew who knew and who didn't. And that made me feel uncomfortable. I wasn't supposed to ask questions and I wasn't supposed to tell. I knew that because the slightest hint would make Mummy tense up with anxiety. Mummy wouldn't look at me. She would start talking about something else or leave the room. I knew that something about where I came from upset her but I didn't know why. My 'other mother' was never mentioned. I grew up with the suspicion that something was bad underneath the silence and maybe the bad thing was me. Sometimes I thought Mummy was angry with me for asking and sometimes I suspected that she was scared. As a child I knew that the most important thing in my world was for Mummy to be happy. If Mummy wasn't all right then I wasn't either. If she was angry or upset I might have to go away. I tried to keep everyone around me as happy as possible all the time. It was very tiring. I still try too hard to do that and it is still exhausting.

When there is tension in the air, the fear of it goes straight to my stomach. I don't always know what the emotion is that I'm feeling but I've always been hyper-vigilant to the feelings of everyone around me. Being that child made me empathic and compassionate and gave me a career as a social worker, a teacher and a therapist but it came at a cost. I learnt to interpret every facial expression, halting breath or silence. To recognise instantly what my Mummy's feelings were and to constantly make adjustments to compensate. Having my Mummy's approval was the difference between life and death. For an infant the attachment to a mother (primary caregiver) is essential. John Bowlby, the British Psychologist, discovered that and first taught the world about attachment from the 1960's onwards. Babies die without that. Death for me had already happened, maybe more than once, so now it became the fear of being cut off and disconnected from my source of comfort and safety. Instinctively I knew that loss could happen because it already had.

There was shame in our house. It ran deep through our interactions like a river. Mummy couldn't have babies herself. She told me that her ovaries were 'shrivelled up like walnuts'. A doctor had once said that to her that and she recounted it with an air of shame. I don't know if her anxiety and insecurity came from her feelings about infertility. I know she dearly loved children. I was a baby that came ready made. Mummy wanted us to be a family just like any other butI don't think she really believed that either.

30 May 1958, I am ten weeks old and I am leaving the foster home where I have been for 10 weeks. I have a photograph with the date written on the back in my Daddy's handwriting. It says, '**3pm 30 May 1958 Victoria Park, London**'. It looks like Mr. and Mrs. Richardson took me for a picnic before they took me home with them to Sheffield. They would become my new Mummy and Daddy.

There is a note in my adoption file that tells me what happened;

```
30.5.58 Julia Anne Newman
Application Number 97047
Went on trial for adoption to
Mr. and Mrs. Richardson,
54 Trap Lane, Bents Green, Sheffield.
```

Dear baby Julia

Your first picnic! I have only just discovered that this picture is the first I have of you. I see your sweet hands and how carefully you have been dressed and wrapped in that blanket. Your new Mummy and Daddy are so proud and they will love you so much. These first few days and weeks you will feel strange, as if you are in the wrong place. But know you are loved.

Love, me. Xxxx

I don't know if Margaret and Stephen Richardson drove down to Kent to collect me from the foster home or if they came on the train

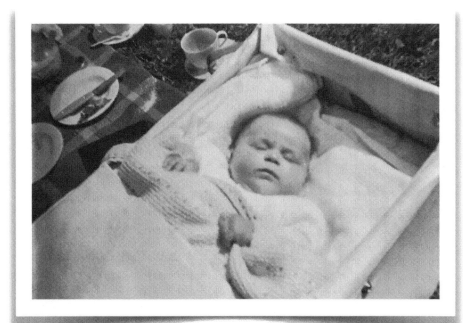

Julia Anne 30 May 1958

from Sheffield to London. That first photograph of me was taken in Victoria Park. Looking at that photo I wish my parents had trusted the true story of my adoption. They collected me from people who had cared for me for ten weeks.. I would love to have a picture of my foster carers from that time. I would tell my little self about the day I met my new parents-to-be and that they took me on a special picnic to Victoria Park before they took me home. I would say how baby Julia slept in her carry cot with her chubby starfish fingers curled round the blanket that Mummy or Nana had knitted. How Mummy and Daddy sat on the picnic blanket in spring sunshine and drank tea from a flask and ate their sandwiches and all the time how they couldn't believe that they were taking this beautiful baby home.

There are many more photos of Mummy and Daddy and me. I am always dressed beautifully. Their faces beam with pride and joy. It is obvious to anyone that I was wanted and loved. But the weeks of my life from birth to ten weeks old are unrecorded. When our boys were born their Dad's and I had taken hundreds of pictures by the time they were thirteen weeks old. I remember watching them change from day to day. In a photo of me at thirteen weeks I am smiling at the person taking the picture. My gaze is focused and I have round chubby cheeks and hands with dimples. When I was born I weighed 6 lbs 13 ozs so I was an average size baby. I weighed less than any of my children did. At three months I am a bonny baby, round faced and wide eyed. I have been bottle fed and I have gained weight. It didn't take long for food to become the primary source of comfort and soothing that would last most of a lifetime. Food took the place of attachment because it was there.

The pictures tell one story and there is another underneath. There is always a story under the story. Mum told me often that I cried and cried and couldn't be comforted. It became part of our family history. A story that told of my greed and discontent. I wonder why I was told this part of the story but not the other part, the part that would tell me about where I came from. My Mummy didn't know why I kept crying. She told me that she felt helpless. Especially in the evening when I wouldn't settle.

I was fed a bottle of 'Cow and Gate' baby milk, warm and sweet. I sucked it down and there was temporarily a blissful silence. My little body relaxed, my rosy cheeks sometimes wet with leftover salty tears and dribbles of milk. Mummy held me and felt relief for a few blessed moments. Then my back would arch and I started to cry again. I couldn't be comforted. Mummy said that she felt like she must be doing something wrong. I could have told her she wasn't doing anything wrong. But she was wrong. She was the wrong mother.

I still find it hard to settle. But full tummy always put me to sleep. I just needed more. Food soothed me. Eventually mummy asked for help. The family doctor came to visit.

What is wrong with her? What am I doing wrong? She cries and cries and won't be satisfied? Is she still hungry?'

I am checked and weighed and inspected. I am healthy. I must be hungry.

"Just give her another bottle," he says. So that is what happens. Full to bursting I settle. I learn that food is comfort, a place of safety, that food will send me to sleep. I always needed more. Warm milk filled my tummy until it was round and tight as a drum. Until it leaked from the corners of my rose-bud mouth and my fat cheeks were pink and wet. Until my eyes closed, the dark lashes I inherited curving in half-moons on my soft sweet-smelling baby skin. Eat and sleep, eat and sleep. Another pattern begins. Warm milk and being full are still a comfort. Cappuccinos or lattes call to me to soothe me.

Adopted babies can cry a lot. It must be hard to settle easily because we know that we are in the wrong place, with the wrong smells around us. The tastes are different, the sounds and the voices. Everything is strange and unfamiliar. We feel wrong. The curve of a shoulder or the soft lap are not the right shape, the hands that touch us are not the ones we remember from our first moments. We wriggle and fidget. Sleep and relaxation can be a struggle throughout our lives. It affects our guts so we have stomach problems. Anxiety is always present. Depression is a thread that runs through our stories and conversations. We have evidence that trauma in early childhood is passed on genetically. Gabor Mate, the Canadian doctor, author and speaker on addiction and trauma, says that addiction is rooted in childhood trauma. The past has a long reach.

I learnt about trauma in therapeutic circles. There is the excavate and deep dive of psychotherapy and the free form flow of person-centred counselling or the in-the-moment solution-focused be-here-now-ness of mindfulness practitioners. All are valuable. To understand myself I needed to know about where I came from, not just information. I needed to understand the relationships, to understand myself, and that took years. There are so many hidden parts. Places that were too difficult for my birth mum to go to, times that she said she had forgotten. And my birth father's side is mostly a mystery to me. I had some bits of information but nothing that gave me a picture of the man he was or the family he came from. There is a part of me that has always felt out of place. I notice it more now, which is funny as I was always too caught up in all the other relationships before to feel I could cope with adding more. Now I feel sad for the lost opportunities.

CHAPTER 3 WATCH WITH MOTHER

When I was three years old we lived in London. Mummy was a stay-at-home Mum, and Daddy went to work in an office. Mummy and I went to the park together and she would push me on the swings. I liked the roundabout best but really I needed someone who could push it round for me.

I can run alongside and then jump on but Mummy doesn't like me to do that because I might fall and she can't run and push me because of her back.

We would walk to the corner shop to buy groceries. Mummy made me boiled eggs with toast 'soldiers' to dip in. I loved dipping the soldiers into the yolk when it is runny but I didn't really like eating eggs. I would have liked to just eat the toast and butter and dippy yellow part. I had to eat up my dinner if I want to have a pudding.

We would read Rupert Bear stories and watch 'Watch with Mother' from the BBC on our black and white television at lunchtimes. I liked 'The Wooden-Tops' best. I had a hamster called Hammy named after the hamster in the programme 'Tales from the Riverbank'. Hammy often used to escape and run up the curtains and under the sofa. I would pedal up and down the garden on my red tricycle. Our small two up and two down terraced cottage had a gate from the pocket-handkerchief garden that led onto the street behind the house. One day Mummy wasn't watching me so I stealthily opened the gate and pedalled for dear life up the street. I was flying to freedom until I came back round the corner and saw Mummy standing there with her arms folded and worried expression. I knew I would have to say, 'sorry' and promise not to do it again. I lie easily. *Maybe she won't find out.*

I played with Linda who lived next door. Our houses were joined together and I could knock on my bedroom wall and she would knock back. We had a wooden fence between our gardens with knots in the wood and we pushed one out so that we had a hole we could peep through and post messages. We made dolly and teddy tea parties on summer days and gave the dolls baths in an old baby bath on the paving flags. This was one of my favourite games. I loved my doll family and making up stories in my head.

Linda's brother, Alan was two years older and sometimes came to play when his friends were busy. Alan wore short trousers and checked shirts and liked boys things like football and The Beano and soldiers and cars. He didn't really want to play with girls but sometimes he would join in our make-believe games. I was shy though, and I preferred it when it was just me and Linda.

Dear little Julia

I see you with your friend Linda. You loved her and you cried when you had to leave her. You made a friend and you will make many more. You are a good friend. I see your knee with scratches on it and I want to kiss it better. You look like your cousin Mary and your sisters here. Love, big me xxx

Sometimes we go into Linda's house and sit on the sofa and can watch the TV when the children's programmes come on at four o'clock. Her mummy makes us sandwiches with meat paste or sandwich spread. The sandwich spread tastes of vinegar and makes me feel sick but I eat it anyway. We are brought up to be polite girls and to eat everything on our plates.

My Mummy reads me stories and I like colouring and drawing pictures with crayons. She plays the piano sometimes and I would like to play but I am not allowed to bang on the keys and Mummy says that I am heavy handed. I look at my hands and they aren't very big so I don't know how they can be so heavy. Mummy says she has a 'light touch' but I am clumsy. I like feeling the piano keys and hearing the sounds they make.

Julia (Fiona) and Big Suzy

Dearest Julia

The joy of Big Suzy! You look so happy. I love your tartan skirt and that cute fair-isle jumper. You have always loved a good cosy jumper.

And look at the bunny lamp. Your Daddy used to love to tell you stories and sing to you. 'The sunny side of the street' and 'Speed Bonny Boat"

Love, big me xxx

Julia (Fiona) as an angel in the Sunday school Nativity with Big Suzy and Baby-Baa Lamb

Dear Julia

You were an angel. I know this picture was posed and you were uncomfortable, but look how proud you were of Big Suzy and Baby-Baa Lamb. Your angel costume had silver ribbon sewed on by Mummy. She wanted to make it special for you. I've got you.

Love, big me xxxx

Big Suzy was my favourite doll. She was almost as big as me when Father Christmas brought her on the Christmas morning of 1961. That December we went to Yorkshire for the holidays which was where my Granny and Grandpa, Daddy's parents, lived. I loved going to stay with them in their big old stone house. There was a Grandfather clock that played a tune when it struck the hour and I loved lying on the sofa underneath it and waiting for the chimes. Granny and Grandpa had a tortoise called Jimmy who lived in their garden In the summer he would come to Granny when she called and I fed him dandelion leaves. He would be so excited he had quite a turn of speed for an old man. But that winter Jimmy was tucked up safe in a box with lots of straw and newspaper because he was hibernating. There was a big snowfall that year and our travel plans are changed when the trains were cancelled. On our eventual journey home from the train station Mummy ties Suzy to me with a big scarf so that I can carry her in front of me. My little legs found it hard to keep up but I held Mummy's hand on one side and Daddy's on the other and Big Suzy is attached to me in the middle. The snow was so deep and it came up over my red Wellington boots as we trudged back together. I remember the journey as an adventure.

We usually went to church on Sundays and I would go to Sunday school whilst Mummy and Daddy attended the service in the church. I liked singing 'Jesus Loves Me' and 'Jesus Bids Us Shine' and colouring pictures of Bible stories. The Christmas after we went to Yorkshire there was a Sunday school Nativity play. Mummy offered Big Suzy as the baby Jesus and I dream of being Mary, but I was picked to be an angel instead Mummy made me an angel outfit with a halo out of wire and tinsel. I had a toy lamb called 'Baby Baa Lamb' and he is in the play too.

My life was quite settled and happy. Daddy would be tired when he came home but he would tell me stories at bedtime. He had created a saga about a bunny family who live in a house called 'Sunny Side'. Mummy and Daddy made me a bunny lamp which sits by my bed at night.

My parents loved making things together. I still have the lamp because I found it when we cleared out my parents house. It is wrapped up on top of a bookcase waiting for another child to light it up again.

Daddy would sit with me until I fell asleep if I was scared. I was scared of the dark all of my childhood and had to have a light on the landing or I couldn't go to sleep. In the mornings especially at weekends I would creep along the tiny landing to my parents bedroom so that I could surprise them. My Daddy always pretended to be amazed that I had appeared but Mummy would always call out, 'Hello, Fiona' when she heard me coming. Once in the bedroom I would snuggle into bed between them. Mummy always had cold feet and Daddy would and laugh when she puts her freezing toes on his hot ones. It made me giggle. When I was in their bed I felt warm and safe. I was much more comfortable when my Daddy was around. Mummy was tense and found it hard to relax. I felt her feelings and they got mixed up with my own so that I never knew whose were whose. Daddy was just himself. When I was with him it was easier to be me.

My Daddy could play rough and tumble games with me, he would give me 'piggybacks' and pretend to be an elephant swinging his trunk while I rode on his back around the living room. He was very ticklish all his life and sometimes Mummy and I would tickle his feet and he would laugh and say, 'Pax, Pax' which meant ' Stop, stop'. I liked making him laugh, it made me feel good inside. Mummy couldn't get down on the ground with me because she had a bad back so I loved those special times playing with Daddy.

Tearing apart

I knew that Mummy had hurt her back. She fell and broke something and needed an operation to fix it. It meant that she would have to go into hospital and it would take a long time for her to be better. My parents decided that it would be best if I were to stay with some family friends up in Yorkshire where we used to live.. Daddy would be working and visiting Mummy but I wouldn't be allowed to. In1962 the hospital wouldn't let children visit on the orthopaedic ward. One day, several weeks after Mummy had had the operation, Daddy took me to the hospital to visit. Because I couldn't go inside he took me into the hospital garden and lifted me up onto his shoulders so I could look through a window. Mummy was in a bed on the other side of the glass and I was told to wave. Daddy lifted me high and I could see several beds in a big room. The beds had white sheets and a green cotton blanket. Each bed had someone either lying flat on their back or sitting up propped on big white pillows. I couldn't tell which one was my Mummy but I wave. Dady keeps saying, 'Can you see her? Can you see Mummy? Wave to Mummy" I say, 'Yes I can see her' even though I don't know which one she is. Afterwards Mummy tells me how she cried because she couldn't be with me. I don't remember any more.

My memory of that time is patchy. I know that Daddy drove me in his car from London to Yorkshire. 'Aunty' Alice's 'house was light and airy and it smelt of rose talcum powder and shortbread biscuits. Dad and Aunty Alice kiss each other on the cheek and they chat as she showed us round the house and especially where my bedroom and the bathroom. I had been to this house before when we lived four houses down the street but I was little so I don't remember. Alice is a sweet and pretty lady with curly light brown hair. She had a quiet voice and a warm gentle manner. She would wear pastel twin-sets and soft tweed skirts which suited her relaxed femininity. Alice was small and neat and comfortable and seemed to just know how to be a mother.

I don't remember my Daddy leaving that first time. I didn't make a fuss. I just walked upstairs. I didn't cry or shout. My head felt strange as if it was floating somewhere above me like a balloon. The next few minutes are etched deep into my memory flash lit by years of unnecessary shame. I walked into one of the bedrooms, but not mine, and I pulled my pants down. I remember squatting and poo-ing on the carpet. It was a big poo. I stood up pulled up my underwear and waited. I don't know what I was feeling. It was too much for me to know. I heard Alice call out, "Fiona, are you there dear, do you need the lavatory? Are you all right?" She came looking for me and I heard her light footsteps as she ran up the stairs and crossed the landing. I heard a door open and shut and then her footsteps coming towards me. "Oh, here you are, I thought I'd lost you," she smiled I remember the look of surprise that appeared on her face. I just stood and waited

She said, "Oh I'm so sorry lovey, did you forget where the bathroom was? Don't worry — we can clean you up." And she did.

Aunty Alice and 'Uncle' John weren't really my aunty and uncle because both Mummy and Daddy were only children. Growing up I had a lot of 'aunties' and 'uncles' who were friends of my parents. I found it confusing. It was hard to know who I was related to. When I had my own children and they would visit their Nana and Grandpa they would came home and say we saw 'Uncle Bob' or 'Uncle Jim' and I would go crazy inside. I didn't know who these people were. I told my parents that they weren't allowed to tell my children that strangers to me were their 'aunties' or 'uncles'. Mum and Dad were quite offended and didn't understand why. I struggled to explain because the rage I felt inside was so great and the lies were crowding in on my own kids now. I didn't understand my own rage. It seemed out of proportion to the situation. But the trigger was the lie. My ancestry was wiped clean by adoption but I was offered fake relatives to make it better.

Alice and John had two teenage children who I looked up to as some sort of alien beings who came and went, friendly and kind to me but busy with their own lives and friends and school. I spent my days with Alice and their beautiful Collie dog called Rex. He was just like Lassie. This was my first experience of being with a dog every day and I loved him. He had a long soft coat and I would sit and stroke him and feel the silkiness slip through my fingers. Alice and I would take him for a walk in the woods behind their house every day. It became a routine that I enjoyed. There was a big old oak tree in the centre of the woods that had fallen down. It made a special place to sit and I would collect acorns and make tea parties for the fairies on the bark. Those walks gave me a sense of being back in my body and a feeling of peace. Alice was quieter than Mummy, she was gentle and patient and contented. Alice was comfortable in her own skin and she gave me the space I needed to just be myself. Those times in the woods she was happy to sit and wait whilst I played my games. She didn't try to interfere or make me do anything — she just let me be.

Daddy would visit me every weekend. He would make the four hour drive up on a Saturday or Sunday and spend a couple of hours with me. I don't remember. He never talked to me about it. I wish now I had asked him. Mummy used to tell me how hard it was for her and how upset my Daddy used to be. She said, "When your Dad tried to leave you would cry and cling to him so hard. Alice would have to pull you off him. Each week he would come back and visit you and each week it was the same."

I wish he had just picked me up and taken me home.

Looking in the mirror.

I am back at home in London with Mummy and Daddy. For the first few weeks my Nana and Granda have been here to help look after us both. Mummy has to lie down a lot of the time and to learn to walk again. I have to be good and be gentle with her because she is in pain and I think she might break if I touch her so I don't. Nana and Granda take me to a lady's house one day because they say I am going to a playgroup. When the lady opens the door to say hello all I can see is her scary face. I scream and scream until Nana and Granda take me home. Nana tells me off for not picking up my feet when I walk and she makes me hold her hand. I'm sure the lady wasn't scary, my terror of being left was the trigger.

A few weeks later I am in the living room of our small terraced house in London whilst Mummy is in the kitchen cooking. I am used to playing by myself. The light comes in through the French windows and I am standing on the little sofa with my back to the window so I can see myself in the big round mirror which hangs over the chair. I

27

stand on tiptoe with my chubby toddler legs stretched so I can see myself. My knees are dimpled at the back under my skirt. My face in the mirror is round and my hair cut in a simple bob. I have brown eyes and long lashes and a button nose that Mum calls 'retroussé' which she says means it turns up at the end. Mummy has a long straight nose but she has a bump in it where it got broken when she was young. I am looking at myself and wondering who I was, just pulling faces and playing. Mummy comes in behind me and she and kisses me exuberantly. "Oh I do love you so much" she says and she reaches out to hug me. I hear her say, "I love you" and I feel myself freeze and it seems as if I float up above my body. I hover somewhere overhead looking down on myself and I hear the voice in my head say, *"No."* The voice is quiet and insistent: *I don't believe you,"* *"No, you don't," "I don't care," "You left me," "I'll never trust you again".*

I shrug as Mummy puts her arms around me and I see myself give a little smile and jump down as I shut off. This is a new feeling and I quite like it. I get small so that I can disappear. I don't trust her but I need her. The pushing her away becomes a pattern. She loves me so much and I know it and I don't.

I want her to be able to hold me very tight and keep holding me and never let me go. And I want her to go away and leave me alone because her love for me is too much and it makes me want to wriggle and squirm and hide. If she holds me tight I will fight and push and then maybe I will soften and cry and be able to be comforted and let it all pour out of me. I will be able to say all the horrible things I think and feel like *"I hate you"* and *"you aren't my real Mummy"* and *"'where did you go?"* and *"why did you have to leave me?"* and *'I needed you"* and *"keep telling me you love me and hold on to me".* I could learn to be able to say what I want and need and feel instead of locking it all away inside until it comes out in other ways.

Our time apart unstuck the glue that had formed when my Mummy and I were put together. The loss compounded my early trauma of severance. I didn't know what to do with my feelings, so I shut them away. My outsides looked the same but my insides were not.

Throughout my childhood we pushed and pulled against each other like a game of tug-of-war. One of us was always falling over

Dear little Julia

I see you with your friend Linda. You loved her and you cried when you had to leave her. You made a friend and you will make many more. You are a good friend. I see your knee with scratches on it and I want to kiss it better. You look like your cousin Mary and your sisters here. Love, big me xxx

and struggling to get back up. We rarely pulled on the same team except when push came to shove and then she was there for me. I knew in a crisis she would be there, no questions asked. I relied on that.

I didn't have the words for what was happening to us and neither did she. Disassociation was the unknown. The flame of connection and love was bright but we kept burning ourselves. We were both trapped by the wounds of birth separation and trauma.

On the surface we managed quite well. We could be silly together

Julia (Fiona) with Linda and Alan

and laugh and I would feel the hysteria build in me until I was almost crying. I couldn't regulate my emotions and she didn't understand what I needed and was scared to push through. I became hard to cuddle and touch, my body didn't bend in to her. I both longed to have that comfort and it made me feel sick to my stomach because the longing was so uncomfortable. She was a sensitive, gentle, kind and anxious person but we didn't always bring out the best in each other. I still miss her most days since she died in 2011.

'Sunny Side' The bunny lamp

Julia (Fiona) with Mummy at the caravan and with Daddy beside a loch in Scotland.

Dear Julia

These pictures show you in two of your happiest places. The caravan holidays and being by water. You will always be an adventurer. Your Mum and Dad gave you the gift of loving travel, caravanning and sea, sky and nature. Both your

Julia (Fiona) aged 5 1963 School Photo

Dear Julia, your hair was so shiny and I see your sweet shy smile and those brown eyes. I remember that dress was pink and white. I have to tell you that you look beautiful and you are safe. I see you. Love, me xxx

Mum's loved to travel and the sea. Your parents gave you wide horizons between them and your true self loves to spread her wings and fly. Keep going, don't despair. Life is good.

Love from the future, always, me xx

CHAPTER 4 SCHOOL DINNERS

At five years old, it was time for me to start school. Mummy had recovered from the back surgery although she would be careful for the rest of her life.We had spent the last few months at home together. The playgroup experiment was not repeated. Mummy had taught me how to read using 'Janet and John' books. School wasn't far away so we could walk there. I remember being excited because Mummy had told me that I would enjoy school. On the first day I was ready to go in my new uniform of a grey pinafore dress and knitted cardigan with yellow edging. I had knee-high white socks that wrinkled down my legs and shiny black Clarks leather shoes. Mummy took a picture of me and there was a big orange cat sitting on the wall behind me. He wasn't our cat but it made a good picture and Mummy had an eye for colour.

I went in to school quite happily with the other new children and we all waved 'Goodbye' to the Mummies and Grannies on the playground.. I would stay for the morning and then go home for dinner. At home we called our mid-day meal 'dinner' because we were a Northern family. In the South they called it lunch. We had 'tea' at six o'clock where they had 'dinner' or 'supper'. But school 'dinners' happened at lunchtime. It could have been confusing but it wasn't. That day I wasn't sure what happened after dinner. I had quite a nice morning. I was shy and like many of the children I didn't know anyone else there. The school bell sounded and Miss Jackson said:

"All those who are staying for school dinner must stand in this line'. I stayed where I was. "And those who are going home stand over here'. I moved to the second line. Miss Jackson looks at her list and then at me and says kindly, "No, Fiona, you should be in this line, you are staying for your dinner at school".

I told her firmly, 'No, my Mummy is coming for me I'm going home'. I know that I am right.

"No, no you aren't on the going home list. You must be having school dinners. Come with me".

The panic built into a wave of terror. I couldn't move but I wanted to run. *If I just tell the teacher she will realise that my Mummy is taking me home.* I kept on saying, "No, I am going home" and Miss Jackson kept telling me I was staying at school. We have reached an impasse. The rest of the class had left in their crocodile. The teacher took me by the hand and said briskly, "Come with me. I will take you to the dining room". *But I am going home for my dinner. Where is Mummy? This is wrong. I want to go home. I am scared. I don't like this place and I don't want to be here any more. I don't like school. I hate the teacher.*

Footsteps tapped swiftly down the corridor. Mummy swept in breathless, "Fiona, there you are! I was waiting and everyone came out but you. I wondered where you were". She smiled. I am rescued and relieved. It is just a mistake but it felt life threatening. We go home for dinner. I said 'I don't want to go back there. They don't believe me when I tell the truth. I said I was going home for my dinner and they didn't believe me. No-one listened. I don't like it there. I don't want to go to school any more.I want to stay at home.'

But I had to go back. Every morning and afternoon Mummy walked me to school. I would get dressed in the morning and eat my breakfast and off we would go. We chatted happily. Every day as we arrived at the school gates the terror overwhelmed me afresh and I sobbed uncontrollably as I glued myself to my Mummy. I hung on to her for dear life until the teacher would come and lead (pull) me down the playground and into the classroom. Some days it took two teachers to get me inside. Everyone looked at me but I didn't care. I cried and clung I learnt nothing in school because I was too traumatised to hear or see. At first the teachers were kind and brisk and sympathetic but then they seemed to lose interest in me and I was left to myself. I didn't make friends. I just wanted to go home.

What I learnt wasn't on the curriculum but it stayed with me for a long time. I formed some beliefs that were built on a shaky foundation of trauma and they went like this :

Crying doesn't work.

It doesn't matter how bad I feel.

You are on your own.

It doesn't matter what I say.

I am powerless here and helpless and school is not a safe place.

Keep your feelings to yourself.

Just get on with it.

No-one will come to rescue you.

Mummy had rescued me once but she couldn't do it again. Everyone believed that I had to go to school. Their commitment to my education was stronger than any emotion I could express. Eventually, I stopped crying. I lost hope and instead I chose survival. I had no skills in that environment, it was foreign to me and I had missed out on the first few weeks of orientation. The other children were playing together in the play-house or sitting on the carpet listening to a story. Some of them were in small groups at tables drawing and reading books. The teacher was busy going from group to group. The other children looked happy. I saw a little girl get the teacher's attention by pulling on her sleeve from behind, so I started doing that instead. I would hang on to a hem or a bit of clothing pulling gently. The teacher wasn't keen on this behaviour either and she was snappy. I saw some children fall over and get picked up and brushed down. Sometimes a child sat on the teacher's knee for a few minutes. I wanted that too. I wanted gentleness but I was good at pushing people away.

The story I understood was 'be a big girl'. My experience in that school wasn't a very happy one. I never really liked school.

Once I stopped crying came the reading. The teacher wanted me to start with Janet and John Book 1. I said, "I've already read that". She didn't believe me. So for the next few weeks I re-read all the books. I was bored. Mummy tried to get me moved up to another class and somehow I got to hang on to this idea. I would follow the teacher round pulling on her hem or the back of her shirt and say, "When am I moving up into the next class?" I couldn't settle and I became obsessive about moving up. My crying became constant whining and eventually they moved me into a higher class. And in that class I struggled. The children were older than me. I didn't understand the maths. I felt scared and lonely. And I started to fail. I felt stupid. I didn't understand the numbers and the teacher didn't seem to want to help me. I couldn't understand what was written on the blackboard so I would sit at my desk and do nothing.

One day I got something in my eye. Mummy always said it was a seed that blew in. It hurt a lot and it got stuck. So she took me to an eye doctor. And they made me better and whilst they were doing that they found out that I couldn't see properly. I was myopic with astigmatism and I had to have glasses. When I got back to school with my pink round NHS frames I found out that things were different. I could see the blackboard. It made life better. I didn't have to screw my eyes up to see. Things improved.

I learnt to swim, literally. Mummy and Daddy had never learnt to swim and they were scared of the water. But Mummy took me every week to the swimming baths and got me lessons. She stood at the side of the pool whilst I floundered and splashed and swallowed several gallons of chlorine-filled water every week. I coughed and spluttered and thought I would never be able to get from one side to the other. And then one day I did. And she smiled and clapped and celebrated my success and I felt like there was something I could do that would save me.

My childhood safe spaces became mostly inside my own head. Swimming was a way to feel free. I disappeared into books and writing stories and in playing families with my dolls and shells and grasses. I made everything into families. I remember sitting on the school fields and playing with the long grasses that had seeds that you could strip off with your fingers. I would play with them at playtime and dinner time. I wasn't very good at playing with other children there. I had missed out on getting to know them because of the early weeks and months and I didn't know how to start again. I played with Linda who lived next door. I played with our dog, Kim. He became my confidante. He was a black beagle cross with little brown spots above his eyes like eyebrows. I could stroke his soft ears and look into his brown eyes and know I was understood. He would sit with me and let me cuddle him. I wanted to marry him when I grew up. He gave me what I needed — attention and unconditional love, listening and understanding. He knew when I was sad or unhappy or scared. I have always loved dogs. I was a bright child. I wanted to learn. I loved books and stories. I could read but I couldn't do numbers. Everything about maths confused me. I didn't understand the patterns and I found numbers hard to remember. I took a long time to be able to tell the time. I remember being sent to find out the time in school. There was a big clock in the hall and sometimes a teacher would ask one of the children to go and find out the time. One day it was my turn. I stood there for a long time looking at the clock. I didn't know what the numbers meant. I felt as if I couldn't go back until I knew. Eventually someone came to find me. I still didn't know the time.

I have problems with spatial awareness, with left and right, and with tying shoe-laces. These things all took me longer than the average bear to learn. Now I know that many adoptees have difficulty with attention, with patterns and organisation. Often it gets labelled as ADD. But trauma looks like that too. Maths teachers often labelled me as lazy.

I was good at English. I could write stories and lose myself there and it got me approval with praise and encouragement. I devoured the children's section in the public library and had to have special permission to borrow books from the adults section by the time I was nine or ten. I read the sides of cereal packets and shampoo bottles. If it had words on it, I read it. I read trashy romantic novels and serious authors. Reading took me to another place. When I read I learnt I could be somewhere else. I could block out the world. I learnt that to bury myself in a book was a way to be private. To find people like me. To see and hear feelings like mine. To be able to cry and laugh and wonder and learn. Books became my best friend. They were also a place that was mine. My Mummy and Daddy didn't read. They said they did but I never saw either of my parents read a book. They valued my reading and supported it and encouraged it and there

Julia (Fiona's) 6th birthday party

Dear Julia

You look happy in this picture, I think you are sharing a joke with the girl opposite. You have always loved to laugh and to make others laugh. You are funny! Your dress was green with a white fake fur collar, it was itchy but you felt pretty in it. You look beautiful. All will be well. I know birthdays are hard sometimes when you are adopted. I love you. Sending hugs.

Love, me. XXX

was a sort of wonder in them at it. Mummy saw reading as an occupation not to be disturbed. If I was reading I was left alone. I remember the first time I read a whole proper book to myself. It was 'The Lion, The Witch and the Wardrobe' by CS Lewis. It felt like magic had happened.

When I met my birth family I found people who read. My birth mum loved books. We talked about reading and bought each other books. My sisters read. They are my people.

When I was a child, birthdays were a special day. My parents always made the day a celebration and I don't remember it being difficult. But when I became a teenager and young adult that changed. I started to have conflicting feelings about my birthday. My Birth-Day. The date of my birth. Suddenly it became full of meaning that I hadn't noticed before. *Where is my mother now? Is she thinking of me? Does she remember my birth? Does she think about how old I am? Does she have other children?* My mood would drop in the week or so before my birthday and I would feel sad. The questions would roll around my head.

CHAPTER 5 SUGAR LOVE AND ALL THINGS SHINY

I loved sugar from the first mouthful. The taste lit up my mouth and sent happy feelings shooting into every part of me. I craved the next bite and the 'hit' from anything sweet or stodgy to my brain and body. Sherbet dabs, fruit salads and penny sweets. Humbugs, those black and cream mints my Nana used to love. Easter eggs that Granda bought. A giant sized bar of Cadbury's Dairy Milk as a present that I ate secretly in my bedroom. The biscuit tin on the top shelf in the pantry. The hidden sweets for visitors or Mummy's diet sweets that would make her thin. The diet sweets were called Ayds and came in two varieties, mint and fudge toffee. The idea was to eat one or two before a meal to fill you up. But they tasted just like sweets and they came in a big box which Mummy hid at the top of the kitchen cupboard. I would eat them by the handful. They never seem to fill me up.

I was seven when my feelings on the inside started coming out in my actions. Looking back I see myself as a frightened, lonely, anxious little girl who doesn't know where she fits in. I can see a child who is insecure and whose attachment is badly affected. I see my little self running in ever decreasing circles crying out for help. But my parents didn't seem to notice. I got sneaky. I didn't show my feelings. I just tried to take what I needed in other ways. We had moved house again and I had moved school. Mummy had started doing some teaching from home after school so when I came home I often had to be 'good' which meant being quiet and amusing myself. I hadn't made any real friends yet. I don't think I could. I was a good girl who did well at school and could keep herself occupied with a book or her dolls. But somehow my needs got left behind.

One day when our youngest son, Joe, was a baby we went to the seaside as a family. My husband was driving our estate car and the children were strapped in the back. I had organised a picnic lunch and all the baby paraphernalia it takes to get out of the house. As we got to the end of our street, one of the boys said, "Where's Joe?" We all looked round. There was a space where the baby should be.

We had left him on the sofa. He was wrapped up in his little red snowsuit, kicking his legs happily and smiling. It took just a few minutes for our hearts to stop and then to turn back and go inside to collect him. It has become a family story and one he doesn't like to let us forget. I feel like I was left behind on a sofa and it took a couple of years for my parents to notice enough to turn the car around. By then the damage was done.

One day when I was seven I was in the local shop with Mum and I saw the orange 'Club' biscuits on the shelf. Self service had just come into small shops so Mum had her basket and was busy looking for tea and bread. Quickly I picked up a biscuit and put it in my pocket. But the trouble was I needed to eat it. I had an incessant and overwhelming craving for chocolate and sugar. My lifelong sugar addiction was starting to reveal itself. Gabor Mate says that addiction has its roots in childhood trauma. I was trying to replace something I couldn't have. I had a hole inside me that I couldn't fill. I didn't need God to fill it, I needed to be seen.

In 2011 I was nearly 22 stone. It was the heaviest I have ever been and I felt horrible. Depressed. Sad. Fat. In the middle of my addiction with no way out that I could see. It has been quite a journey from there. Food has been my comfort and solace, my secret pleasure, my companion, my number one sleeping pill, my avoider and obligator since I was tiny. Food is easy.

There is a space between what I crave and what I can get, it is liminal space. This is a space between wanting and having, a space between me and myself. There is a space in-between. Most of my life it has been a place to escape to. A run away place. A numbing out, obliteration of sensation. A place to not have to feel. To elude the rage and terror and grief that lives in my gut. That is where the addiction lies. It is a friend in the dark.

But it is also my sworn enemy, it wants to take me down. To leave me in the gutter, broken and bleeding and oh so small and tired and finished with. And it takes me there with seductive glances and whispers. "You deserve this". "Just a little somethin' to take away the pain" "I'll just have one and save the rest for later…". Mostly it tells me "It's OK, this is just too hard for you right now, take a little easiness". Eat. Sleep. Repeat.

I learnt that I could climb up into the cupboard to find treats whilst Mum was tutoring in the dining room. The treats were for the other children. There were treats in our house but these seemed to be special, and they weren't for me. I started to steal. I stole other children's sweets from their bags or pockets in the cloakroom that were meant for playtime and a chocolate orange 'Club' biscuit from the Spar shop. I used to climb up on a chair in the kitchen and find the treats in the cupboard whilst Mummy was teaching. I was always careful to only have one or two from a packet so there were some left. Eating became a secret pleasure with an adrenaline boost as I tried to be quiet as a mouse in the kitchen. I would take my treasure into the bathroom and sit on the floor and eat it.

I took a purple pot of 'Potty Putty' from another girl's pocket in the cloakroom one playtime. She had told us in class that her brother in America had sent it over.

She has a big brother who is so grown up he lives in America. He must love her very much. I wish I had a brother like that. Why don't I have someone who thinks I'm so special?

I stole marbles. I learnt how to lie. I was deep into the feelings of not having enough. And I found comfort elsewhere. I found other made up families. I was like the magpie collecting to myself everything new and shiny and taking it back to my nest to hoard. Comics for girls were becoming popular in the sixties here in England. I had a longing to read 'Bunty' and 'June' like the other girls at school but Mummy thought that reading matter should be educational so she favoured 'Treasure' which she put into a blue binder for me every week. Eventually I won the battle to have a girl's comic but Mummy insisted on 'Princess Tina' rather than the 'Bunty' I had set my heart on. She didn't approve of Enid Blyton either, "not 'proper' books." I loved them in all their easy accessibility. Enid Blyton fuelled my burgeoning inner white-trashy self in the days before consciousness raising and I had met. The children in those stories had agency to have adventures. They were largely free of parental influence or interference. Their relationships with each other were what mattered. Those children made their own 'families' in schools and on camping trips. There was a girl called George and a dog. And in the school stories the girls were brave and funny and always had cake. Mummy thought they were common. Being 'nice' was very important. Now I have learnt to indulge my inner need for sparkle and frivolity. Having to be 'sensible' is overrated. My wife Teresa watches 'Countdown' on TV to relax but I will stealthily binge-watch 'The Real Housewives.' I don't have to do it secretly but it confirms the pleasure. I wasn't deprived as a child but my personality was different to my parents and I had interests and desires they didn't see as important. Learning to make my own choices and that they are acceptable is hard. I have Princess tendencies under my hippie earth mother exterior. When I was older Mum would often say to me in exasperation, 'You will argue black is white just to be right'. She had a point, although I would argue her down every time. I am contrary and difficult and argumentative when I am not trying to keep everyone happy. I am high maintenance emotionally even when I aspire to be low, but no-one is more critical or harder on me than I am myself.

I believe that children need fun and frivolity as well as education. When I had children we enjoyed or suffered various crazes such as Pogs, Tamagotchi and Top Trumps games. I knew it mattered that they had some of what other children had. It is a form of belonging and fitting in. That is what it meant to me.

Barbie clothes and other people's treats.

The Christmas I was eight, I had a deep and burning desire for pretty dresses for my dolls. I didn't have a Barbie, I had the English version Sindy (Mummy's 'nicer' choice again) and her little 'sister' Patch. I adored them especially Patch even whilst still coveting the more glamorous Barbie. I had seen outfits in the shops in their plastic wrapping, with tiny plastic shoes and accessories like a comb or a handbag, even a newspaper or a mirror. I was entranced. I just wanted one set of cheap plastic gorgeous-ness to fulfil my inner pink Princess. Christmas morning came. We sat by the coal fire opening our presents. One at a time we opened a present and Mummy watched every moment on my face. I knew she was watching and she would be miserable if I wasn't happy enough. *Which outfit will it be? Will it be the evening dress with the little 'fur' stole and the high heeled shoes? Or will it be the slacks and polo neck sweater with the black shiny flat slippers.? This is a big box! Maybe there is more than one?*

A small plastic box with clip together fastenings like a suitcase was inside the wrapping paper. I opened the box. I knew it wasn't going to be what I'd asked for. I prepared my face. Inside the box was full of clothes handmade by Mum for my dolls. She must have spent hours making them. A little knitted yellow jumper with a polo neck, a smart dress and several tops and skirts, a little coat. I knew I had to be grateful and smile and say, 'thank you'. I didn't know whether she knew. I felt misunderstood. It was symbolic of our miscommunication. We were both trying, maybe too hard. She put in hours of love and attention on those dolls clothes But it wasn't what I wanted and I didn't feel listened to. Mummy made assumptions that failed her and me. And I tried to keep her happy because her happiness was essential to my wellbeing. If she was happy I was safe. Our needs were polar opposites. And mine often got lost in the swamp of hers.

I don't like saying this about me or about my Mum. I feel mean and whiny and spoilt. I don't believe that I should have had everything I wanted. But she wasn't attuned to me and that is what this is about. It affected my sense of belonging and my identity struggled to emerge without fighting every step of the way

On my 7th birthday I came downstairs early. My dad was an early bird and already up and about. I had been desperate for a bike and there was a big object wrapped up in the hall.

"Happy Birthday love" said Dad. My eyes must have lit up. I looked at him and at the present. I held my breath.

"Open it, then" he laughed and I did. It was a bike. I was so happy. A little while later Mum came downstairs.

"You've let her have her present" she said through gritted teeth and wet eyes. I knew something was wrong and I suspected it was something I had done.

"Yes, love, why what's wrong?"
She started to cry.

"I wanted to see Fiona's face when she opened it" she said. *It's my fault.* Dad apologised to Mum but the innocent excitement of my birthday leaked out like the air from a pricked balloon.

New school.

It is 1965 and we are moving Up North. We moved from London, leaving behind my best friend Carol, the girl next door. Dad had a new job and my parents wanted to be nearer to their families. Both sets of grandparents were getting older and some health problems were creeping onto the horizon. First we moved for a few months to a house provided by Dad's employer. We settled in there and I made friends with a boy who must have lived nearby. He liked playing with dolls and I loved my Barbie and the doll from the 'Sugar Puffs' cereal pack that Granny and Grandpa had bought me one Christmas, collecting tokens from the side of countless packets as they ate their morning Sugar Puffs with prunes. Visiting Granny and Grandpa in Sheffield meant eating Sugar Puffs and Granny's apple and blackcurrant pie. When we had dinner there was 'Tizer' to drink which we were never allowed at home. 'Tizer' was a fizzy sweet red pop loved by both Granny and Grandpa. Grandpa read me Bible stories and took me for walks through the 'jungle', an overgrown piece of ground behind their house. He would use his stick to beat down the thistles and he would tell me about his childhood. I have my Granny's 'Be-ro' recipe book that she gave me when I was fifteen, but I never got my pastry to be as nice as hers.

I spent hours creating stories around the dolls, lost in my own little world. And the boy was like that too. I think we must have moved over a summer holidays because I remember long days of playing before I had to start school. The boy was also at the school but a year older and in a different class. I couldn't understand why he didn't want to know me in school. I thought we were friends but boys and girls didn't play together on the playground. Being an only child is a double-edged sword. One of its gifts is self sufficiency. School was stressful. I didn't fit in. My voice was wrong.

The way everybody spoke was like a foreign language. I felt like an alien with my soft vowels and London girl ignorance of Manchester United. One day in class I answered a question and said, "bath" in my London accent. The teacher said, "Baaarth?" And everyone laughed. "Do you say 'graaarrss as well?" he smiled at me. My little London self went into hiding fast. I started to change the way I spoke. Anything to fit in.

I wore glasses. And then I started to bite my mouth. I always had mouth ulcers and when they got really bad the doctor prescribed some Gentian Violet to coat the inside of my mouth. One day I got told off in the class for "sucking on a pen" because my mouth was purple. I was struggling to make friends. I didn't really know how to do that. Everything had changed again too fast and the ground was shaking underneath me.

Our little family lived in that area for two years from when I was six and we moved twice. Once to another house round the corner and the second time to live in a caravan whilst our new house in a new town was being built. I was doing well in school. I tried hard to be liked and to fit in. But I was scared and lonely and my attachment issues were leaking out in my behaviour. My rebel child was screaming inside but she learnt how to do it silently and discretely so that on the outside I conformed. I didn't feel like I belonged. This is where it started. That recognition in myself that I didn't quite fit, in my family, in my life, in my own skin. Trauma was in the house but no-one knew its name.

I started to behave in ways that would now be called 'acting out'. I had accidents and injuries often. I trapped my fingers in doors and fell over and fell off my bike. I bumped my head and split my lip and needed patching up. Mummy said I was 'accident prone'. I started to have nightmares and would often end up in Mummy and Daddy's bed in the night when I couldn't settle back to sleep. The stealing caused me the most pain and also the most satisfaction. It gave me an instant feeling of comfort. For a few brief seconds when I had something in my hands that didn't belong to me, I felt happy. I felt like I had what other children had. I just wanted to be like them. I wanted to be someone else. I wanted to be like the popular kids. The ones with the shiny hair. The one who did ballet and had the perfect little outfits. I wanted the potty putty that had just become a craze and the marbles that were the big thing in the playground. I wanted the new colourful felt tip pens and the Orange Club chocolate biscuits. So I took them. I stole the other kids 'tuck' meant for playtime and I ate it, stuffing it into my mouth in the girls' cloakroom or I hid it in my pocket for later. I spent a lot of time feeling sick and ashamed and frantic. I knew that what I was doing was wrong. I was terrified of being found out and getting into trouble. But something was missing and taking something shiny and special made me feel like a little bit of their life would rub off on me.

Marbles

Colin had red hair and a dusting of freckles across his open face. He loved football and especially our local starring team, Manchester United. He was friendly, kind and eminently likeable. Colin was the possessor of a collection of marbles that came out every playtime. There were small marbles with different coloured swirls inside and several king-size beauties. The coloured spirals inside the green might be one or two colours. Each one seemed more beautiful and desirable than the last. I imagined how those smooth cold globes would fit into my palm. My fingers would long to curl possessively around them.

51

Marbles seemed magical, like a ship in a bottle or a kaleidoscope. Colin loved those marbles. He was the sort of boy that would play with girls as well as boys. I watched him play and sometimes would join in with the game. One day I went into the cloakroom to get my coat and bag at the end of school. I went to the toilet first and the chatter

and laughter had faded to silence by the time I came out. I washed my hands slowly. There was a distinctive smell in the cloakrooms of the stringent green soap and sweaty plimsolls. Each child had their own peg with their name printed on a white card stuck in a little metal slot above the hook. The empty cloakroom showed a line of empty hooks with an occasional forgotten jumper or PE bag. In the middle row was a handmade drawstring bag with Colin's name embroidered in yellow thread. The bag was weighted down with forbidden fruit and hung heavy and ripe. I reached out and touched the bag gently. It swung seductively and chinked gently. I held my breath, looking round to see if anyone had heard. No-one came. I put my little hand under the weight of the bag. The marbles were heavy in my hand and the wanting was so big it was like a drug rushing through my system. In seconds I had freed the bag from its lonely isolation and tipped the contents into my own PE bag. Colin's empty bag swung quietly on its hook as I ran out of the school to find Mummy who was waiting to walk me home. The excitement was a little buzzy feeling that made me feel good and bad at the same time. The acquisition was the drug. It was a foretaste of compulsive shopping. The pleasure was only a little bit spoilt by my feeling of guilt.

Retribution hung over me in my dreams but nothing happened. I wondered if I had got away with it. Then one morning in the classroom Mr Houghton started to ask questions. "Has anyone seen Colin's marbles?" "If you have taken them come and tell me and own up". "If you come and find me and tell the truth, you won't get into trouble. It will be better than being found out" "Tell the truth". 'Mr Harris, the Head Teacher, is coming down to speak to the class'. The words went on and on. I tried to keep my face blank. The Head Teacher called me into his office to question me. I wished I could give Colin his marbles back and it would all be over but I didn't know how to do that without getting caught. I denied everything and that was the end of that. I wish I could change the story back and give Colin those marbles. I'm sorry Colin.

The childhood years between six and nine were full of change. Our family moves meant we kept criss-crossing England in a game of cat's cradle. It was hard for me to settle. I carried that pattern into adulthood. It gave me a sense of adventure and a wanderlust that meant I am always ready for a new adventure. I get twitchy when I have lived somewhere for a while and feel it's time to pack a case and go. This is a double-edged sword .

My nemesis was coming and it came in the shape of a rubbery plastic toy with a cute ugly troll face and long hair in a range of colours. Everybody had to have one and my little trainee-addict self was no exception. Trolls with hair all colours of the rainbow and hard pink bodies with baby bellies. Small trolls and big trolls. Trolls that would sit on top of your pencil or attach to a key ring or pencil case. I had one with orange hair, chosen by me with breathtaking nail-biting care one Saturday, but one is never enough.

It was the season of birthday parties. A clutch of hot over-excited, barely socialised, sugar-fuelled children gathered in a middle-class home one Saturday in Cheshire. What could possibly go wrong? Izzy was in my class at school. Mummy dropped me off at her eighth birthday party and I felt shy. I am wearing a party dress, my hair is brushed so it shines. I have clean socks on and I am clutching a present wrapped by Mummy in shiny paper. *I don't know what to do or what to say. What are the rules?.* I am an observer, a people-watcher already. *She has sisters. I wish I had sisters, what would it be like? Izzy is so lucky.* I am always envious of other people's families. I can sense an atmosphere in this house, it is like a new scent called 'We Belong Together'. They all seem to fit like pieces of a jigsaw. It is alien to me and darkly deeply desirable. I didn't want to be alone with my parents.

This party house was busy and lively. There were games and a 'tea' with cakes and jellies and sweets followed by a cake with candles on. All the children stood round for the cake ritual and sang 'Happy Birthday' and then the cake is cut and we all had a piece to eat. I loved the soft sweet buttercream icing in the middle. That sweetness in my mouth is soothing and I could stay there and eat all the cake all day. After the sugar high, there was a game of 'sardines.' I am too shy to ask what to do. *Everyone else knows. It's just me. I'll look stupid. I'll just copy everyone else. I wish I could have more cake. I want to go home. I don't know what to do. I don't belong here. I want my Mummy.* I use my super-power skills. I watch and follow the cues. In the helter-skelter running round the house I am anxious and uncertain. I loved the idea of getting away but as soon as it happened I wanted to be back at home.

Izzy had already showed a crowd of excited girls around the house. She was so proud of her big sister's troll collection. I heard her talk about her sister and it gave me a pain in my tummy. I wanted a sister to talk about me that way. There was a family of trolls standing on a chest of drawers in the big sister's bedroom. There was one with rainbow coloured hair. I wanted him badly.

He is so beautiful. And he's so much bigger than the one I have. She has four and I only have one. She won't notice if I take one. I can just borrow it for a little while. No-one will know. It will make you feel better if you can hold him. You will have a friend.

Go and hide somewhere, you are supposed to be hiding and playing the game. But I don't know where to go. I don't know anyone. He is looking at me. Oh I want him.

In a flash my little fingers scooped him up and put him in my pocket. My heart was thumping hard and I was scared of getting caught but for a moment I am caught up in the joy of possession.I know that what I have done is wrong. I have guilt and shame mixed with the adrenaline of the capture. It is a heady mix.

Soon Daddy is there to pick me up. As we stood on the doorstep I could hardly breathe. My tummy hurt. I wanted to escape. It feels dangerous and urgent and exciting and wonderful and terrible. In one hand I have the troll clutched so tight it hurt. His hard little body wasn't comforting but it is solid and real in my hand. It made me feel grounded. I belonged to the troll. I was real. His hair is soft and long, stroking it through my fingers made me know I was there. I clutched Daddy. He looked slightly surprised by my affection but he squeezed my hand and we are about to leave. Suddenly Izzy appears. Her face was flushed from running, her long hair damp on her forehead. She angrily grabbed hold of me by the shoulder and shouted

"That's my sister's troll, you've taken it from her room, what are you doing? She's stolen it! Give it back!"

Her Mummy was standing right beside her. She looked puzzled and as she looks at me I saw the question forming in her eyes. Before it could reach her mouth I say:

"No it's mine, I brought it with me"

I kept on repeating it until they stop. Izzy's mum looked at Izzy and at me and I knew that she knew. *I fear that everything will come crashing down. This is it. It is over. I am finished.* She told Izzy to be quiet. She bent down and said quietly,

"Are you sure it is the one you brought with you? Perhaps you have just made a mistake and thought he was yours?"

She was kind and tried to give me a way out. I hesitated for a moment but it was too big a leap. I felt like I might die if we didn't get away. All the magic had gone, the glitter turned to ashes in my fingers.

Several weeks passed. The troll stayed hidden under my bed. I couldn't play with him or even take him out and look at him. His image burnt through the mattress and the covers and stayed in the back of my mind all day. At night my sleep was restless and I woke with nightmares of being found out and taken away. I felt sick a lot and my earaches kept coming back. I wonder why no-one says anything. One day at school my worst nightmare came knocking in the form of an eight-year-old with freckles, long curly light brown hair and a determined expression

"My Mum knows you stole that troll and she is going to tell the police and then you will go to prison. You have to give him back".

"But I didn't take it, it's mine," I keep saying hopelessly.

Inside me, the shell I had built to keep all thoughts of discovery out, shattered. Back home I cry in my bedroom until Mummy hears me. It seemed to take a long time and I am lonely and scared. *I know that this is it. Now they will take me away and I will be sent to prison and I can never come home again. Mummy is going to be angry with me. She will think I am bad. I don't know what to do.*

I told her what I had done and I showed her the troll. I didn't like having him any more. Mummy listened and said gently,

"You are going to have to give him back you know".

She hugged me. I like it and I don't. We walked to Izzy's house and her mum met us on the doorstep. She was alone and I felt grateful that I didn't have to see the girls. I gave her the troll and said, "I'm sorry I took him" and she smiled at me and said

"Thank you for bringing him back." That is it. It's over.

We turned around and walked home. I don't remember any more being said about it. I felt lighter. There is no extra punishment.

I know this can't ever happen again. I can't bear the shame. We don't talk about difficult things. But when push comes to shove Mum will be there for me. I stopped stealing from other children after that because I realised that it made me feel worse than the reward. But the longing remained. I had just learnt to layer shame on top of need.

Writing about the troll for this story I bought myself a set of mini trolls. I have them in front of me now and they remind me that this story is not about shame, it is about understanding and compassion. Ibsen asks Peer Gynt to work out what is the difference between a troll and a human being. The troll's motto is "Be true to yourself, and to Hell with the world". I quite like that.

My early trauma and my childhood sowed the seeds for patterns that continued long into my adult life. I am one of the lucky ones. Not all adoptees make it out the other side. The incidence of suicide and depression is high. But healing and hope are possible. I don't regret my life and I wouldn't change it now if I could. I can't pick and choose what to keep and what to give away. My experiences led me into a career in social work and teaching and as a therapist. They made me want a family of my own. My hidden past made me want to find out who I was and where I came from and that search for my identity has been like opening a treasure chest of new family and of new adventures. I wouldn't be the woman I am today without my history and I wouldn't be able to share how I came out the other side.

Moving again

When I was eight we moved again to a new area and my third school. I remember sitting on my bed not long before the move and making a decision that this time it was going to be different. I wasn't going to steal any more. I didn't like who it made me and I hated being found out. I was going to make friends and find a way to be liked. I wasn't going to be bullied any more and I wasn't going to hurt other kids either. I was going to make people laugh. I was learning to perform. I can see and feel my eight year old self deciding to change who I was. I learnt that I could become someone else. I became a chameleon.

There was a girl in my ballet class. Middle class girls had ballet lessons but I was clumsy and had no sense of balance. I loved the idea of dancing, of being a dancer and the music. The class was on a Saturday morning in a church hall. I thought that eight year old Essie was everything a ballerina should be. She had long dark hair that she swept up into a bun at the back of her head In the class she wore pink tights and a black leotard and those pale pink ballet pumps. I watched her. She was friendly and polite and easy to like. Essie always smiled and could chatter with everyone. I wanted to be like her. She seems to fit effortlessly in her own skin. Essie had this little knitted white bolero in soft Angora wool, it seemed the height of luxury and not the sort of clothing my Mummy would ever think of for me. I wanted the prettiness. Essie was a perfect sized girl in her perfect ballet body, everything about her just seemed to be right sized. I was self-conscious of being chubby and clumsy and somehow not right. I felt ugly. My mummy used to tell me I had "an interesting face". I just wanted her to say I was pretty.

After we had moved I asked if I could see Essie. I had used my own money to buy some sweets and chocolate and put it all in a bag to give to her. I didn't know how to say I missed her or that I was sad. Money or food were easy currency for love. The winter afternoon was turning to dusk the day my parents drove me to Essie's house. We weren't expected and I walked up the path alone with Mummy and Daddy waiting in the car. A man answered my tentative knock. I looked up and said, "Is Essie in?" He said, "No love she's busy". So I handed over the bag of sweets and I left. I felt lost. The front door had a glass panel which the light shone through onto the path. It felt like a long walk back to the car. My Daddy drove us home and I never saw Essie again. I needed some help to learn how to say, 'Goodbye' . My parents had no idea that Essie mattered to me so much but I felt that I had lost someone special again.

Moving on, and on, and on

Moving house. Moving school. Moving on. Always moving.
I would have another childhood if I could.
Mine would make me a Yorkshire lass
Living in that house with the rocking horse
And staying there
Being with my Mum and Dad, not moving
Or transitioning
Not being dug up and transplanted
My roots getting weaker and weaker.
Now they snap easily.
Or I would have been the oldest of four
Girls with a Mum who was practical
And clever and loved to read.
We would have learnt to protect each other
And I could have been the one that Mum practiced on
Until my youngest sister got away with everything.
I can move at the drop of a hat
I have to be forced to stay in one place
My internal world of anxiety pushes me
Into a new space
Discomfort and adrenaline addiction.
I learnt how to perform In every group and situation
In each new class and school.
In each new family group
With each new mother.
I lost myself along the way.
She is scattered in pieces like a jigsaw

Shards of broken glass under my
Naked feet
I leave bloody footprints
Smears and lines that show my path

And my pain
But I wipe them up obsessively
As I go along
Not wanting to reveal too much
Not willing to be seen.
Being me, coming home

Iain and Julia friends and compadres 2019

CHAPTER 6 IT'S JUST A PHASE

I always wanted a brother but a dog came close. Growing up as an only child meant that I developed the skill early of being able to amuse myself happily for hours. I can escape into a book and not notice the time go by. I was independent and over-protected in equal doses. I never felt lonely but I got tired of trying to be a good girl. I didn't have someone to fight and argue with. When I had children I knew I wanted a houseful. I would watch the boys roll around together on the floor fighting and playing like lion cubs. Sometimes it ended up with hurt feelings and bruises. Being an adopted only child means not having the edges rubbed off. It is being an only child on steroids. I was too much and not enough. When I was in my twenties Mum said to me, 'It was hard to discipline you without breaking you. You were such a bright strong willed child'. She made it sound like a bad thing.

I just knew that life would be easier if I had a sidekick. Kim the dog was my substitute brother. He was my confidante and also managed to behave badly enough for both of us. I remember being on a walk with my parents somewhere in the countryside with sheep. Dad had let Kim off his lead chasing sheep. Dad chased after him shouting and Kim was brought back in disgrace. I was crying. I remember Dad saying "He's going to have to go. We can't keep him if he does this". Kim stayed but the fear of one of us being sent away stayed too.

My friend Iain became the other brother I never had. Our Mum's got to know each other and Iain and I were forced into playing together as seven year olds. He wanted to watch Top Cat on TV whilst I was desperately attached to Robin Hood and Maid Marian. Through the sixties and seventies as we grew up alongside each other, we argued over Monopoly and who was cheating and we played endless games of table tennis whilst our parents had dinner and watched mind-numbing slide shows of holidays. Two only children we became friends, there for each other no matter what. Iain's Mum Mary was another Mum to me, one of the nicest women I knew. She died too young after years of early-onset dementia took her away. I can still see her smile and hear her soft Scottish voice. Iain is still my kid brother although I am very bad at making contact. He was there when Mum Margaret was deteriorating with dementia and he still says I cheat at Monopoly. He thinks he is my big brother now. We understand each other although I don't know that I have ever talked to him about adoption. It amazes me now how many times I didn't speak up. A lifetime of observing for the slightest signal of disapproval means I have found it hard to claim my identity.

Tia

When I was seven or eight Mum and Dad decided to foster another girl for weekends and holidays. I wanted a sister but having Princess Tia to stay was not the answer. Tia lived in a Children's Home nearby and was a few months older than me. She had long thick wavy blonde hair and blue eyes. We were similar in height but she was more of a girly girl where I was what Mummy called a 'tomboy.' I liked to climb trees and jump over ditches and often came home scratched and muddy. Tia kept her clothes nice and was careful how she sat. I was told that she didn't have a family to live with and I felt sorry for her, but it wasn't the whole story. Tia talked about her Dad and her brothers and sisters. Her family lived near to the children's home and she visited them regularly. Tia had her own story about why she and her little brother were in the home but I thought she was lucky to know who her family were. Tia seemed down to earth and practical. She saw the world in black and white and liked to know what to do and how to behave. I was much the same it just showed up differently. I was a rebel and she was a good girl. I lived in my own secret world with my books and doll families. Tia just wanted to stay with my Mum and do some colouring in. We didn't realise that we had much in common and neither of us wanted to be friends. We didn't like the same TV programmes and she didn't read books. She shared my room when she came to stay and when we went in the caravan we had to top and tail in our sleeping bags on the bed. It was like having a pretend-friend. I had a collection of pretend relatives now there was Tia. I liked not being alone with my parents but I wished it wasn't Tia. She stayed with us for respite for years. I wonder what she thinks about that now?

On holiday Daddy gave Tia and I some spending money. We took it in our hot hands to the small shop in the Welsh village we were staying in. I bought a book of paper dolls and Tia bought colouring pens. Back at the caravan I spent hours cutting out the dolls and their outfits which had little white paper tabs all round so that you could attach them to the doll. Each doll had an array of skirts and coats and hats and trousers and jumpers all made of coloured paper. I loved that book. I loved the way the doll could be a different person in a flash. There were cut-out hair-pieces to could change hair colour and style too. One day a doll could have a blonde pony-tail and the next a curly brown bob. It was like magic and it made me so happy. I was always a chameleon, I learnt to merge with the color of the background I was in. My dolls gave me a way to have different lives.

I didn't know what to do with my feelings of jealousy anger and confusion whilst feeling obliged to be nice. I had internalised the message to be grateful for what I had and that meant I should be happy to share it. Sometimes when we took her back to the home I wished I could just go and live there too. I thought it might be easier and I envied the way she talked about her family. I devoured books about boarding schools like Mallory Towers, The Chalet School and St. Clare's. I wished I could go away. Tia loved her family with a passion that was the strongest part of her. She knew who she was and where she came from. And she knew she was going back. Tia was just herself. I was a paper doll version of myself.

Accident prone

I was what Mummy called 'accident prone'. She made it sound like a personality trait. It is one I have kept into adulthood. The last two summers I have given myself concussion, once by banging my head on a hotel bed head and secondly by walking into a branch of a tree in my own garden. I shook up my brain and it didn't like it. As I left the house one morning I slammed the front door leaving my right index finger behind between the door and the jamb. The tip of my finger was severed and lay on the floor on the other side of the door to the rest of me. Toby was seventeen and a recently qualified Life Guard and that morning he had a rude awakening to be my first aider and hospital escort. He carefully wrapped my finger-tip in paper towels and ice. He carried my finger and the rest of me leaned on him as we made our way to the Accident and Emergency Department. Toby is great in an emergency because he stays calm and strong and gives the best hugs. The doctors managed to sew my finger back on so I still have all my digits although one is a bit bumpy. I had been on my way out of the house to a work event. My boss said she thought it was an extreme way of avoiding going on an away day. I am good at avoidance.

I fall up stairs and down. I have torn ligaments coming downstairs and going for a walk is often a dangerous occupation. When I am tired or upset my brain disconnects even more from my body and it is as if I cannot feel my feet. I can't count the times I have ended up flat on my face in car parks and outside buildings I am leaving. We go to the cinema with friends and come out in the dark and I trip and fall flat. I always go down hard because I never see it coming. Once I went to an AA meeting in a nearby town and as I left there I fell in the car park, sliding along the gravel and ripping the skin from my arm and knees. I had to sit in my car and cry before I could drive home. I'm sure that anyone passing must have thought I was drunk but I don't need any alcohol to fall over. I can come home covered in mud and bleeding from a trip to the corner shop. I am clumsy and I fall over my own feet. I drop things in the kitchen and burn myself on the oven. It is worse when I am tired. My spatial awareness is dodgy, and I struggle with left and right and putting lids on saucepans. We used to have a set of three pans that all looked the same but in different sizes. I always had to try a lid on all of them to find the right one. I struggle with alphabetising and organisation, with numbers and detail. I am a big picture girl, right brained and creative and I am good with words and images. I am skilled with people and groups because I learned to survey my environment in detail and observe everything. I always find out what the rules of the group are, unspoken and overt. I longed to be elegant and balanced. It took me longer than usual to learn to ride a bike, tell the time or tie my laces. I wasn't good at sports or the sports that you were supposed to do like tennis and netball. But I love yoga and Tai Chi and dancing and swimming in the ocean. I also love walking because I love to be outside but really I need a risk assessment and knee guards.

As a child, I fell over a lot and had permanently grazed knees and elbows, I fell into barbed wire fences, I slammed a car door shut on my fingers. The day my parents were trying to sell our house for our next move I got my head cut open on a metal swing in our garden. I had been sent to play outside whilst Mum showed a couple round the house. I was anxious. I stood behind the swing just pushing it backwards and forwards. I pushed it harder and harder, higher and higher it went. It was green metal. Solid and heavy. On an upswing it came back fast and I didn't move out of the way. The seat hit me square in the middle of my forehead and knocked me over. The pain made me cry out and when I brought my hands to my head blood was pouring down. I staggered into the kitchen like a child from The Omen. I was always being taken to the doctor or the hospital for minor injuries. Mum said I was 'accident prone'.

Once, in High School, a teacher said I looked like I might be able to run fast or be a good long jumper because I was tall. I felt flattered and excited. Maybe this was my chance to shine. I might be picked for a team. It didn't work. I can't run. My jumps were solid and I landed heavily and inelegantly and at a shorter distance than was acceptable. I wasn't usually the biggest kid in the class but I wasn't one of the girls who were the same size as her age. My clothes always had to come from the bigger section or Mum made them for me. I hated that. I decided to be the funny girl.

But underneath it all I was sensitive and desperate to be liked and loved. I had vivid dreams and nightmares. I was scared of the dark. I was terrified of death and dying. I didn't like to be left alone at night, I couldn't sleep without a light on.

Angel Delight

When I met my friend Susy I couldn't believe that she talked about being adopted. She could say it right out loud and in front of her mother. And her mother would say it too. "Susy is adopted, so we don't really look like each other". Susy's mother was a single parent in days where this seemed unusual in our village. She was divorced. She wore short skirts and tank tops and knee-high shiny patent leather boots. Dad referred to her as "a dolly bird". Mum wasn't too keen. I never told my Mum that Susy was adopted too, I don't know if she knew because she never mentioned it. That would have been nice. At Susy's house we ate 'Angel Delight'. It came in a packet and we were allowed to just make it ourselves. We ripped open the paper packet and tipped the intensely sweet smelling powder into a bowl then whisked it with milk. It set into a sort of glorious blancmange and we could eat it with a spoon straight from the bowl. Butterscotch was our favourite, and also banana or chocolate. As I write I can smell it and the taste is almost there on the back of my tongue. It was one of my favourite things. Susy's mum had darker skin than Susy and her hair was an amazing Afro. That was when she wasn't wearing her wigs. She seemed to have several of these. One day it would be long and blonde another day she would be a redhead with a 'perm'. She seemed impossibly glamorous. Susy was tall and athletic. She could run faster than anyone I knew. She was funny and we laughed all the time. I loved her rebellious streak and her air of freedom. We would lie in the long grass behind our house where the garden backed onto fields. A derelict army base remained there from World War II and we found old tin hats with holes in and clowned about with them on our heads even though bits of rusted metal would fall off into our hair. We made dens where we could hide and talk. Sometimes we held hands and we would lie in the sun with our arms around each other telling stories and watching the sky and the clouds roll by. Then Susy's mum got a new job somewhere else. When Susy told me she was leaving I felt like something really bad was going to happen. I didn't know what to say. Susy was laughing and telling me how she was moving to a new flat in the city and a new school and I felt bereft. It seemed like Susy didn't mind so I had to pretend it was all OK with me too. I smiled and said, 'Goodbye'. One week in the long summer holidays Susy was there and the next she had gone. When we went back to school in September she wasn't there. I missed her a lot.

Anger, childhood

I never knew what to do with my anger as a child so I kept it hidden.

I lived in a fantasy world in my head. I told myself stories. Everything was a substitute family. The grasses on the school fields, acorns and conkers on the ground. My dolls. The sets of plastic tumblers I played with at bath time from when I was a baby until nine or ten. The square set and the round set. I can still see them and remember the shape and feel of them in my hands and in the warm water with Mr Matey bubble bath. The dog would come in to the bathroom and eat the soap.

Every toy or game was divided into sets. I read and re-read books, losing myself in sagas with characters I loved like kin. The Chalet School, Mallory Towers, The Chronicles of Narnia, Ballet Shoes and The Secret Garden The Little House on the Prairie, What Katy Did, The Weird Stone of Brisingamen. Swallows and Amazons, Heidi and Little Women and so many more. I have a bookcase in my study with them all here behind me. A comfort blanket I have read them all over and over and I still do sometimes.

When I was a baby I had a real blanket too it was wool and I chewed it so it got smaller and smaller. Mum had to cut pieces off it as it disintegrated and nearly disappeared. Even now the smell of wet wool brings saliva to my mouth, I feel warm inside. I love it. Wet wool carpet or woollen coats. It's not so often now I get that scent because most fibres are manmade.

My youngest son loved his blanket too. He would go to sleep with it stuffed into his mouth. His started off white and beautiful made by a relative of my adoptive Mum's in Canada. He didn't like it when I washed it because 'It didn't smell right'.

Becoming beautiful

We are walking down the street, Mum and I. Mum is tall and imposing looking. She has blue eyes and her hair is dark brown. I don't know this yet but she dyes it that colour because she went grey early. She has it permed at the hairdressers and then she puts it up in curlers every night and wears a scarf over it to keep it nice. The curlers are fun to play with because they come in pastel colours, green and pink and white and blue and they clip together with little pieces of paper in between. It is a grown-up mysterious process that seems glamorous but I don't like the smell of the setting lotion. It tickles the back of my nose and makes me sneeze.

I am short because I am only seven and my hair is straight and a lighter brown colour. When I go to have my hair trimmed the hairdresser says my hair is 'fine' like a baby's. I think this is a good thing to have the way the hairdresser says it but Mum says she has 'thick' hair and that she is lucky. Mum has long slim legs with elegant ankles. I wouldn't know this but she tells me so quite often. Even when she is eighty she will say, "I have always had slim legs that look good in boots". For years my legs were too chunky to fit into boots. I have big calves and strong thighs. When I started going for reiki and shiatsu massage the therapist said to me, "You have strong legs". I had never thought of my body as strong before and it felt exciting and new. I can do yoga and swim.

As we walk a woman is coming towards us. We live in a quiet suburban town where people stop to say, 'Good morning' and to chat about the weather. The woman is wearing a red coat with a black velvet collar and she has a black hat which matches. I am looking at her because she is colourful and different to Mum who is wearing muted colours. The woman says, 'Hello' and looks at me. She smiles and says to Mum, "I love your daughter's eyes, they are so beautiful and that gorgeous chocolate brown. And such long eyelashes!"

No-one has ever said anything so astounding about me before. I feel myself blossom. I had no idea that my eyes were special. I look up at Mum, she is smiling but looks uncomfortable. I sense that she doesn't know what to say. Mum's eyes are blue and so are Dad's. My eyes are not like theirs.

Mum Margaret would say to me, 'You have such an interesting face. It's so expressive'. I want her to tell me I am beautiful. I didn't want to be a princess but I wanted to be her princess.

When I had my boys I knew that they were the most beautiful babies in the world. I marvelled at their perfection. Feeding them I spent hours gazing at their faces and feeling their tiny fingers clutch at my breast and burrowing deep into my heart. I saw myself reflected back in their beauty and how they surpassed me. I don't think Mum could see herself in my face because she wasn't there. I couldn't be her mirror and it was too hard for her to bear that. I grew up feeling plain because my face wasn't good enough to be beautiful it was just interesting.

No-one ever told me I was beautiful so I didn't believe it. When I met Teresa she told me all the time. She still does. Now I know that I am because she sees me that way and I believe her. She mirrored my beauty back to me.

CHAPTER 7 GETTING BY

When I became a teenager I started to notice something about myself that I didn't understand. I would have intense relationships. I fell in love or became attached hard and fast. Everything in me was connected to that person. And then I would panic and withdraw. It happened with my grandparents. I was closest to my Granda. I had always been his girl. I loved him. But as he got older and frailer I started to feel angry with him. He had the bedroom opposite mine and I would hear him cough. It was a horrible sound rattling and wet and he struggled to breathe. Mum told me it was because he had been 'gassed' in the War. She meant World War I when he was in the Red Cross Ambulance service and would carry injured and dying soldiers back from the front at Ypres and on The Somme. Granda had only one lung that worked because of the gas. He smoked Players No 6 and drank whisky every night so he could go to sleep. He never talked about the War and he would turn off any mention of it on the TV.

I used to stand up for him to my Dad. Dad wanted to watch War films like The Dambusters and Granda would get upset. I would shout at my Dad and tell him to turn it off. I could speak up for Granda. I have always been able to speak up for other people. Sometimes Mum and Dad would go out in the evening and I would sit with Granda and we would watch TV together. He would smoke his pipe and I loved the smell of the tobacco and the way he tamped it down in the bowl of the pipe. It would take him few puffs to get it going and then he would sit and smoke and we would settle in for the evening. I would get snacks from the kitchen and listen to him breathing.

Usually he would fall asleep by nine o'clock and sometimes his breathing would stop. I would hold my breath until he started again. Many times I thought he had died. I would be frozen in place on the blue sofa waiting, just waiting. I never told anyone how scared I was that I might be there when he died.

So cutting myself off from him made me feel horrible. I hated myself for being that way. I left home when I was eighteen and he died that same year. I rang my Mum from a cold phone box early one November morning because I hadn't been able to sleep. The red phone box smelt of piss and cigarettes and she told me he had died in the night. I felt sad and I felt guilty because I didn't think I had loved him enough.

Joe was seventeen and I was fifteen coming up sixteen and we spent every moment together. Everyone thought we are a couple. I loved him because he was funny and clever and kind and sweet and different. He was a rebel. He looked like a hobbit and he was a brilliant musician and lived with his Gran. We went to the same school and started to hang out together because we got the same bus every day. We recognised something in each other. For months we were inseparable. We went to the same church and youth group. We spent hours on the phone to each other. In the school holidays we were together all the time. We held hands and hugged. He had small hands and sensitive skin so in the winter they were often chapped and flaky. When he played the piano and sang he was transformed. One day we took the day off school and got the train to Manchester for his audition for a TV talent show. I was so proud of him when he played. We sat around for hours waiting for his turn to come. He didn't get chosen, but I knew he was going to be a star. The famous host was an asshole.

We were close for a couple of years and then the fear started. My body said, "No I can't do this, I can't be this, I have to run, to escape". There was no sexual relationship. We were just friends. I loved him so much but I couldn't be near him any more. I stopped taking his phone calls and I tried to avoid him at school. Our friends thought we had had a row. I had no idea what was going on with me so I couldn't explain it. I didn't want to hurt him but I did. It was horrible. Cut and run, fight or flight. I felt ashamed and scared and I hated myself. I kept trying to make it all right and to be friends again but I just couldn't do it. I knew he would be leaving soon because he was going off to university and I would lose him. I had a sneaky feeling that he might want more than I could give. Everyone thought we had broken up. So many people told me they were sorry. I didn't know what to say. I felt so sad that I didn't have the words and I'm still sorry that I made such a mess of it. Forgive me.

At eighteen I left home for university. It was the easiest way out. I couldn't wait to escape. I knew I would never want to live 'at home' again. I wanted a place to call a home of my own. I found it in a thousand bed-sits and house-shares and rooms. I have friends who still live in the village we grew up in. The roads we used to walk down now seem like a foreign land. I was always in the wrong place. People often ask, 'Where do you come from?" I don't know. The place I was born means nothing to me. I had no roots that connected me to a place. I have grown my own roots. My accent is a mixed up collection of northern midlands and people can't quite place it. I don't have an answer. I usually say, 'I moved around a lot" which is the truth. I envied people who had a connection to a piece of land.

I got rejected by two of the universities I applied to. I settled on a place as far away from home as I could imagine and still be in the same country. Dad drove me there in our family camper van. I had boxes of new stripy towels and bedding, saucepans and spoons and some tins of food. My clothes and books from a reading list and a new green jumper which I thought was cool. I had put on weight in the weeks before going away and my jeans felt too tight as I sat in the passenger seat on the long drive. I had been eating obsessively and secretly. Crackers with slabs of butter and cheese whenever I was in the house by myself. I bought chocolate and sweets in the newsagents along with cigarettes 'for my Granda'. I smoked cigarettes from a gold pack because I thought they looked sophisticated. The smokers were always the cool gang. It was like getting drunk. Being out of my own body was a relief. I was anxious but had no way to say it. My skin had broken out with little blisters all over my fingers which I scratched until they bled. That summer I had hay fever for the first time and my eyes streamed all summer. I cried all the time but it was an allergy.

1976.

I met a boy and decided that he was 'The One'. He was an artist
and I knew that because he had long hair and a beard. He looked like
a hippie and I thought he was sensitive and caring. He seemed to me
like a beautiful, liberal rebel but I was mistaken. Months later he
shaved off the beard and cut his hair. He had a weak chin and his
conventionality had just been hiding under the hair. He was a control
freak disguised as a wannabe missionary.

I met him on a beach near the retreat centre where I was working
for the summer again. I sat on a small stony beach on the island writing poetry and looking out at a pilgrim's trail and imagining the
Vikings and early Christians. I was ripe for a romance and filled with
a craving for someone to belong to. Getting ready to leave home
tipped me into his arms and then into bed.

Two weeks at that university were enough. It wasn't the place, it
was me. I needed a safety net and I thought I had one ready and waiting in my new boyfriend. I was anxious all the time and my nervous
system was on constant alert. I couldn't sleep and was smoking far
too many cigarettes. I tried to make friends and find a group I could
belong to but it didn't happen quickly enough. I needed something
immediately that would make me feel safe. One morning after another sleepless night I packed a bag and got on a train and several hours
later I arrived at the boyfriend's door. I sat outside in the hallway until
another boy took me in and made me cups of tea and fed me toast
and jam. Within a week I had signed up for the Sociology degree
there and found myself a bedsit near the park with a landlady who
insisted that all men left by 10 p.m. The sense of relief was enormous. I had found a way to belong and I didn't have to go home.

I persuaded the boyfriend to come with me to tell my parents. No
mobile phone, no email or text then. Once I left home I rarely saw
my parents alone. I took back-up. Friends, boyfriends then husbands,
kids, my wife. Anything to deflect the intensity of our disconnection.

I could no longer bear to manage my relationship with them alone. Food, alcohol and drugs had been a buffer when I lived with them, once I left home the food took over.

Island boy didn't last although we got engaged that first Christmas and I kept insisting to everyone that I was happy. I was caught up in the need to be needed. He was a little bit too controlling and when the relationship ended he cheated on me with another girl. He tried to tell me what to wear, objected when I had my hair permed and my ears pierced, didn't like me wearing make-up and wanted me to dress 'modestly'. Alarm bells were ringing even through my desire to be in a couple. He tried to persuade me to give all my possessions away and his mother once gave me an iron for a Christmas present. They had no idea who I was and I wasn't sure enough of myself to object. He asked for the teeny-weeny ring back when he dumped me. I still had sex with him a couple of times until he raped me with my skirt up over my head and I never told a soul because I was too embarrassed. After we split up he wrote to my parents asking them for money to help him to become a missionary. They didn't contribute as far as I know. God help the mission. I never let anyone control me like that again.

I lurched from relationship to relationship throughout my twenties, I was always in love within weeks of a break up. He was always 'the one'. My friend Janet always said that she imagined me married with several kids and a Labrador retriever piling everyone into an estate car. Earth mother and hippie. There was truth in that image but it was just one turn of the kaleidoscope. I was all or nothing in relationships as in life. I dived off the high board straight into the deep end. I always wanted my own family. I wanted a home and I didn't know what that was until I made them myself. Even now I have a tendency to want to move on from the place I feel safest. It is hard for me to fully invest because I expect people to go away and I expect to move on.

In my twenties I started working with children and young people and families. I loved being a social worker. It felt like my insides and outsides matched up for a while, and I had found my way home. I felt like I had found my people.

Social workers get a bad press. Sometimes they deserve it. But the social workers I have known have been brave and kind and work their socks off to try to do the right thing. They care about the kids and support and encourage the parents, and they care when they have to remove children from those parents because of abuse and neglect. I cared. But the toll it took was too much. I found myself in work that used me up and I could never find a way to put enough back in.

I loved to work with young people who were struggling, the more difficult and troubled the better. I knew I could listen and engage with them. 'Naughty' troubled boys would talk to me. I could hear their stories of abuse and neglect and pain and I wouldn't run away. For the young people I worked with I had no desire to leave them. I wanted them to all be safe.

I found my way into more therapeutic work as a social worker and counsellor in young people's mental health services and there it was possible to work with people towards healing. I loved all the jobs I had in social work for a while. I poured myself out in them and sometimes I felt the resonance of my own experience starting to knock on the door. I was in the fog of my adoption. I didn't know that there was a way out of the denial I was in about its impact on me because I was in denial that it mattered that much. Everyone around me seemed to think I was fine so I went along with that. I gave everything I could to keeping up that image. Marriage, kids, work and ambition and studying and learning more, being liked, being good at what I did. My authentic self was in there somewhere but she had a hard time surviving.

Thinkin' bout drugs and alcohol

As a teenager I had started to self medicate with alcohol and nicotine. Other drugs didn't appeal so much although I dabbled briefly. I am eternally grateful that I didn't take the slide down into the pills and poppers and heroin that other people I knew sank into.

Some of them died young, on motorbikes on dark winter nights speeding crazily through the country lanes where we lived. They were high on pursuing a feeling of connection, even of spirituality that was different from the boredom of just being ordinary. Some got into dark magic and that frightened me so I stayed away. But my addictions were enough to take me into oblivion every night. Sugar and alcohol are potent mix if what you want is to escape from your own brain. I learnt how to drink to knock me nicely into a woozy and warm state of well being. Some nights I went too far and drank enough to knock myself out. I would stagger my way home, usually supported by the boy I was then dating. A disreputable future alcoholic who had a reputation for being the bad boy of the village. I was so lacking in self esteem and confidence I would take any form of affection. And it really pissed off my mother.

I would do anything to get out of the house in an evening. I stole money and cigarettes from Granda's drawer in his bedroom. Not much, a couple of cigarettes here and couple of pounds there. I felt guilty because I loved him but it didn't stop me. I would hound my two best friends to come out. Landing on their doorsteps and persuading them 'just to come out for a walk'. Inevitably we would end up at the pub. There were two main pubs in our village. One was nearer to where we lived and was a big establishment, usually full of couples and young people from the village. Some of us had 18th birthday celebrations there, ignoring the quizzical looks of the bar staff who had been serving us for months beforehand. It was a relatively safe place and the popular 'nice' kids from school are usually in there too. I was slightly envious of their easy self confidence and assurance. I told myself they were boring and pathetic whilst flirting with their boyfriends and drinking more than they did.

The other pub was further away. This one was tucked away in the older part of the village. It was tiny and full of regulars. My way 'in' was through Disreputable Boyfriend. He was different to the school boys we generally hung around with who were busy studying for college or University. They went out on a Friday and a Saturday night and they were home by curfew of eleven or midnight for a special occasion. I had a curfew too. I just ignored it. He bought me drinks. We smoked and talked about life in our alcoholic haze. He kept me safe. He always got me home. Sometimes I fell over on the way and lay in the grass at the side of the road. I would wake up some time later and he would be sitting next to me waiting patiently. He would pull me up and make me walk on. The walk home should have taken us about 25 minutes. Often we left the pub at closing time, eleven o'clock and I didn't get to my front door until two or three in the morning. He could have just gone home. His house was across the road from the pub, but he never did. He looked after me.

There were other boys. I trod just on the side of safety by grace rather than intention. I was a mess and I was busy pressing a self-destruct button as hard as I could. As long as I got home eventually and I did my school work nothing was said. Inside the house it felt stultifying and death by boredom, outside I was a flakey chaotic wild child. At school when I went I did the work and passed the exams and I had friends. I had a different persona for every situation. I was trying to break through to find myself but I couldn't do it whilst I was there. Sex was the best way to stick two fingers up at my Mum. She found it impossible to talk about and pretended that everything was fine. I didn't want to have sex with any of them but I made it look as if I did so it kept her at bay. I just wanted another life.

A Family Tree

People told me their life stories in a queue at the supermarket or on the train. My face said, "You can talk to me". My body felt like it was saying something quite different but that didn't seem to get the message to my face.

It was in a social work class that I first learnt about Family Trees. The tutor used her own family as an example. It was obvious to me that her parents were her biological parents. "Now draw yours and then share it with the people at your table." My mind off to the races, anxiety flooded my system. I felt sick. What could I do? By this time in my twenties and with two children of my own drawing a family tree of my adopted family felt wrong. I felt like my family began and ended with me and my children and their father's side. Anything else felt like a lie that I didn't want to perpetuate. I didn't yet know anything about my birth family so my tree would have no branches just my small circle of attachment at the bottom of the page. I didn't know if I was ready to share my life in such a vulnerable place. I felt fear and anger and I wanted to cry, to run out of the room. Firstly I froze, then the urge to fight or flee switched on. Now I know that is a trauma response, then I was caught up in the adrenaline. I felt blindsided and ambushed with no safe place to run. Somehow I muddled my way through.

As an adoptee the family tree is just one of many questions that sneak up on us unexpectedly. Some of the others are:

"Do you have a history of cancer, strokes, high blood pressure, mental health problems in your immediate family?"

"How the hell would I know?" Do I tell him I am adopted? Or do I just say I don't know? Quick, quick, choose one. Answer her!

I still flip-flop between the answers.

"Who do you look like? Your Mum or your Dad? Or "Who are you most like?"

"It's complicated".

"Where were you born?" This question sneaks up on me. It might be in general chat in the pub or with friends. It might be a more formal question from some sort of government agency or a security question. The familiar anxiety kicks in. *What is the right answer? What did I say last time? I don't remember!* This leaves me in the position of not knowing the answers to my own security questions. Adoption makes life messy in the little things.

Being an adoptee and 'coming out' about it is often a big deal. This is especially true for my generation of adult adoptees from closed adoptions. A closed adoption was one where all contact and knowledge of our birth families was legally erased from us. We had no right to information and our adoptive parents were told that we were theirs as if we were a blank sheet of paper they could write their new family story upon. Often I had a feeling of being disloyal or of betrayal. That I was doing something wrong if I talked about being adopted. I always felt an obligation to portray my childhood as picture perfect. I knew they loved me but it's not about gratitude for the life I was given. To have that life I had one taken away first. There is a deep sense of something being missing. I didn't know anyone else who was adopted until I met my friend Susy when we were nine or ten. For years after she was the only person I'd ever talked to about being adopted. My way of crossing a bridge from acquaintance to friend was to tell them I was adopted. It was a test.

Teen Spirit

I was a teenage dreamer, someone who wanted to know the meaning of life. I was brought up to go to church and sent to Sunday school. My dad had been brought up in a very religious family where he was expected to go to church three times a day on a Sunday. He didn't want that for me. As I became a teenager, the staid Church of England that we did attend felt more and more alien to me. My friends' families were only occasional church-goers. One day the Vicar told me about a Gospel meeting just for young people in a different church. I persuaded my two best friends to go with me. The event was run by young men and women who all seemed to have long hair and beautiful faces. I thought I saw love there and the face of Jesus. I wanted to belong and this was a ready made family with acceptance on offer for the price of a leap of faith. There was emotion and love and joy and music. It felt like something joyful and exciting and emotional and somewhere my parents wouldn't go. It felt young and fresh and different, something of my own. It was love and peace and incense and a woman who talked about working on a Kibbutz in Israel. It was hugs and singing on a Sunday night in a little house. Sometimes there were twenty teenagers packed into a room after the church service. It was like a youth club but better. We sat on the floor and prayed and sang and talked about life and love and the world. The church was excited at the explosion of young people in its midst. I loved it and subsumed my self into belonging there until one day I just couldn't do it any more. Their values and mine were not the same but for a while I was all in. That is me all over. I am in or out. No half measures. I have to belong.

Getting Out

I survived those years between fifteen and eighteen somehow. My saving grace was having friends and leaving home. I took the easy route and went off to University. I picked one that was as far away as possible I thought this would prevent my parents from turning up at a moment's notice. I could be free. I had opted for a mixed Social Sciences degree because I had become enamoured of Sociology by doing an A level at a local college. My parents let me go there as long as I stayed on at school for my other subjects. The deal was that my Mum came with me and did the evening class too. Every Tuesday evening off we would go in her car to do our 'A' level together. I was mortified. I didn't get to know anyone in that class. But I loved sociology. I sucked up the ideas and politics and philosophies. My Dad would say, "I don't know where it's going to get you doing this." And Mum would say how interesting it was. Both of them annoyed me. I was a teenager after all.

My relationship with my parents was complicated. At eighteen I just wanted to get as far away from them as possible. The outside I presented to the world said two very different things. I was the nice girl and the rebel. I didn't have the language to talk about the demons inside. The depression. The secrecy of the adoption. My desperate need to know who I was and where I had come from. My insides felt like there was a gaping dark hole in there that I didn't know how to fill. Alcohol helped. So did bingeing. I just wanted to be wanted. I managed to steer a course just short of going the whole way. A couple of times it turned darker and I came a hair's breadth from it going bad.

With Mum my relationship was heading downhill. I was defiant

Dad Stephen and Kim

and rebellious and compliant and manipulative. Our relationship was messy and complicated and fraught with guilt and shame and trauma and resentment on both sides. The adoption fog stopped us from working out what was wrong and we couldn't talk about it. Most of the work that I have done in relation to adoption was after Mum died. We both tried our best with what we had. Our DNA was an issue, another adoption kick in the teeth. Nurture built our relationship and nature ate away at it from the inside. Mum would have liked shopping trips and being close, to able to hold each other, to phone each other every day and to be linked psychically as if the umbilical cord that never bound us was still in place. I would have loved that too but we couldn't make it work with each other.

The Stories She Told Me

We are visiting Mum's friend from church. Amy had just had her second child at home and she was in bed with the baby and the toddler was playing with building blocks on the floor. Amy was a rather vague pretty woman, slightly faded looking with curly hair and a sweet smile. Her little girl was a bundle of energy and I have been asked to babysit in the school holidays. I have had no experience of small children and no particular interest in them at fourteen. Mum thinks this is a good idea. I have no idea how to talk to Sally, the two year old, but I sit on the floor and help her to build a tower. Mum sits by Amy on a chair by the bed and the two women chat whilst I listen to them and try to look as if I have the patience to play with Sally.

"Oh it took for ever, and it's so painful isn't it, when it came time to push I just didn't know if I'd be able to get him out … Well Margaret, you know what it's like, you never forget do you! Men have no idea have they? They think that we forget the pain when it's over. I'm so glad he's here now. You'll know from when you had Fiona. What was that like? Did you have a hard time with her?"

I looked at Mum. She smiled, shifted slightly uncomfortably and changed the subject. The unspoken lie lay between us like a cold lump of porridge. She never acknowledged it. I realised that Amy didn't know I was adopted. I never knew who knew. It was like a

Tarot deck where you have to wait to see what the next one will reveal. Mum's fixed smile never wavered. I felt her shame and made it my own. It seeped through like blood from a wound covered in thin gauze. She wasn't part of the club so maybe I wasn't either. I recognised that she was ashamed that she hadn't given birth to me. I watched Amy with her new baby. I couldn't stop looking at her with him. She held him in the crook of her arm. He was less than two days old and he had dark curly hair that was slightly damp from being pressed against her. They looked like they were meant to be together. There was something different there. The look on Amy's face belied the words she spoke. She was gently dismissive about him saying he was a 'such a big lump and look at the size of his head! How did he manage to come out? What a bruiser he is,' she laughed. But her face shone with joy and pride and the way she held him was so tender. I could see she adored him and that they were just right together. It felt alien.

He had been born at home in the bed they were cuddled up in now. She fed him whilst we were there. She pulled her cotton nightie to one side and I was appalled and fascinated to see a breast appear as she deftly held her nipple and guided it into a searching mouth. The image burnt into my brain. It was my first experience of someone mothering a new baby. It felt foreign and magical and I wanted it. It unsettled me. I wish that Mum and I could have talked about it. I wish we could have talked about my mother and when I was born and what it was like. I wish we could have made some connection between the parts of me that were split between mothers. It was like I was two different babies and we didn't talk about one of them. That was the bad baby because she came from the bad mother. But in my mind she was a girl like me. And I think that's what terrified my Mum. She was always panicking about sex and drugs. She seemed to see me as someone I wasn't. At fourteen I was still compliant and a 'good' girl. I was only just beginning to try to push the boundaries.- To my Mum I was always an unknown quantity, potentially risky and unmanageable because of where I came from. Still that 'strong willed' child she had to control but not break.

The Stories I Heard

It is the nineteen seventies and I am at home with Mum in the kitchen. I can see that she wants to talk. We sit down with coffee at the big table. It feels cosy and safe. Mum gets some biscuits out. This is a treat. Whether we have nice food or not depends on whether Mum is on a diet. Apparently this week we can eat.

Mum says, " I've been talking to Deirdre "

Deirdre is in her fifties, a bit older than Mum and someone Mum looks up to I think. She goes to the Church and they go to the Women's Institute together.

"You know her daughter Christine, she is 15, just a bit older than you. Well, Deirdre is so upset because Christine is pregnant". Mum pauses for appropriate sounds of shock from me which are not forthcoming

"She has been going out with this boy for over a year and they all liked him very much but of course she can't keep the baby, they are just too young".

I am frozen to my seat.

'What is going to happen then?' I say.

"Oh she has gone to the city to a mother and baby home until she has had the baby and then of course the baby will go for adoption".

"But what does Christine want?" I say. "And what about him, what does he say?"

Mum looks at me as if I'm speaking a foreign language.

"Oh well it's very sad but she is too young to have a baby."

Hmmm well, apparently not.

"She needs to finish her education. Deirdre and her husband always hoped that Christine would go off to University so this means that maybe after the baby is born she can carry on with her life. Christine wanted to keep the baby of course but it's just not realistic.

The boyfriend has offered to marry her but she isn't 16 yet so her parents would have to give permission"

"Well, can't they do that?" I say.

"No, no this is wrong, can't you see? How dare they. This is cruel and wrong. Why are you telling me this anyway? Are we going to sit here and pretend that I am not that baby? That my mother is not that mother? Are you telling me what would happen if I were to get pregnant?"

I couldn't say any of it though. I got up from the table and went to my room. I had to get away from her.

"Let her keep her baby".

I could never look Deirdre in the face again. I hated her from that moment. I didn't yet know how to hate my mother. But I felt angry for my birth mother. I knew that somehow she was implicated in the story. It was a warning. "Don't be that girl."

Years later I asked about that Christine. She had married her boyfriend as soon as she could and then they had emigrated to Australia where they went on to have other children together. I hope that stolen baby found them again eventually.

Living in Sin

Another day and another kitchen sink drama.

Mum: " I was chatting to Aunty Molly on the phone last night."

She isn't really my Aunty. She is Mum's friend from college.

"Oh yeah, how is she? " I say politely but disinterestedly. I didn't like Aunty Molly very much. She told me I was getting to be a 'big girl' when I was eleven or twelve. She said that I should 'slim down'. She may have been right but it hurt and I didn't think it was any of her business. I have never found that telling someone they are fat is helpful.

"Oh she is so upset, she was just devastated"

"Why what's happened?"

"Well, George" (her younger son aged about 22) " has moved in with his girlfriend. They are Living Together".

I laugh, "Well, it is 1975 not 1955!"

"Yes but they aren't married and Aunty Molly is so upset".

"I don't understand why" I say, "That's ridiculous".

This is very daring. I am beginning to say what I think.

Mum talks for some time explaining why I am wrong and Aunty Molly is entitled to be so upset. I tune her out. I get the message. 'Don't upset your mother'.

My rage was building. Each story added an ember to the fires. It took me a few more years to be able to let it out. For now I turned it on myself. My rebel parts were getting activated. I was about to become a 'difficult teenager'.

I wish we could have worked through the messy misunderstandings and miscommunication in our relationship but I didn't know how. Why would I? It is expecting too much. I needed an advocate. I needed help. To clear up the brambles in the path before they turned into the thickets of thorns that tore us both to shreds.

CHAPTER 8 DYING FOR CONNECTION

It is August 2020 and I have just come home from two weeks holiday in Norfolk with my wife. Covid-19 had apparently come out of nowhere in March in the UK and all our lives changed in a million ways. My birth Mum Mary died in December 2019 pre-Covid and we were able to have her funeral and my sisters and birth mum made a plan of what to do with Mum's ashes. A few months later I had a phone call from one of my sisters. She told me that our Mum had left me something in her will. And I just felt shocked. I didn't know what to say. When she died and my sisters cleared out her flat I chose a couple of things that meant something special including a bronze hare that I love and so did she and he sits on our fireplace. My wife bought me a print of a painting of a hare for Christmas from the cafe we all ate in on the day we made her funeral arrangements.

I feel acknowledged and seen. The gift of being unexpectedly remembered. Re-member. To put back together. With memories we bring the past back to life.

Nana, Humbugs and Dying

When I was eleven my Nana, Mummy Margaret's mum, died. She and my Granda had lived with us since she had a stroke when I was nine. Nana was bed-ridden and didn't speak. She lay in bed and watched television and my Granda would sit with her most of the day except when he went to the club to play bowls or dominoes. I was nervous around Nana because I had never really got to know her and sometimes she made odd noises. She had to be fed liquid food like Farley's rusks mashed up with milk like a baby. Mummy was often stressed and unhappy and then everything in our house felt tense and awkward. One summer Mummy and Daddy and I went on holiday and Nana had some respite care. When we got home the tension in our house had ratcheted up. Mummy said, "I've cared for her all this time, and not one sore. And I leave her for two weeks and now she has bed-sores." After that home felt more fragile and wobbly. I worried that something bad was going to happen soon. Nana would shout out and cry and Mummy and Daddy argued. One Sunday Mummy cooked a chicken in the oven for dinner. The Pyrex dish the chicken was roasting in exploded in the oven and glass shards were everywhere in the kitchen. Mummy cried and Daddy shouted. I felt as if my parents were shattering under pressure.

One day in March I came home from school and Mummy said that my Nana had died. I was told to stay downstairs and keep out of the way. The atmosphere felt crackly and brittle. Daddy came home from work and said to me, "I'm going up to see your Nana to pay my respects." I didn't know what that meant. No-one I knew had ever died and we had never talked about what happened. Daddy said, "Have you been (sic) up to see her and said Goodbye yet?' I said, "No". "Come up now then with me, we will do it together " he said. I didn't want to go and see my dead Nana but I didn't know how to say, 'No' to my Daddy. In the bedroom Nana lay with her eyes open staring at the doorway. She looked strange and yellowy and her eyes scared me. Later that night Granda and I sat in the living room whilst the men in black took her away. Granda didn't speak and he looked sad and I thought maybe he was angry. Mummy was crying. I didn't cry because I didn't feel sad. Mostly I felt anxious.. The sight of my Nana staring at me from the bed haunted me.

Nana had dementia before the stroke and had often accused me of having stolen her handbag or eaten her sweets or having kicked her under the table. Nana loved humbugs. They were striped black and white sweets, hard on the outside but when you sucked them they became chewy on the inside. Humbugs were minty and sweet and they came in a white paper bag from the shop next door to my Nana's house. On the shelves were big glass bottles with sweets and toffees that the shopkeeper would weigh out for pennies. I loved the sherbet that came in a white paper cone with a twist at the bottom to stop the fine fizzy powder from falling out. I loved the sparkle of it on my tongue and the rainbow colours.

I was often just "She" to Nana, when she used my name it felt like an accusation. Mummy told me that Nana wasn't very well but I thought that she didn't like me. When the funeral happened I didn't go because my parents didn't want me to. So my ending of that relationship was in our house, not at a graveside. The graveside would have been easier. I had nightmares and started wetting the bed. I didn't want to go to school and kept having tummy aches and ear-aches and wanting to stay at home.

I remember our family doctor coming out to the house to see Nana not long before she died. I was home with another tummy ache. The doctor was young and interested in psychology. He sat by me and asked me how I was. I was a well-brought-up child so I said, "I'm very well thank you." He said, "Don't worry it won't be long until your Nana dies and then this will all be over". I felt ashamed.. *He must think I'm making it up, but I do have tummy ache..* And then when she died I wondered if it was my fault. Mummy kept crying and saying how much she missed her mother and that 'We never had a cross word'. Even then that seemed unlikely.

The vision of Nana's dead face haunted my dreams. For months I hated going upstairs, especially at night. I would look to see if she was there still lying on the bed and then dash into my bedroom and shut the door. When I got into bed I knew that she was still there on the other side.

Mummy's grief was an uncomfortable presence for months. One day though Mummy talked with me about death and dying. We lay on their bed together and she cuddled me and I let her, and she told me that it was normal to be sad. It did help because she noticed, but I wasn't sad. I was just scared.

Pete and Charlie

I struggled through my twenties. I was a contradiction in action. Emotionally fragile and messy with a mask of sparkle and perfor-mance thrown over me like glitter. I wasn't sure who I was or who I wanted to be when I grew up. I had identity issues but I didn't have the language to say so. Some therapy would have been useful if I had been a) American b) self aware and c) rich. I hated my adoptive parents and I loved them, we were bound together and I was desperate to get away. I didn't know how to navigate relationships with them or with anyone else so I was angry and compliant, rude and kind. I was caught up in intense relationships with men whilst unaware of my true sexual orientation. I thought love was expressed with gifts of money and food and I practiced self-love that way even when it turned to chalk-dust in my mouth. Mum and I would bond best over cake and shopping. I was lonely although I had friends. When relationships I had invested in ended I let them go as if they meant nothing to me.

I didn't know how to ask someone to stay. I had sexual relationships with men because it was a way to feel like I mattered. I searched for belonging in things and I wanted to be wanted. With sex I felt seen and unseen because the person who was there wasn't really me. I held up a mirror hoping to see myself reflected back but I didn't recognise my own reflection. I had no-one in my life who knew that I looked like them. I tried hard to be a good person, to be kind, to be a good friend. I was always there for other people when their lives were falling apart but I didn't know who to turn to when mine spiralled out of control. I had big ideas and I wanted to help people.

With a BA degree in sociology I started work in a new city in a hostel for homeless men. I loved all of their broken, messy, addictive craziness and I felt useful. I was surrounded by addiction, whilst deep in my own with food and later alcohol. The residents were often dirty and messy with poor physical and mental health from years of neglect and being invisible. Few of the men had friends or family connections outside their own small community. Loneliness was endemic but so was loyalty and a dark vein of humour ran through every day's interactions. The small hedge outside our hostel was a hiding place for various bottles of cider or cheap wine. I learnt about life in a way that I had never known before. I learnt to give and to listen and to do things for other people. I loved them. Several of the residents died whilst I worked there. One died whilst I was with him. This was my second death, but now I was an adult if only just.

Peter was tiny and wizened like a walnut. At nearly eighty he had survived far longer than was usual. He had been living on the streets for many years before he had made his home with us. He looked like a friendly goblin and had a big grin, the bluest eyes and not very many teeth. When he smiled his sweetness and kindness shone out. He was a long established alcoholic of the well pickled variety but usually managed to stay just on the side of sober enough not to be evicted. Booze wasn't allowed on the premises but interesting combinations of alcohol were created including a lethal concoction made from home-distilled boot polish or meths. Peter was one of those drinkers. Every summer when the warm breeze tickled his whiskers Peter would decide it was time to go for a wander and he would disappear for several weeks. He never said goodbye — one day he wouldn't be there for breakfast and we would miss him for a while until he walked back in again as if he had just popped out for a roll-up.

Peter died suddenly one Sunday evening. I had gone to find him when he didn't turn up for dinner. He never liked to miss a meal. I heard a strange noise and heard a thud and found Peter collapsed on the bathroom floor. He had had a massive stroke. I held his hand and sat beside him whilst we waited for the ambulance. His hand was little in mine. His skin was so dry and a bit flaky but it still felt warm. He squeezed my fingers and I was conscious of how small he seemed. He didn't seem afraid. His blue eyes twinkled at me and he smiled when I squeezed his hand. He died in a breath that just didn't start again. Peter had left the building. He gave me a gift when he went. I saw the difference between living and dying. And I stopped being afraid of death. Being with Peter in that moment of transition was a privilege.

Most of the men were unable to read or write. Some of them had had wives and families in the past. All of them had had mothers and fathers somewhere. I felt drawn to them because of their fierce independence and their humility. Some had worked and owned houses. Pat was reputedly an ex-tailor who had worked in some of the top establishments in London. He mended everyones trousers and could sew an invisible hem.

John was with us because he had had a mental breakdown and lost his home. He had a psychotic episode where he jumped out of dustbins naked and upset his neighbours. Before coming to live at the hostel he had been hospitalised for years. Most of his time with us he stayed completely silent. His aura of depression was a grey overcoat that swamped his personality. John was slow in walking and moving, sedated to extreme by the medication he was prescribed. The treatment then was fairly brutal. One day John woke up like Sleeping Beauty and he started talking. He talked and talked and talked and just couldn't seem to stop. I didn't understand what was happening. John's mood swings continued until a new doctor began to take an interest.

Charlie was Polish and had fled the Nazis as a refugee in World War II, travelling across Europe by foot. He had no family left living and he loved to talk. He was diagnosed with terminal cancer. One day at work he presented me with a beautiful tortoiseshell kitten who he said had come in through his ground floor window. He told me to take her home and look after her so I did. Not long after, he died. We were the nearest thing to family for Charlie when he went. I kept the cat until she died years later. I called her Freya because she came in the window on a Friday.

I learnt in that job that I had empathy and people would talk to me. I learnt that I had an ability to relate to people and to love them. I also learnt to take on too much, to give until I was empty and I had no idea how to fill the reserves up that I needed. I threw everything of me into the work and outside of it I was drowning in my own addiction and despair and loneliness. I had started to learn to build a shell around myself called professionalism. I learnt to put my feelings into boxes, or rather I honed that skill. I was authentic and false. My authentic self was emerging as I found what I truly loved but my false self held me back as I drowned out the voice that wanted to shout out what I had lost.

Those men taught me that death was just an ending and I saw how it could be peaceful and profound and sacred. I discovered that the shell that was left was nothing to fear. The spirit was the essence of the person and that had flown freely on. Peter and Charlie taught me that death was a passing place, a doorway they just stepped through.

Dog Food, Dementia and Loving What Is

The last two years of Mum Margaret's life were challenging for everyone. She developed vascular dementia slowly. Sometimes it was obvious and at other times it was only when another bit dropped off the edge of her abilities. Her confusion and delusions reached a point of apparent psychosis very quickly. I learnt to recognise it happening. There was a look in her eyes. She disappeared and I saw this stranger looking out. It was chilling. And it terrified me because sometimes I thought that I was seeing how she really felt about me.

When it started happening I became the target for her rage and frustration. She didn't trust me. Several times she nearly called the police on me for 'stealing the dog' or the dog food. She thought I was trying to poison her and that the water system had been poisoned. She believed that people were in the house and walking round above her at night when she was on her own. We got used to phone calls at all times of night and day. She would leave messages arguing with the answering machine for "stopping me talking to my daughter". Sometimes the calls came from neighbours who believed Mum when she said I never visited or didn't do anything to help her. At the time I was often visiting three times a day. Sometimes and then more frequently it was the emergency services in response to her red call button being pressed. We made a lot of visits to hospitals and outpatient appointments including geriatricians and psychiatry. Social Services got involved. Eventually after another nasty fall she was kept in hospital and after a few weeks we managed to secure her a place in residential care whilst she was assessed for her ability to manage at home. We knew it didn't work to have her live with us. We had tried it briefly after another late evening call from a tearful and scared Mum but she just got angry and difficult and I knew our relationship wouldn't sustain her living with us. I couldn't have done it.

Julia and newborn Toby

CHAPTER 9 MOTHERHOOD AND BECOMING ME.

It is the autumn of 1983 and I long to have a baby. I shouldn't have married my first husband but I had convinced myself it would work. I wanted to be safe and 'settle down.' *Note to self: I shouldn't have married 'husbands' at all.* More than anything I wanted to belong. I thought marriage and a baby would fix me. I felt lost and lonely and sad most of the time on the inside but I appeared fine on the outside.

I was working as a teacher in a college but I had a longing for something different. I thought maybe I could be a social worker and after a few false starts I found a job that felt like it fitted like a glove. I was hard-working and passionate and committed to fighting for the best for the families I worked with. I was good at my job because I cared. On the outside I was functioning and I had a foot on the ladder of living an authentic life.

Inside though I was still grieving the loss of the baby that I let go. It was a physical yearning for replacement. I hadn't known for sure who the father was and I knew that adoption was never going to be an option for any baby of mine. My body was grieving. Every month when my period came I was sad and disappointed. Sex was just a way to get pregnant. My marriage was a disaster and neither of us had a clue what was happening. The adoption fog was wearing thinner and thinner and I felt angry all the time. I wanted to smash and break and crash and burn. I needed the sound. I thought of using that glass to cut myself open but the thought was enough to bring me back from the edge. I kept going by working hard, drinking wine, smoking to excess and running away to my girlfriends. When I was with them I felt safe. Especially the mothers. They taught me how to be mothered so I could feel it. I learnt from those friends how to be a mother to my own children.

I see much better now how my attachment and abandonment issues affect me. I find endings hard. I'm most likely to make them happen if I see them coming because I can't stand the transition and the 'in between' feelings. I leave groups I have been part of easily. Sometimes I feel guilty about leaving and I worry that other people

Julia and Toby 2018

are angry with me for 'breaking up' the group. I often take on responsibility for other people's feelings. I am a mediator and a caretaker in many situations. It is the role I most naturally gravitate to. I do it in my family, between the children, between the adults. I try and explain people to each other and smooth out the connections. I find conflict difficult and I have a Brownie-Guide badge in Avoidance.

When my first son, Toby, was born in 1984 I was catapulted into new feelings. A fierce love and the overwhelming need to protect him. I didn't know much about attachment but direct visceral experience taught me what it felt like. I could see what I had missed.. I will never forget the feeling of holding him. The scent of his round, hard head and the softness of his skin and his sight of his dark hair. His eyes were dark blue and he gazed at me with an intensity that reached into my heart and squeezed it tight. The midwife said his eyes would change colour and probably be brown like mine. And they are.

One day in school, in my early teens, the Human Biology lesson was about eye colour. The teacher explained how it was impossible for two blue eyed parents to have a brown eyed baby. One of my parents at least had to have brown eyes. I remember tingling all over. I felt hot and cold at the same time. I already knew I was adopted, it wasn't new information. But here was a tiny piece of the jigsaw puzzle handed to me in a lesson. Somewhere out there were people who looked like me. Even if it was just the colour of their eyes.

I was fascinated by other people's families. I studied them constantly looking for family resemblance. Sometimes people said to me that I looked like my Granny, my adoptive Dad's mother. We were the most alike in colouring in my adoptive family. She was much shorter than me but she had brown eyes and dark skin like me. We might have been related, but I knew we weren't.

When I was pregnant with my second son I started to bleed after my first scan at 16 weeks. I had gone back to work and realised I was bleeding so my boss drove me to the Doctor's office and waited until my husband arrived. The doctor was unsympathetic. He said, 'Oh well you are probably having a miscarriage. There is no point me examining you because I could just make it worse. Go home but you will probably lose the baby". I was by myself in his office. I came out and started to cry and scream. The receptionist looked shocked and I was crying and trying to explain and say, "I can't believe he just told me that". We went home and rang for the midwife and she came and listened for the heartbeat and reassured me. I had to stay home and stay off work. I knew it meant I could lose the baby. I was at home or in hospital for the rest of that pregnancy. At the same time, we moved house. A couple of months later my boss was visiting me at home. He was a good friend as well as my boss and we were talking about work when I got up to go to the bathroom. As I stood up I felt blood gush between my legs and I had to sit down. He rang for an ambulance and got hold of my husband again. My boss friend came with me to the hospital. I thought I was losing the baby this time for sure. I was about 5 months pregnant by now but still too early to have the baby. At the hospital the nurses and doctors were efficient and kind. They said, "Your husband can come in with you". I laughed and said, 'Oh he's not my husband". "That's Ok, " they said, "your partner can come in." "No, my husband's coming, but this is my friend". There was a raised eyebrow or two but later when I was in a bed on a ward for a few weeks my friend the boss would come and visit me in an afternoon and then my husband would come after work in the evening. It made us laugh but we were all best friends. Later boss friend would help me in the searching for my birth family. He was the person who spoke to my birth mum first. He helped me to write a letter to my half sister when I had found her.

In the hospital I had a scan and they examined me and admitted me. I was told I had placenta praevia and had to stay in bed maybe until the baby was born. If nothing changed I might have to have a caesarean section. But baby number two stayed put. We hung on to each other. I wasn't going to let him go if I could help it. The worst part was not being able to be at home with my first son. He was there coming up to four, the same age that I was when my Mum went into hospital in London and I was sent away. I was frantic for him. I felt like I was being torn in two. But I was adamant that he wasn't going anywhere. My parents offered to take him and look after him but I wanted him to stay at home. I knew he had to see me every day. My husband and friend who lived down our street brought him to visit and we made it work. I persuaded the obstetrician that I would not move a muscle without permission and I was allowed home. We moved house during that pregnancy and I didn't do a thing. I hired a removal firm to pack us up and I sat on my hands. I had been warned that if nothing changed I would have to go in to hospital at 34 weeks and stay there until I had the baby. I was determined that I would at least be at home until then.

I felt exhausted and unwell for weeks and plagued with nightmares of bleeding out and my baby swimming away in a red sticky sea whilst I tried to claw him back. I would wake gasping for breath and patting the bed to try to find him.

Two days before my twenty-eight week scan I had a dream that the baby turned around. When I woke up in the morning I knew I felt different. I felt well. I didn't dare hope too much but I trusted my inner knowing. When I went for the scan I learnt that the placenta had shifted and I would be safe to have my baby vaginally.

A few weeks later Jonathan was born safely, beautiful and healthy and weighing 8 lbs and 3 ozs. I watched his father hold him and saw his face transform with love. I had the baby blues after his birth. I think the trauma of nearly losing him made it hard for me to trust my feelings but I held on and cuddled him and fed him and cried and his sweetness and beauty seeped into me and we bonded. As parents we navigated parenting and step-parenting with two children. My parents would come down and help but our relationship was tense. Mum believed in routine and bottle feeding and I was a passionate about breast feeding which meant I spent most of my day with a baby attached. Mum never experienced pregnancy or birth and those early weeks and months of motherhood and it must have all seemed intense and messy and strange. She would say, 'You are a natural mother' and I felt both proud and uncomfortable at the compliment. Dad would get embarrassed when I whipped my top up to attach a baby to the breast. I wanted someone to look after me and mother me whilst I was learning to be a mum to two children but I didn't trust her enough to do that for me. Mum told me that when I was a baby she had potty trained me from a few months old. Nothing she said to me about mothering made sense to me.

How to have a baby

Mum was a good 'Nana' but she found me having babies hard. My third child was due sometime at the end of December 1992. We had invited Mum and Dad to stay for Christmas. Now I wonder why we did that. I kept trying to do 'the right thing'. In this case the right thing being what I thought made other people happy. It was a big mistake. My determination to be the good girl meant we were all upset. The plan in my head was for them to arrive on Christmas Eve and then to depart gratefully, full of turkey and stuffing sometime just after Boxing Day. The problem was that plan was *only* in my head. This baby was to be born at home. On Christmas Eve, my midwife came to visit and announced that I was 'fully engaged' and that the head was down. A Christmas baby became a real and worrying possibility. I decided that my legs would stay firmly crossed and no baby was coming out until my parents had left. I didn't share this plan either. Boxing Day came and no-one moved from the comfort of turkey sandwiches and endless cups of tea. The Christmas cake was cut. Mum and Dad seemed to be settling in for the long haul. I was getting worried. 30 December came and went. My blood pressure was going up. Something would have to be done. I delegated the husband to the task, which he duly carried out over breakfast. "We just wondered when you were setting off home?" He enquired politely.

Tumbleweed rolled across the living room. Words were said. Bad words. Mum and Dad departed in high dudgeon. I had a lie down and sent the husband to go and buy an answering machine to screen calls.

Ben arrived safely as I knelt by the bedside on the second day of January. A peaceful home birth. My friend Jane took the older two children out whilst I was in labour. My coccyx cracked a little as he came out, all eleven pounds and two ounces of him. I heard it crack but didn't know what had happened until a couple of days later. It still catches when I sit on it on my yoga mat or on a floor. He was perfect. Beautiful and loved. I drank tea on the sofa and held him and his brothers came home and met him for the first time. A couple of days later Mum and Dad came to visit and meet their new grandchild.

Nothing was said.

Hindsight is a wonderful thing. I see Mum's insecurity. I see how my whole life the narrative was 'Don't upset your mother' and then I did it anyway by default. I also see how I was unable to set any boundaries or to state what I needed calmly. Our relationship was as messed up as my attachment. Mum was caught up in her shame about infertility and guilt at having left me when I was three. Mum later confessed her anxiety at being present when I gave birth We could have made life so much simpler for ourselves if we had both been able to be honest instead of making assumptions. Nothing was ever resolved.

"When one has been traumatized at the beginning of life, there is often very little awareness that coping behaviors are a result of that trauma, rather than indigenous aspects of the person."
— *Nancy Verrier*

Truth teller

Ironically, what matters most to me is to find the truth. Finding what matters to me made me feel real and finally I was able to sit in my own body and just breathe. When I can step out of my own ego and insecurity, when I can put aside shame and fear and all the little irritations and bitternesses that crop up during an ordinary day, then I can breathe and be grateful. Being adopted gives me an awareness of identity and belonging. I was stripped of the assumptions that other children make about their own place in the world. I knew that I came into this family by myself. There was always something significant in knowing that my biology was not the same as the family I grew up

L-R: Son Jonathan, Mum Margaret/Nana, Toby holding newborn Ben

with. There was no physical connection that meant I knew that when someone says, "You look like your Mum," there is a sense of right-ness about that statement.

A couple of years ago one of my adult sons told me how his brother used to tease and make fun of him when he was young and that one of his weapons of choice was to tell his younger brother that he was adopted. Younger son said that he almost believed it but then all he had to do was look at me and his oldest brother and see the family resemblance and he just knew it wasn't true. I envied that.

Babies

Loving and bonding are not the same thing. Gratitude doesn't ce-ment broken back together.

Phrases like "You were lucky" or "Be grateful you had lovely parents" are silencing. Silence is for secrets, and most secrets are full of shame. Shame tells us not that we have done wrong but that we *are* wrong. Shame says, "I am bad". Being adopted meant that someone gave me away. The reasons for that are immaterial to the wounded child, to the baby me who was left. I knew that being given away meant there must be something wrong with me. *How bad do you have to be to be given away as a baby?*

Taking a baby away from a mother is an act of violence. Choice is only possible for someone with power. A mother's choices may be limited by age, disability, skin colour, poverty or the conventions of society at the time. A baby needs its mother to thrive. The smell of her body, the feel of her skin, the touch of her hands. The baby already knows and is familiar with the tone and sound of her voice from being in the womb for nine months. Wherever that baby goes next, no matter how kind or wonderful her next carer or mother is, they are not the mother she belonged to in the beginning.

If you adopt a baby or a child you can be their parent. You can love them and give them a wonderful life with you and your family. But you are transplanting that seedling. Be gentle. Recognise the trauma. Seek out those who have been there before you. Listen to the voices of adult adoptees. They will show you how to help your child know who they are. Recognise that adoption is trauma. Accept it and live with it and then you will be able to give your child the understanding and compassion and knowledge that they are not wrong, not out of place but a beautiful human being who has the gift of knowing where they came from and that they belong because they are themselves.

You will be the mother who loves her and cares for her and stays up at night when she comes home late. But there is a difference. The bond is different. The baby is like the ugly duckling in the swan's nest. There will be discrepancies and moments of disconnection, moments when you don't understand each other. The mirroring has to be learnt. When that bond between the birth mother and child is broken the child can't just be transplanted onto another mother without any feeling of dissonance. The glue that will bind you together is real and made up of every moment of blood, sweat and tears that you go through in your parenting journey but there is a fragility to the bond that the adoptee recognises.

The search for identity is about finding that lost bond, the search for self.

You won't love me. You will leave me. I will be kicked out of the family. I am the cuckoo in the nest or the ugly duckling of my respective families.

I am ungrateful. Selfish and narcissistic.

I go in and out of the fog, it hurts my brain

Having my own babies made me angry with my mother for giving me away. How could she?

TV programmes that re-unite adoptees and birth parents are sanitised, sweetened fairy tales and I love them and hate them. I want the happily ever-after as much as the next abandoned baby. There is another story under the story and the dark threads are necessary to show up the light.

I feel everybody else's feelings. Sometimes I feel other people's feelings much more than I feel my own. I grew up as an only child surrounded by adults who I watched for every clue. I thought I hid my own feelings because they didn't seem to be noticed. My face however gives me away. My kids always know. So does my wife. I was the only one who didn't.

I asked Teresa, "What do you notice most about me being adopted?' She said, "It's not obvious because you are so good at pretending to everyone that you are okay. You are adept at changing with the situation. But it comes out in your anxiety and your obsessions and your generally being unsettled. You are brilliant at covering it up but because I know you I see it". The people who know me, see me. That is interesting to me.

I became a social worker in 1985. It seemed I fell into it almost by accident. I worked in children's services for more than twenty years, dealing with child protection and abuse cases, adoption and life story

Toby, Jon, Ben and Joe c.1997

work and therapeutic social work with kids in care. I trained as a
therapist and counsellor and added those skills and worked with children, young people and families in a specialist service for mental
health work. There I did family therapy and individual work with
young people and I managed teams delivering the services.

My own adoption experiences, depression and mental heath issues
and my struggles with food addiction and weight stayed firmly tucked
into the bottom of my bag where I hid them from view — mine as
well as the world's. Of course these issues had an uncomfortable and
annoying tendency to leak everywhere. I'm quite sure that many of
the people I worked with, never mind my fabulous and insightful colleagues, were perfectly well aware of my flawed-ness. It's taken a lifetime so far to understand my own demons, recognise them and then
be brave enough and lucky enough to be blessed with loving friends
or families or networks that have helped me heal. I have been in recovery programmes in groups in church halls, read self-help books or
websites, done therapy and counselling, practiced meditation and
yoga, spirituality and politics and I tried to change the world and save
the planet in my own disorganised way. I am glad that I reached the
utter bottom of brokenness more than once and I knew there was no
way out except by surrender and hope.

Four boys Joe, Jon, Toby and Ben (L-R) 1994

Parallel lives
Parallel lives
Parallel lines
Will we join again at infinity?
Searching for love we do our best
Coming into the light one soul
At a time we connect
Parent and child
Sisters, brothers, cousins
Wives and husbands and lovers
And friends
Weddings and births and deaths
Sex and love

Joy and pain
Intimacy and disconnection

I love you, love me, love you, love me, love you, ad infinitum, for ever and ever and ever, on and on and on and on…. Connecting… in parallel lives.

How to be a mother

My friend Sara taught me how to be a mother. I met her on a course I took at a University. She had had to bring her small daughter in with her to a lecture because she had no childcare that day. Nicole sat and coloured in whilst we talked. She was a dark haired and beautiful child with an air of self containment and seriousness. Sara was petite and strong and dressed in soft colours. She had a wide smile and an intensity in her attention that I noticed. She was a bit older than the eighteen-year-old me who was in the first weeks of newfound independence. I liked her immediately but we didn't really get to know each other until much later. Our lives were different. She was married and lived in a house in a village in the countryside. I lived in a bedsit in the city with four other women and a landlady who watched our every move. Sara seemed like a grown up to my scattered and fragile self. I was a student with a boyfriend who was doing an art degree. I was deep into a hippie look, all long skirts and Jesus sandals. I walked everywhere. She had a car and could drive. We bonded over cigarettes, women's studies and music. We drank wine and talked politics of Marx and Durkheim and Women's Liberation. I wanted to be her and she was the mother I hadn't had and the one I wanted to be. She was beautiful, clever and sharp witted. She read everything and we could talk for hours about anything. I loved her and I imagined we would always be friends. She had two more children during the years we were friends. We spent all our time together or talking on the phone. I helped with the children and I learnt how to cuddle and speak endearments, how to play with them and talk to them. I learnt from her patience and openness. She was my best friend and the sister I hadn't had. I lived with her and her husband for a few months later on. Her children felt like my family. I imagined they would always be in my life. I would be at their weddings and when they went to High School.

My best days then were with Sara. We would go swimming with the kids in the Peak District and take them for picnics in the summer and sledging in the winter. She taught me how to make snow angels and we stood outside her house in the country lanes one cold January day with snow drifts six feet high and fell back wards laughing. We sat by a stream in the woods and dangled our toes in the cool water. We ate homemade bread and cheese and drank wine and smoked cigarettes surreptitiously when the children weren't looking. We listened to Leonard Cohen and Bob Dylan and I learnt to be a real person with her. I felt like she was another part of my soul.

She understood me. Or so I believed. We sat in her house in front of the log fire, the dog at our feet and the children around. When her youngest was born I spent hours walking her up and down when she wouldn't settle and my friend was struggling with post-natal depression.

When husband number two came along Sara went away. She wouldn't stay around. She dumped me like a hot potato burning her fingers. It crucified me. She blamed me for being inattentive and unavailable. I thought that she maybe had a point and I said I was so sorry and promised to do better. I begged. I wrote letters. My heart broke into a million shattered pieces and I bled internally haemorrhaging grief whilst outwardly behaving as if nothing had changed. She wouldn't answer my calls. I wrote letters again. This was before the advent of email and social media. If we had been on facebook she would have blocked me.

Years later we tried to reconnect. Several times she agreed to meet me and then cancelled. Once I was at the theatre with husband number two and I saw her across the aisle. Our eyes met, but she turned away. At the interval I tried to find her but she was nowhere to be seen. I stood in our garden that night smoking a cigarette, and shaking.

It took me years to understand that it was a bereavement. That I had loved her and lost her. I got through it by keeping it inside. I didn't have the words.

Once she contacted me and we met a couple of times. Our lives had changed. We struggled to make the connection. She wasn't surprised to hear that I was gay, it made sense she said. But our relationship was just love. She taught me to become the mother I am. I loved her for that.

Pregnancy and Children

In my early twenties I had become unexpectedly pregnant in messy circumstances. They were messy because I was. I didn't carry on with that pregnancy. I was completely unprepared for motherhood. I didn't even know if I wanted to have children at all. I had no idea what I was doing with my life. I'd just ended a relationship with a boy I loved but had no sexual feelings for and I had been throwing myself into experimenting with sex as if I could find out what was wrong with me. I didn't find that out, I just got pregnant. A small collection of cells implanted in my womb did not make me into a mother. But the hormone surge after and the grieving of the loss started me on that path. There is a psychological state called 're-placement baby syndrome'. Taking a baby away from its mother creates a deep need to replace that baby. I had a physical yearning as well as an emotional drive to have a baby. For me adoption was never an option. I might still have been in in the fog but at least I knew that.

I felt guilty for my messiness and getting drunk on cheap wine every night just turned into me ineffectively stalking my ex-boyfriend. I would hover outside his flat hoping to see him, then walk home alone in the early hours of the morning across the city. The next night I would do the same again. I was thin for a while as alcohol had temporarily replaced food in the addiction stakes and nicotine was a close second. I flirted with trying to feel better through a fairly toxic mix of church, sex and feminism and eventually I moved cities, jobs and my life to have a fresh start. The church grated on me more and more. The language was archaic and the hierarchy was patriarchal. It didn't feel like a safe place.

Within a year I was desperate for children. I got married to my first husband. The urge for children felt essential and primal. I wanted babies that came from my body. I needed a genetic connection. Being pregnant felt like the best times in my life. I adored it. I felt incredible, satisfied and whole. My urge to binge disappeared entirely whilst I was pregnant. I stopped smoking, went off caffeine and took care of my body with those babies inside her.

My first child was born in 1984. I had felt so attuned to the baby growing inside me. I loved feeling him move, from that first flutter like butterfly wings, to the sense of pushing and turning as an arm or leg or bottom pressed outwards through the skin on my belly. The sensation of knowing this baby inside of me was growing and becoming. On the night after my first son was born I lay in bed in the hospital with him in a cot beside me. He was dressed in a soft cotton blue gown that the ward provided and wrapped in a blanket burrito to lie on his side. I was high on the after effects of birth and adrenaline, and he was awake too. His round face with the slight sun tan of baby jaundice, his dark eyes met my gaze with a serious concentration. That was the moment I first fell in love. Irrevocably, indisputably and for ever. I knew him in my soul. From that moment we were bound together. He was mine and I was his. That moment my life began again. My identity shifted as if my whole life was shifted apart and back again into its rightful places. I had a new identity, one that I could claim as mine. I belonged. We were both exactly where we were meant to be, the stars had aligned and we had come together. From that moment on, nothing else would really matter. He looked like me. He always has. It healed me. Three more sons, three more moments of belonging. They saved me from myself.

I found my meaning in being a mother but I wasn't perfect. I was caught up in my own messy life and a lack of awareness of who I was in any other way. Two things saved me and crucified me at the same time — being a mother and becoming a social worker. Both felt like vocations, a calling to be who I was meant to be. I didn't know what I really wanted until it found me.

My kids look like me. There is a clear family resemblance when you see us all together. They have inherited physical characteristics like my clumsiness, and emotional traits like depression and addictive tendencies. We understand each other, there is a shared language and knowing how the others tick. When my son was born suddenly I had a blood relative. He came from me. We shared our DNA and our genetic heritage.

I wasn't always great at either but I put my heart and soul into both. I didn't always get it right but I tried my damnedest. I agonised over conversations and decisions, made commitments and broke them but I always tried to tell the truth and be honest. I had a temper and some rage issues. I smacked and shouted and apologised and cried. I drank too much sometimes and smoked too much a lot of the time. I argued with their fathers and then I left and broke up the family home and broke all of our hearts for a while.

Little by little I had to put myself back together and learn to be the Mum I wanted most to be to them. One who told them the truth about who she was. One who did her best to be kind and compassionate. One who tried to teach them to be the best version of themselves they could be. One who was always there for them no matter what.

The trouble was I didn't always know what the truth was. And I didn't know how to be honest when I didn't know what I felt. In relation to my children I never had any doubts. I loved them passionately and unreasonably. I understood what it meant to know that you would die or kill for them. I was a Tiger Mum and I still am. I will fight for them, stand up for them and go down for them. I think they know that. Sometimes that has left me broken and bleeding on the floor. Sometimes it has got me into trouble. Sometimes the co-dependence has been something I have had to work on day-by-day, moment-by-moment, bank loan-by-bank loan, relationship-by-relationship. I didn't always know how to say "No".

Transitioning from my role as the mother of children into a mother of adults has been challenging for me and I'm sure for them. I never thought I would experience 'empty nesting'. I thought I was living a busy fulfilling life of my own with work and relationships and interests but what I didn't see was how much my identity had been founded on that role for myself of being a mother. It felt fundamental. And it was hard to start to unpack that and recognise the loss whilst knowing I had to find my own essential identity under all that.

CHAPTER 10 HIDE AND SEEK, SEARCH AND FIND

I am sixteen or seventeen and Dad and I are in the car. We are heading towards London and I am excited. London is so full of life and a world away from our village. London is diverse and colourful and trendy. Fashion and art and life and colour. I say, "Was I born in London?" I take my chance because I know Mum would shut me down. He waits a few seconds and then he says, "Yes, I think you were". "I thought I was" I say. The conversation goes no further. He is embarrassed and I know where his loyalties lie. They are always with Mum. She always comes first. I cradle this secret knowledge to me. It is a treasure I hoard and polish and take out to look at and imagine. *I am a Londoner.* And it makes me feel different. I feel something new, special. It is a tiny piece of jigsaw. It is a little nugget of truth about me.

Later when actively searching for my birth family, I am on the London Underground and walking through the streets in the East End. I look at faces. *Am I related to you? Are you my mother, my aunty or grandmother? Are you my brother or sister or father? I could be sitting opposite you right now. Would we know?* I search for people with brown eyes and hair like mine. For skin that browns easily in the sun. When I met my birth mum she told me proudly how she never ever used sun screen because she just turned brown in the sun. She talked about skinny dipping in the sea, even the cold North Sea in Norfolk where she had retired. She was a water baby sun worshipper and I knew where I had got it from. It was so satisfying to find that recognition. I stare at the faces surreptitiously trying to find a similarity, a moment of recognition. So many things that if you were a kept child you just grow up knowing.

I heard what she meant.

It's ok if you find someone else
She said
All is as it should be and everything is perfectly
In its place.
And I heard, 'You can go'.
'I love you enough to want the best for you' she said
'I want you to be happy'.
And I heard, 'You don't matter enough to me to keep'.

'It was the times' she said,
'They were different then'.
'Single mothers couldn't raise a child'.
And I heard, 'You were too much trouble'.

'I love you enough to want the best for you' she said
'Every child deserves to have two parents'
And I heard, 'I didn't want to keep you'

'I love you so much' she said
And I heard 'But'
'I want you' she said
And I heard 'For now'.

'I need you' she said
And I was lost.

I heard what you said
I heard the words

Of loss and grief
I heard the words
And I said
'It's OK'
'Everything is as it should be'
But what I meant was
I don't believe you.

Julia's Adoption file notes 1958.

This baby is offered for adoption as she
is illegitimate. The mother nursed the father in hospital and their friendship lasted
for two years. They intended to marry this
year, then, when the baby was expected the
mother realised that they were not suited
and broke the engagement. She is anxious
that Julia should be adopted and have a father as well as a mother.

Mary and her parents are all very nice
people. The family health history is good.

Mary belongs to the Queen Alexandra
Nursing Service. She is known to be of good
character and reputation. She is of good appearance with dark eyes and hair. She likes
music, swimming, amateur dramatics and reading. Her height is 5'4"

The putative father is healthy, so are his
parents. He is interested in motoring and
gardening as hobbies. He is 5'11, has light
brown hair and brown eyes.

The baby is of placid disposition, has

normal intelligence for age, has good health. She has dark hair and dark eyes — considered suitable for a professional home, mother is well educated.

(Note: This is the sum total of my family medical history)

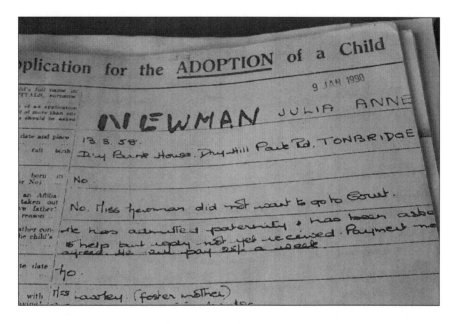

Adoption Papers

So it seemed that everyone concerned in my conception and birth were 'very nice people'. Apparently I came from 'good' stock so I could be placed in a 'professional family'. I wondered what if the opposite were true? I was marketable. Not me, just a commodity. Maybe I sound bitter and angry. Some days I am.

Days were filled with normal life and bookended with The Search. Trying to find my birth parents was a journey into the unknown. I researched UK Adoption Acts, birth, marriage and death records and I met with social workers. I joined an agency called NORCAP (now defunct) set up by the indefatigable Pam Hodgkin, which helped to mediate and give information to adult adoptees and birth parents. The stories written by adoptees about their own search in NOR-CAP's magazine were the first contact I had with adoptee voices. I recognised them. They sounded like me.

Searching meant travelling to London. The internet was not the familiar option it is now. London meant organising my life to fit around the search. I had to have someone to look after the children and I couldn't ask Mum and Dad because they didn't know what I was going to do. My husband took time off work so that I could have the time. In St. Catherine's House in London I found huge books of black and red and green records in governmental buildings. I searched alone, scared and excited. I was afraid and hopeful. Is my mother dead or alive? I searched the records a decade at a time. I stopped and started the decades with my own process too. I couldn't do it all in one go. The searching was exhausting but I was persistent. I still hear adoptees say that they don't know where to begin. Adoptees helped other adoptees. I am eternally grateful to those who helped me. The official channels were clunky and slow and formal. It required a level of determination and obstinacy that is tough when you are making a journey into the unknown.

How it started

It is 1975 and I am seventeen and home from school. I was ironing my dad's shirts in the kitchen. Mum and Dad are at work. The radio was playing. Unusually I am listening to Radio 4 rather than Radio 1. I hear the word 'adoption', then 'those people who were adopted before 1975'. The hairs on my arms quite literally stand up as I get goose-bumps on my arms. *This is me they are talking about.* I have literally never heard anyone talk about it before. It is in public, on the radio. I am riveted to what the presenter is saying and I am holding my breath. *"Please don't let anyone come in, please don't let anyone come in".* I know that if Mum or Dad appears the radio will get turned off and I will miss out on hearing this. It feels life changing, and it will be. "From next year children who become 18 will have access to their original birth certificate. This means that they may be able to trace their birth mother or birth family." *I didn't even know that I had an original birth certificate, I think.*

I am in the process of applying for University and I have to send off a copy of my birth certificate *as proof of my identity. This is my opportunity.. This will be it. I will know who my mother is, I will know her name, maybe even my father's name. I will know who I am.*

I pick my moment when Mum is busy doing something elsewhere and I know that she won't hear me and I ask my Dad, "I need my birth certificate because I have to send it off in my UCAS application". There is a long pause, then Dad smiles and says, 'Yes of course love, I'll find it for you.'

I know he will have it. I know he will know where it is. He is very organised. There is a drawer in my parent's bedroom that is always locked. I think there will be information in there. I have tried to open it of course.

It takes him a few days to come back to me. *Why it is taking him so long? Surely he has it in his drawer. I know my Dad, he has everything organised and filed away.* I am anxious but also have a small sneaky feeling of triumph. He hands me a piece of paper. It is very short. It just says my adopted name, Fiona Margaret Richardson, 'Girl' and my date of birth. It doesn't say anything else. No parents. It is a short certificate. I am gutted. Literally I feel as if my insides are going to fall out. I don't exist. I am nothing at all before I was this person. The disappointment is crushing. I take it and say, 'Thank you'. I don't know what else to say. *That's it? Why is there not more? This tells me nothing. It's a dead end. What else can I do? They won't tell me anything. I will have to wait until I can find out for myself.*

I feel like my life has come to a standstill. I am powerless. It is a moment of devastation but I can't show it. My origins are not mine, they seem to belong to other people. It is not my story so I am not allowed to know how it started. I began at three months old, and anything before then is a blank sheet. I don't know all the things that other people know. I don't tell anyone about the birth certificate. I am ashamed because it makes me feel I'm not real. Other people have this information. They can ask their parents and they can see it written down. I thought this was my chance. But the system was designed to protect the adoptive parents. It says, 'You have no right to this information because you didn't exist until you were adopted. This is your name and these are your parents'. The space for parents was blank. My original birth certificate was a sealed record that no-one could access, especially me. A door had slammed in my face and I was expected to not care. But I did. I cared a lot. I held on to my knowledge from the radio. One day I would be able to find out. I just didn't know how. This was before the internet. No Google to search. It seems impossible.

Adoption Act 1976

In most of the UK, children who have reached the age of 18 have the right to see their full birth certificate, which may reveal that the child is adopted and give the name of their biological parents. In Scotland children have the right to see their birth certificate from the age of 16. A record of all children who have been adopted is now kept on the Adopted Children Register.

Adopted children who have reached the age of 18 may use another register, the Adopted Contact Register, to find their biological relatives. By adding their details to the Register an adopted child indicates to their biological relatives that they wish to contact them. However, the biological relatives must also have registered their details for this system of contact to be effective.

The Search

The first social worker I met gave me my original birth certificate. In the UK the Adoption Act of 1976 had set a protocol for adoption agencies to follow in dealing with enquiries from adult adoptees. I had to apply for my records and then wait for an appointment at an office near to where I lived for 'counselling'. I was nervous and excited and alone. *This is it. This is it. Now I will know. Don't get your hopes up. What is counselling anyway? I hope they are nice. I'm sure they will help me. After all, the law has changed now. They know that we need to know.* I told no-one what I was doing.

The Social Services building was tucked away at the back of the town. Outside, it was an imposing big brick building with huge sash windows. Inside, it looked grey and institutional and had a faded air of budget cuts and outdated posters. I arrived far too early and smoked cigarettes round the corners I waited. My mouth dry and tasting of stale tobacco, I had to sit and wait. *Does the woman behind the counter know why I am here. Does she think I'm in trouble? Do I look ok? What are they going to ask me?*

A middle-aged man called out my name. He barely made eye contact. He was untidy, a badly ironed shirt strained at the buttons over his beer belly. I expected someone dressed more smartly and then felt bad for judging. All my senses were on high alert. The social worker took me into a small room with dingy green walls. The paint flaked on the ceiling and there were two ancient office chairs and a desk. The social worker sat down and put a brown envelope on the table in front of him. *Where is my file? Aren't there notes? When do I get them? Maybe he has to talk with me first? I don't feel very comfortable. Stop making judgements, relax, just go with the flow.*

He says, "So why do you want to have access to your birth records?" *What? Are you completely stupid? I'm fucking adopted. I know nothing about my origins. Wouldn't you want to know? Oh God this is not going to go well is it? Be nice, be nice.*

I stammer something out about wanting to know where I came from. He says, "You must understand that when you were adopted times were different. Your birth mother wouldn't have expected to be found. When she gave you up for adoption she believed that that was the end of it and she would never have any contact from you. Her life has probably moved on. She may be married or have children You will have to be careful because you could cause her a lot of upset. You don't want to upset her do you?"

Fuck. But what about me? So I have to be the one to consider everyone else's feelings again? Of course I don't want to upset anyone. But maybe my mother would like to see me? I would want to if I was her. I'm not a bad person. I nod and smile to show I understand. "And your adoptive parents too, how do they feel about it?" he asked. Seriously what? Well, I haven't told them of course. I am 26 I don't have to have their permission. Do I? Ok pull yourself together here. Don't cry. Don't get upset. Just tell him what he wants to hear and get your information and get out of here. I answer his questions. I tell him I don't want to upset anybody. I just need to have some information about my birth. I don't tell him how I long for my birth mother, how I think about her and imagine meeting. I pretend it isn't emotional, just a process of information seeking. Inside I shut down on the bubbling rage. I feel silenced and wrong. *Does he think I am being selfish? I thought they were supposed to be helping me? I thought counselling was meant to help me. This isn't counselling. This feels like being warned off or inspected to see if I am sensible enough to be entrusted with this information that is about me.*

It wasn't about me. It was all about everyone else. Their feelings had to be protected. Mine didn't matter. The interview took about twenty minutes. At the end he hands me the brown envelope unsealed. There is no file. I open it and pull out my original birth certificate and a short piece of paper with the the name of the Local Authority where my adoption happened and the address of the adoption agency through which I was placed. I want to just sit and hold that piece of paper and gaze at it. But I also want to get out of there as fast as I can. The names were unfamiliar but this was me. My name was Julia Anne Newman and my mother's name was Mary Patricia Newman. That was the first time I had seen our names together. My father's name was a blank space. *I have a name. She has a name. Julia. Julia Anne. Mary. Mary Patricia. We are real.*

I got up and smiled and said, 'thank you' and left the office. I had no words for how I felt. That was to become a much more familiar experience as my awareness of my adoption grew. Words are often not enough. I walked home and sat in my front room looking at my mother's name and mine and the place I was born. Gradually I absorbed them into me.

My real name.

That piece of paper was the first link to my birth family. I knew that behind it lay the story of how I came to be. I was disappointed that there was no mention of my father but not surprised. I kept looking at my name. *Why was I called Julia Anne? Was it a family name? What does it mean?* I loved the fact that it felt like a name that had been chosen. It wasn't just plain and ordinary. I loved the fact that the Anne had an 'e' on the end, it made feel special. I had never liked 'Fiona'. It didn't feel right for me, it just didn't fit. I felt it made me sound 'posh' and I didn't like that at all. I hated that my middle name was the same as my adoptive mother. I didn't want to be like her. Most of my life I had shortened my name to 'Fee'. That was what my friends called me. I was insistent about it. 'Fee' felt friendlier and more quirky, I felt like it suited me better. I loathed having to give my full name in official situations. I didn't like to see it written down. When I started work I thought that I had to be grown up and use my 'official' name so I became Fiona again in my work environment. It always grated on me.

When I saw my birth name I felt something new. I had always loved the name 'Julia'. Something about it spoke to me. I felt like I belonged to it somehow. It felt like me. From that moment I often thought of myself as Julia. Knowing my name changed me. I kept it inside like a treasure I carried with me. I would take it out sometimes and rub it down like the magic lamp and hope that a genie would appear. Julia made me feel seen. Much later as I started to put the jigsaw pieces together I started to wonder. How did I recognise my name? When I had babies myself I started to understand. By the time they were four months old their names had been cooed and whispered and spoken a thousand times. As babies they knew the sound of my voice and the cadence of their name.

Being adopted doesn't happen overnight. It took a year from my birth until my legal adoption. I don't know when my adoptive parents started to call me by the name they had chosen for me. I assume it must have been when they took me home. Much later and with anxiety crawling in my belly at my nerve, I asked Mum and Dad 'Do you know what I was called when I was born? What did it say on my birth certificate?'. Mum said, ' I have no idea. I don't think we ever knew you had another name.' *But that couldn't be true.* For four months at least I was Julia. When my adoptive parents met me Julia was my name. They took me home as a Julia, but somewhere on the journey between London and Sheffield my name got misplaced. But the miracle is that my name was in the neural pathways laid down in my baby brain. It was embedded deep in my memory and my psyche. It was like a muscle memory it seems my body knew. Pre-verbal knowledge and sense is real.

From the moment I saw my name written on my first birth certificate I knew that it was me. It felt like who I was on the inside. It took me a long time to make the shift to using my real name in every situation but I always knew it was who I was. When I changed my name I knew that I was taking back what was already mine. Some people continued to call me by my adopted name. Some people refused to call me my real name. My adoptive parents always called me Fiona and I accepted that. My Godmother said to me, "I will carry on calling you Fiona, because that's what I have always called you and that's the name your parents chose for you". She didn't ask my permission, she just told me. I smiled. I should have said, "No".

Julia is my name. It is me. Now I am Julia everywhere, inside and out. If anyone asks I tell them, 'This was always my name, I am just taking it back.' I get anxious revealing my adopted name. I kept it as my middle name for the sake of Mum and Dad. It doesn't feel like it belongs to me at all and I don't want to put it back out into the world as if we are connected.

My brain and body always knew who I was. Gabor Mate says that 'Recovery' means to find. I thought I had lost my name and my identity, but if we can find something it wasn't really lost. I recovered my name and I recovered myself piece by tiny piece. But it took a while.

My real authentic self was always there. I knew my name and I didn't feel myself until I took it back. I am Julia.

Brené Brown, the social worker and inspirational speaker and writer, says that the opposite of belonging is fitting in. When we are desperate to fit in we lose ourselves. The paradox is we can lose ourselves in the fitting in and in the not fitting in. For me there is an upside to being the chameleon who adapts to my environment. I can morph from one place to another and find a way to be comfortable and to make others comfortable too. I easily navigate new groups and I developed an ability to navigate and support a new group by revealing my vulnerability or using humour. I learnt those skills being the new girl in my childhood. Being the new girl is familiar and so is fitting in. But staying, that's something else. Staying in relationship. Staying in a group. Staying means learning to tolerate discomfort. To belong to someone I have to let myself be seen. And it's hard to be seen if I am always changing. Being seen means being real.

Sometimes I would like to be able to put all the feelings away in a cupboard and shut the door. I used to have an old fashioned airing cupboard with wooden slats for shelves to store towels and bedding. Everything would start off in neat piles but then more would get shoved in on top. Some days I didn't want to do anything but get the laundry out of sight. When you opened the door you had to stand close to catch things as they fell out and just hope it was a small pile and not the whole lot. My feelings pile on top of each other in the cupboard until one day they all fall out on top of me or anyone standing nearby.

CHAPTER 11 JIGSAW

After first obtaining my original birth certificate it took me another thirteen years before I got the energy and strength to continue searching for my birth family.

In 1988 I gave birth to my second son, having divorced husband number one and married husband two. We went on to have three children together alongside number one son. I wanted children so much. In 1989 I started social work training having worked in the field for a few years. The combination of another baby and feeling relatively settled at home and having some space whilst studying gave me the space I needed to apply for my adoption records. I contacted the adoption society and eventually a social worker came to visit me at home. This was a very different experience from the first time. She was young, professional and empathic and she came carrying a file full of papers for me. She talked me through what was in there and helped me understand the paperwork. She showed an interest and warmth in the information about my birth parents and recognised similarities to me in the descriptions of their characters and appearance. She shared my excitement. The information was still limited and sanitised but it was beginning to form a picture. Now I knew that my father was called David and he came from Birmingham. Some of the information was a shock. My parents weren't teenagers when I was born. She was twenty-eight and he was twenty-nine, a nurse and an ex-naval officer who met when she nursed him. They were engaged to be married but the notes said that she had broken off the engagement. *What? Why? You could have kept me! Stop judging, wait, find out more. This is hard.* I loved finding more about my birth Mum. The notes say that she loves reading, swimming and amateur dramatics. I begin to see her as a person. *That's like me! She likes what I like.* There are no photos in the file. That would have made a huge difference. *I want to know what they look like. Who do I look like?*

I do some research. I keep dancing around the edges. I want to know more and I am scared. Are they still alive? The voice of that first social worker still rings in my ears. I don't want to cause any trouble. And more than that I don't want to find them only to hear that they have died or worse — that they don't want to know me. The fear of rejection is huge. I find an address for the foster carers who looked after me for those first few months. They are still alive. I am too nervous to contact them and I leave it too late. The next time I check they have both died. I am sad at another missed opportunity. I wish I had met them.

I am in St. Catherine's House in London in February 1997. I have come down on the train for a day from the Midlands. This is where all the Records of Births, Deaths and Marriages are kept. I am ready to try to find my mother. I can feel the years ticking by and the awareness that time may be running out. *I will be 40 next year. My birth parents will already be in their 70's. I want to see if we can meet. I need to know more. I need to see her. If I leave it any longer it might be too late. They could already have died. Don't get your hopes up.* I have found huge shelves of registers. They are in bound books of different colours. Red for births, black for death, green for marriage. There are some blue books too. There are so many people here looking through records. Researchers come here, genealogists and professionals. *How many of these people sitting at the tables are doing what I am? Trying to find out who they are. How many are adopted?* I have come to London alone. My husband would have come with me but I said, 'No'. I wanted to do it by myself. We had four children at home and he was happy to look after them. I came down with excitement and hope but I quickly felt lonely. I didn't talk to anyone else about what I was doing. I was still searching surreptitiously so that I didn't rock the boat. I didn't want to upset my parents. I had my mother's name and her address at the time of my birth but I couldn't find her. I spent hours searching and finding nothing. *This is too hard. It feels like a dead end. Will I have to go home with nothing? I might have to give up.*

I checked electoral registers for my father. No luck.

At the last minute just as I was about to pack my bag and head back to the station I turned a page and there I found an entry in the register that might be my mother and her sisters, Olive and Margaret. They were all born in London in the East End. I remembered how I had been sure that I came from London and the conversation with my Dad when I was a teenager. It gave me a little spark of hope. I was searching in the dark with so little to go on. I fill in the forms and pay to order the certificates. *Fingers crossed. It is time to go home, I have to get the train back and I want to see the children before they go to bed. I am tired and disheartened but maybe I will get somewhere with the birth certificates when they arrive.*

In March 1997 I returned to London and to a museum in the East End. It felt so much more concrete to see electoral registers in person and not on microfiche. I found my mother on the register for 1959 in the area, but with an 'S' by her name. I had to ask one of the elderly ladies who managed the records what that meant. She told me it meant 'Service Voter'. So my mother was in the Forces? What could that mean? I had a clue in my adoption records which told me that when I was adopted she was a Queens Alexandra's nurse. I wondered if she gone back into the service? Maybe she had gone abroad? I tried to find her older sister in the records. In my adoption records Olive had been named as the person who would adopt me if no-one could be found for me. I wondered why she didn't just have me anyway? She was married and a housewife in 1958 when I was born.

Back and back I went through more and more records. I travelled back and forth across London. Sitting on the Tube I looked at faces and wondered. I found a record of my grandparents who were registered at their family address in 1945, but only my grandmother was there with the children. What has happened to her husband, *my grandfather?* Later I learned he had been a Prisoner of War in Japan.

Back to St. Catherine's House. I checked for a marriage for my aunt but found nothing. I felt as if my search had been spectacularly unsuccessful. I was sad and low as I sat in a coffee shop on a busy London street drinking a cappuccino and eating a croissant with cheese and ham. I looked at the people passing by and I felt alone. I bought chocolate because I wanted some comfort. *Are the bits and pieces of information that I am collecting relevant? Are these even the right people?* I had no way to know. I was tempted to just go back to Euston Station and get the next train home. I wanted the security and familiarity of being back with my children and husband. I made a phone call instead to hear his voice and plug in to my 'normal' life. *Maybe I could go back to St. Catherine's House for a couple of hours. If I don't do it today I will be stuck.* I had found out that the records were due to be moved from there soon and then public access was not going to be possible. I would have to apply for certificates without being able to search in person. It felt like I was being stopped just as I might be getting somewhere. Pulling myself together I walked back and started again.

I remembered what the museum curator in Walthamstow had said about 'S' meaning a Service Vote. I had seen the big blue registers on the shelves at St. Catherine's but not known what they were for. Now I knew they were overseas records. Pulling the book down for 1959 I found a marriage record for my birth mother. She had married in Gibraltar; 'I may have struck gold!' I wrote. I remember the excitement along with the exhaustion in my over caffeinated, sleep deprived state. I felt breathless.

Next I tried to trace any births from her marriage, but this was tricky as births abroad are difficult to trace until 1966 when they suddenly start to appear in separate registers. I applied for five birth certificates. I had to pay for each one and fill out a form to explain why I wanted it. 'Family record search' was, I found, an acceptable answer. Everything was a paper document then. The certificates would take up to four weeks to arrive which felt like a lifetime. Ordinary birth, marriage and death certificates took fourteen days to arrive after paying six pounds or you could pay twenty-seven pounds (I couldn't) and get them in twenty-four hours. I had already spent quite a lot of money on the search.

I checked English birth registers in the vague hope that my mother and her husband might have returned to England. It felt very strange to think that she had married a man who wasn't my father. I almost felt jealous on his behalf, or maybe on mine. It was all guess work and intuitive leaps. I found four possible entries but only applied for one because her name and initials were the same as my grandmother's and I thought this might be a clue.

Piece by piece the jigsaw started to come together. I was talking about it more now. I had one or two good friends who understood my need to know. I had started to come out of the shell of my compliant adopted self and risk allowing myself to find out. I was beginning to reject the narrative that told me I should just be grateful for what I had and accept it. The world was also moving on and social workers and academics were thinking more about the concepts of attachment and bonding. The learning around neuroplasticity was still in its infancy but the ideas of how babies were affected by pre-birth experience were starting to be accepted. I knew from my own experience that babies respond to the environment in which they are born. My children recognised the music they had heard in the womb, even the sound of the theme tune for an episode of 'East Enders' that had played every night.

Notes I wrote before our first reunion meeting:
What I want:
To know who I am, where and who I came from
Who do I look like? Who am I like?
What do they look like?
I want to know why, to understand
I want to be told she has always thought of me and loved me

First letter from my birth mother

My dear Fiona

Your marathon letter arrived yesterday, it has already been read several times. It is impossible to tell you how happy you have made me and how wonderful that you have made contact. Already quite a few of my friends here have been told. In sharing this news with them it's amazing how many tragedies and joys have been shared with me by them.

Like you I should love for us to be friends and I am prepared to play things any way you wish. It is wise I think to get to know more about each other first but of course I would love to meet you. How do your parents feel? Just to know that you are there well and happy with a fulfilling life and work gives me great happiness. My life has so many areas you will want to know I expect. Meanwhile bless you for your kind letter and lovely album.

Love Mary

PS. Arrangements to meet.

It would be lovely to see you at your friend's home if that's Ok. I shall go down to K's …Saturday the 21st is it? I think we will both be a little nervous. Anyway I shall be going to K's for a few days to see…. My family and other daughters are all very excited and pleased for both of us.

Love Mary

Tomorrow I send the letter. 1996

I have an address for my sister. I have written a letter to ask her if she knows where my Mum is now.

What will happen next? It feels like I am jumping off a cliff, like waiting to give birth, to know if someone is going to say, 'Yes' to me.

I am afraid. I am excited.

It all feels very near the surface, the cutting edge of me is raw and fragile, I am letting it all out of the box. A butterfly going free, delicate shimmer of wings, let me fly. I could so easily be crushed.

My father may be out there somewhere too. Maybe that is my next step?

What I rely on: Love and support from family of my own that I have made. Friends, (This still holds true today)

CHAPTER 12 REUNION

21 March 1998 and I was in London again. It was the day that I would meet my birth mother Mary for the second time in forty years. Letters and a couple of awkward telephone calls had been exchanged. I had arranged to meet her at a friend's house who would be away for the day. People had offered to come with me but I had turned them down.

I was excited and terrified. I thought I knew what I was letting myself in for. I told myself I had no expectations but really I wanted an instant connection. My heart wanted her to say she was sorry whilst my mind rejected my own longing.. I wanted her to say that she had always missed me and that she wished she'd kept me. I wanted her to remember me. I wanted her to have treasured a photo of me as a newborn, to have kept my baby blanket, anything that reminded her of me. I wanted her to love me. I wanted her to have always loved me. I wanted to know her. I wanted to see myself reflected in her, to meet someone who looked like me. I wanted to belong. I needed her to like me. I didn't know how to be, what to wear, how to speak. Should we hug? Should I buy her a present?

I did.

It was awkward. She was a few minutes late and by the time she arrived I didn't think she was coming. I nearly ran away. I wanted to just leave or not answer the door. And then she was there. She was shorter than I had imagined, and plump with a round face and short fine grey hair. And she sounded like a Londoner. It threw me. I knew she was from London even though she now lived in Norfolk. But I had a strong sense of dislocation. I had grown up in mostly Northern towns. My accent was flat northern imposed on the English Midlands where I had lived for the last twenty years and I sounded like my adoptive parents and most of my friends. I didn't instantly recognise the sound of her voice and I felt sad because I had longed for that moment. In truth I had no instant moments of recognition on that day. I felt like I was a needle inside a bubble unable to pierce through to the outside world where *my mother* sat on a sofa drinking tea. For once I couldn't work out what the right thing to do or say might be. My chameleon colours didn't help. I tried to fall back on the known: *be nice, be acceptable, don't rock the boat but I didn't know what that would look like for her. Who are you to me? Who am I to you? Do I look like you? I can't see it. Tell me who I look like please. Please see me.*

I think my eyes were broken by my fear and hers were broken by her shame. Our cracked gaze got in our way.

I had so many questions. I thought she would want to tell me what had happened but really she didn't, because it was too hard. Mostly Mary claimed to have forgotten. *"How could you forget?"* Trauma is a wound to the body or soul that can cause amnesia. Remembering can be too much. I know this because my memory fails me too. Mary wanted forgiveness but it took until she was dying in 2019 for us to talk about that.. I wanted acceptance and love but I found it hard to recognise in her response to me. Neither of us could ask for what we needed. *If you loved me you'd know.* I didn't know what I was looking at. I don't remember much of our reunion conversation. We spent a couple of hours together and we talked all the time. I know I told her about my life and the children.I remember her asking,,'What are your parents like?' The question grated on me. Mary said, 'They are your real parents, they brought you up. I am sure they were good people.' *Don't say that. Claim me. Say I am your daughter. Yes, yes they are. But they aren't my real parents. You are my real parent. You are my mother.*

She said, 'We are two strangers meeting. It will take us a long time to get to know each other'. She was wise but I found it hard to bear the idea of us as strangers. It hurt.

I made several cups of tea. Neither of us wanted to eat although I had brought food. I remember stark moments of disassociation as emotions raged through me. Later I recognised shock and grief and loss and rejection overpowering me. I kept my feelings tamped down inside as I allowed my mind to float off leaving my body behind to smile and nod.

Some moments stand out clearly: "It's a good job you never tried to find me when I was married to G. I wouldn't have been able to see you. I wouldn't have been able to come and meet you then. I never told him about you."

Ouch. What do you mean? Why couldn't you? Did I matter so little that if I'd found you then you would have rejected me? So you wouldn't have met me at all? How can you say that?

"Have you been in touch with your father? Have you found him too?"

Why are you asking me that? It feels like you want to know about him more than me. Are you hoping I've found him because you'd like to know him again?

I told her, "No, I wanted to find you first".

She said, 'He was a nice man. I don't really remember what happened. I broke off the engagement because I realised we weren't really suited'.

What do you mean not suited? What was he like? How did you meet? Why did you get engaged? Did you love him? Why didn't you just marry him when you found out you were pregnant with me? Didn't he want me? Or was it you that didn't want me? Why couldn't you just keep me? I have always wanted to be with you. I wish you would have kept me and married my dad and we could have all been together.

I wanted to know so much more but I never really did. Now I think that I knew enough. That box was closed. I always felt that there were parts missing to the story Mary told me especially about my father. On other occasions she changed the subject if I brought him up. That day in London I was glad when the couple of hours together were over. I just wanted her to go but I wanted so much more. I was exhausted and we were both re-experiencing the trauma of the past. I couldn't remember and she had forgotten how to.

Mary left to drive to her friend's house and I gave her the plant I had bought and the little book of photos I had made for her. I felt empty. I walked to the station and caught a train back into London and then home

This doesn't seem real. I wish that someone would just come and get me and take me home. Why did I think it was okay to do this by myself.? It's too much. I want to be looked after. I want my Mum but not the ones I have.

On the train I ate sweets mindlessly and drank coffee as I sat in a corner seat praying no-one speak to me. I had my book open in front of me all the way but I didn't read a word. *Just let me get home and into bed. I just want to sleep for a week.*

When my husband picked me up at the train station with all the younger children in the car he wanted to know everything I felt like I had nothing to say.

Mary told me years later that meeting me was hard. I took her forgetfulness personally. 1 thought it was all about me. But the trauma of giving up your child is unimaginable. Mothers who lose a baby never forget. When a child dies they can be grieved and remembered and even celebrated. But with adoption everyone tells the mother to get on with her life. She is told she has done the right thing for her baby. That it would be selfish to keep her. That children need two parents.

The next day was a Sunday. I woke up in pain. My body went into shock and my mind followed. My shoulder had seized up and I couldn't move my arm. I wanted to sleep but I didn't want to be alone. We spent the day doing ordinary things as a family. We walked to the allotment and picked some flowers. We ate lunch and played with the kids and watched TV. I sorted out school uniforms and lunch boxes and homework. I took painkillers and went to bed not long after the kids. I didn't cry. Some wounds are too deep for tears. Neither of us cried when we met. I never saw my birth mother cry. Maybe we had both done all our crying when we were separated. My body made me stop and gave me an excuse to rest. I shut down. My birth mum and I didn't speak again for months.

I needed help but I didn't know how to ask for it or where it might come from. My social work colleagues often talked about adoption but it made me feel angry because I had such complex feelings. I didn't want to be worked on, I needed to be held and heard as I poured out all the grief and rage that was building inside me. But I couldn't let it out. I talked to one or two friends and I kept behaving on the outside as if everything was the same. I was working as a trainer in Social Services and I "job shared" with another woman. We had become good friends outside work as well as colleagues. We made each other laugh and shared a lot. But this part I didn't share. I never mentioned my meeting with my birth mother. A few times I almost spoke but the words got stuck in my throat. I had two weeks off work sick and I took the kids to school and picked them up after and in-between I slept and watched TV and ate chocolate and ice cream. I knew that I wasn't functioning but I didn't know what to do about it.

I waited for Mary to contact me. I kept hoping she would say the things I wanted her to. It wasn't the fairy tale ending I had hoped for in my heart. I kept telling myself that I was lucky to have found her. That I was lucky to have made contact with my birth family. I was starting to get to know more about my sisters and their families although we hadn't yet met. They were welcoming and accepting and that was an unexpected gift. It took my birth Mum and I years to work it out.

The following year I went to stay with her for a weekend. Some of it was difficult and some of it was like coming home.

I drove down to Norfolk by myself. It felt like a very long way as the road goes on and on from Stoke-On-Trent to Nottingham then on through the never-ending flatness of Lincolnshire. Arriving in Norfolk feels extraordinary. I am going to stay with my mother! I need to take a gift. What shall I get? Flowers would be nice? Maybe this weekend we will talk more. Perhaps she will tell me about my father.

There seemed to be no flower shops, no garages, nowhere to stop and buy flowers on the endless roads. There was nowhere to buy a

Mum Mary and Julia (F) Kate (B)

coffee and breathe before I met her again. I saw a sign and stopped at Norfolk Lavender and bought her some soap. I was at least an hour too early so I had coffee and a sandwich in the cafe. I look like an ordinary person just sitting in a cafe with my book in front of me. But this is not an ordinary day. I am going to stay with my mother. For the first time.

When I hand over the soap she laughs, "Oh I can get this any time, you shouldn't have spent your money on it".

Well, thanks, no problem! What do I have to do for you to approve of me?

I feel snubbed but I smile. I learn later that this is typical of Mary

She doesn't believe in 'wasting money' and she doesn't feel like she deserves gifts from me. She says what comes into her head and it can be tactless and cut like paper.

My *mother* Mary lives in a small terraced cottage with a forecourt. It is not far from the beaches of the North Norfolk coast. I have the small bedroom with a single bed made up with proper sheets and blankets and an eiderdown. Everything is spotless and her home is lovely. I love the pictures she has on the walls. On her sideboard and bookcase are photos of the family. My sisters' wedding pictures, their children, school and baby photos. The pictures change every year. I am not there. I notice but don't comment, although I am hurt. Every time I visit I surreptitiously check the photos. It is one of the first places my eyes go to. I send her pictures. I even send her pictures in a frame. They don't appear. *Why don't you have a photo there of me or my family? Are you ashamed of me? Do people not know about me? Do you think your other daughters will be offended? I feel offended when you say, 'My Daughters' and you mean them but not me.*

We both try really hard. We have fish and chips from the chip shop in the village for our tea. We both love to eat. Mum is always trying to lose weight. We have both been to Weight Watchers and I am in a thin phase at the moment but it won't last.

She has a friendly collie cross called Mitzi. We take Mitzi to the beach and we walk along the dykes looking out to sea. I fall in love with the coastline. It is wide and wild and beautiful with endless skies. It reminds me of Northumberland, which is my heart place. I fall in love with places easily and I always want to move and live in them. I wanted to live in Norfolk because my birth mum lived there.

Mum drove quite fast, she nipped about in her little old car, dashing through the Norfolk lanes with abandon and tearing round corners. It made me slightly nervous. She had a nice laugh. I knew she was nervous because she tried to keep us busy. I do that too. She took me to visit her sister and brother in law. Her sister Margaret has written to me already, and she said she had met me before. That must have been when I was born. We didn't talk about that though. I wish we had. I felt touched that she wanted me to meet her sister. She told me that she had been telling her neighbours and some friends from church about me. She said that she stood up in church and told them about me and how she had had me when she was young and I had been adopted. It sounded like a confessional. She seemed to feel grateful that the church had been accepting and kind and her friends were glad for her. I felt uncomfortable because there was a shroud of shame around this story that I didn't like. But I was glad she felt better. I thought that maybe this will help her to move on.

I realised I liked being with her. I liked hearing her talk and watching her. I liked the fact that she wore clothes that I might wear. We both had a pair of black velvet pull-on trousers. We both have red toe-post Birkenstocks.. Her hair is silver and frames her head. She has it cut as short as possible because it is baby fine. Just like mine. She has dark, thick eyebrows. I am still waxing mine but they would look just like hers if I let them. I want to stay longer and I want to go home. Home is where I feel safe and everything is familiar. The tension is hard.

On Sunday I plan to leave after breakfast. It is a long drive back and I am so tired. I want to ask her about my father. We haven't had a chance to talk about him. I want to know more about when I was born and what happened and how she felt and all of it. *Maybe now. Maybe now. Or now. Now I'll ask her. If I don't ask her now it'll be too late.*

I ask.

She says, 'I think I've told you everything I could last time. I don't really remember much about that time.'

But it's not enough. Please tell me more.

I ask, 'Do you have any photos of me from then? Or a photo of my father? What did he look like?'

"No, I didn't have any. He was dark haired and had brown eyes like you. He was a nice man. You look like my other daughter because you are both dark."

When I leave she stands on the doorstep to wave me off. I take a photo of her there. We don't have any pictures yet of us together and

Julia, Jane (B) Kate, Mum Mary and Sarah (F)

I am desperate for them but there is no-one to take them. I want to have pictures I can look at over and over, to absorb her into me or me back into her.

The car crunches on the gravel as I reverse out onto the driveway. I wave and see her in the mirror. I turn left and drive along the village High Street for a couple of minutes then pull in to the Co-op car park. I have a long way to drive back and I am exhausted before I start. I know I will need supplies to get me through. I load up with chocolate and cookies and crap to soothe me going home. By the time I get to Nottingham I just want to stop the car and stay there. I don't feel like I can possibly drive for another minute. I get coffee and keep going. The next day I am back at work.

This is not the way to self care. Don't do it the way I did. Take someone with you. Allow someone else to drive or take the train. Let yourself be looked after. Stay overnight on the way back. Be gentle with yourself. This is the biggest thing you have ever done in your life. It is huge. Don't minimise. Don't pretend you are fine. You are not fine. Eventually you will find a way to do this or you won't. One way or another you will be able to decide if you can bear the pain this reunion enough to keep going until you have a relationship. But it will not happen overnight. It took us years and years and then we needed help.

Letter from Margaret, my birth mum's sister. 1 March

Dear Fiona

I am Mary's slightly younger sister Margaret. Most of my married life was spent in Kent, the past 11 years in Norfolk. Mary was, of course, in ..... for many years until she came to Norfolk some years ago. We both live in villages about 15 minutes apart. Her family and mine were pretty close in spirit in spite of the distances and although our 5 children are scattered we still remain so. (That is five children minus me)

I know you will be coming up (or down!) later in March and I would love to meet you — also my husband P. Your time with Mary will be short so we will understand if this does not happen — you may not even want to extend your knowledge of this family yet.

I met you once, so many years ago but it has been a great joy to me that there is now contact between you and Mary. It cannot be easy for either of you but you do have time now to get to know each other and we would not wish to intrude in the early days of this relationship.

I think you will have a happy, if emotional, time with Mary and perhaps you will like Norfolk if you do not already know it. I can imagine your husband will be having a busy time with the boys!

If we don't meet in March we certainly will later. Welcome into your unknown family.

Margaret

After the visit I wrote this letter to Mum although I never sent it. I am glad now that I didn't but the feelings were real.

October 1998

Dear Mary,

It has been several months since I've heard from you — not since I came to stay with you before Easter. I have a feeling our relationship was over before it started, that you never really wanted to get to know me although curiosity and duty made it hard for you to say 'No'. I feel that you believe I ruined your life, taking away from you whatever your hopes and dreams for the future were.

I suppose I had so many hopes and dreams for our reunion. I dreamed you would welcome me with tears, love and open arms and heart. That I would be a blessing and a joy and I suppose in you I looked to find a mother who would fill the other half of my heart

The letter stops there. Later we had a conversation on the phone. I told her I was hurt and angry with her because I felt she didn't want me in her life. She told me that wasn't true but she felt she couldn't contact me because she thought I should be the one to contact her.

But I just want you to be my Mum. I want you to be the grown up. I want to be able to be the child, your child. I know it's childish, but can you show me that you wanted me because I don't think you did. I think you were glad to get rid of me because then you could move on with your life. How could you say that you would never have met me if you were still married to him? It made me feel worthless when you said that. You gave me away before. How can you give a baby away? I could never have given my babies away. Other women kept their babies, why didn't you? I'm angry with you because I want you to tell me you never forgot me and always hoped I would find you. I feel that if I hadn't found you, you would never have done anything about finding me. You knew of the Adoption Contact Register but you never put your details on there. Why not? Did you not want me to find you? It hurts.

Mum Mary talked of my boys and their 'real' grandparents, just as she referred to my adoptive parents as my 'real' parents. But my 'real' parents are all my parents. The reality is we are still connected even if we can't find each other. All those myths and stories about epic journeys and seeking the Holy Grail and finding a way home are about belonging and identity. It matters to all of us as human beings. We are who we come from and we are also where we grow up. We can be loved and wanted and given a new life surrounded by a loving family and still need to find our roots. We have been transplanted and we still want to go home.

Mum Mary at home in Norfolk

Mum Mary (L) and her two sisters Margaret and Olive as evacuees.

Mary (far right) and her two sisters 1950's.

CHAPTER 13 SISTERS

Reunion with my birth family isn't over. We have spent twenty years together now getting to know each other and being a family. I love my sisters and their husbands and kids, my nephews and nieces. It still makes me smile when we are together and we start to talk and the same words come out of our mouths or we have the same response to a situation. I can never get over the ways in which we look alike. I still study their faces and notice our similarities. We have the same eyebrows — they come from my grandmother's side of the family. We all have chunky legs. I have a photo of us all sat in a row on holiday in Devon. We are all wearing shorts and our knees are the same. We all love reading and walking and swimming and animals. Three of us are vegetarian. We like the same books and we all have worked in jobs that mean helping people. Jane is a librarian, Kate a teacher of the deaf and Sarah works in a hospital and trained in shiatsu massage. Our mother was a nurse. So many likenesses that make coincidence seem a fantasy. We understand each other.

My three sisters, all younger than me. When I see them together they have always seemed to me like sisters should be. They look after each other and keep in touch and go away together with their kids. I love the fact that they aren't perfectly in harmony. They get cross with each other and they know what makes each other tick. They stick by each other through thick and thin. Family rules apply. Kate tries to look after everyone and mediate, Sarah is the rebel and the adventurer and sometimes the family scapegoat. Jane is anxious and kind and has an occasional flash of temper but keeps it firmly hidden away. We all have the temper. We battle with food and weight and diets and every time we get together we have to work out who is on what food plan. Usually it's me with my no alcohol, no sugar, no flour that they accommodate unless I am in a drinking and eating phase. I hope that is done with. One day at a time.

I trust them. Trust is a big deal if you are adopted or experienced trauma. What is it anyway? Trust seems to be connected to belonging.

Now our mother isn't here any more we are on our own as siblings. Often they were the glue that held my birth mother, their mother, and I together. It often feels odd to me that *our mother* is also *my mother*. Our experiences of her as a mother are different. They grew up with her. She wiped their noses and took them to school and listened to them read. Their story is different to mine and it isn't mine to tell. Our shared story intersects only after we had all grown up and formed lives and even families of our own. Sometimes I found it easier to talk with a sister rather than our mother and they would tell me what was going on and pass on my news to her. For years we danced around what to call her. For them she has always been 'Mum'. For me she was 'Mary' with 'Mum' as a subtext inside my head. My sisters interpreted between Mary and I when our communication got muddled or I was hurt by my her throw away remarks. I needed that buffer to be able to feel safe. Some days it was all too raw to navigate another phone call with my guts clenching and the fear of not getting what I wanted from Mary again. I wanted her to love me wildly like I love my children but she didn't have me like I had my children. She didn't birth me in hope and fear and raise me with all the daily joys and irritations. I was desperate for a reassurance that she had regretted letting me go., but that wasn't in her to give. I needed her to tell me that she had always wanted to find me. I didn't hear those things from her. It took me years to believe a little in the possibility that she was glad that I had found her. Whilst writing this book I have re-read our early letters and I read her words on a page She said it had made her happy. I don't think I ever saw that before. Those words just disappeared.

In the early years of our reunion I spent too much time focusing on what we didn't have and not enough on what we did. It is hard as an adoptee not to get caught up in the loss because it is deep and real and often denied by everyone around us. The overarching narrative about adoption is that adoptees are saved and lucky. That adoptive parents are superhuman super parents and that biological parents.,especially mothers, are invisible. So as an adoptee when I realised what

I had lost and how it had shown up in my body. I needed time to feel the feelings. I wanted my feelings to be seen and heard but my birth mother was not the person to lean on.

My sisters always say, "Mum was a very strong woman". They see her from their perspective and experience. Her marriage to their father was complicated and their childhoods were too. I saw my birth mother differently to their mother. To me she was kind and polite as if we were distant relatives. I thought that it might have been easier for her to not know me. She told me that she would never have looked for me because she didn't have the right. That hurt me. It felt

Sisters. Jane, Sarah, Kate, Julia.

like another rejection but I think it was created by the system that severed us. Our shame was toxic like our trauma.

I met Jane and Kate separately because when we first made contact we all had young children. Jane was pregnant with her youngest child and when she was in labour she was so excited she told all the staff, "I've just found out I've got another sister". I wondered how these new siblings would react to a stranger coming out of their Mum's past. *Would they be jealous or suspicious of my intentions? Would they hate me?* I managed to consider every possible negative option but the reality was that they were welcoming and friendly. They took me into their lives and hearts and homes and we make each other laugh because we have the same sense of humour. They are clever and caring and kind and beautiful. Sarah was living abroad when I was first in touch so it took several months before we could meet. When she came back to England to visit she was only home for a short time before she went abroad again to start a year long massage course. We managed to squeeze in a meeting one evening in a pub half-way between and we talked like we had known each other for years. A few days later she flew out of Heathrow and it was several years before we could meet again. The year's course turned into a romance and a baby as well and that sister has lived on the other side of the world

Mum Mary, Julia and cousin Mary

ever since. Every two or three years she saves up enough for her and our niece to come back and visit. It is a whirligig ride of visits for them and we catch up when we can. Last year they came in November because we knew that our mother was dying. We visited her together and then we had a a cold wet winter day in a National Trust coffee shop talking over lunch and too many cups of coffee until we knew we had to say goodbye. In December she came back for Mum's funeral and we all had the day together. The four of us sat with our partners on the front row at the church. The nieces and nephews and three of my boys sat behind us.

Kate told me, 'When she was in hospital the Minister asked Mum how many children she had and she said, 'I am so proud and blessed to have four girls.' She was clear that she had four daughters. I learnt that Mum used to sit and read a dictionary because she loved words so much and that no-one could ever beat her at Scrabble. She loved singing and had a lovely voice. She liked to cook especially baking. She was creative and artistic and it showed up in her love for her garden, in knitting and in the pictures she chose for her walls. Jane said that Mum always wanted to be useful — as a nurse, a Mum and a Granny.

I have just discovered that I have a photo of my maternal grandmother, Hilda. She is standing next to my birth mother in the only picture I have of my parents together. They are at a wedding sometime in the year before my mother got pregnant with me. I had wrongly thought that the woman next to my mother was her older sister but she was my Grandma. I have a picture of the woman who held me first in my biological family. The woman who gave me my name. I am searching her face for signs of our shared heritage.

When you live with people who come from your body there is a mirroring. When I had children I experienced that for the first time. It was like magic. I see it now in my half sisters and in my nephews and nieces and cousins from my birth family. I see how my sons look like their cousins and aunties. It is not just the obvious physical characteristics, but also how we all think and speak. My sisters talked to each other after meeting me. Kate told me they said "She thinks like us".

A turning point in our connection to each other was a holiday we took together by the sea in Devon. I was invited me with my kids. It was a sisterhood retreat of our own making. Four sisters, our cousin Mary and a collection of young children. My youngest two boys Ben and Joe came, but the older two stayed home. It was the first time the group of us had been together in one place and the first time we had spent more than just a few hours in each other's company. My car broke down on the motorway going down so the boys and I arrived in a giant tow truck and walked the last mile to the house as it was too steep and windy for the tow-truck. It didn't feel like an auspicious start to the week. I wanted to appear together and calm not car-less, frazzled and anxious. Having the boys with me helped, it made me feel more myself. I knew who I was with them. I was Mum. We were still the first to arrive. My sisters had had their own dramas and mine just mixed in to the mix. We fitted together.

That week we got to know each other as sisters. The kids played and swam in the sea and the freezing clod pool and we all made food together and ate fish and chips and they drank wine. My sister Sarah had come from Australia with her daughter. That week was the second time we had met. People often say we are alike. I feel protective of her. I learnt that Mum said things to all of us that took our breath away. Our mother could be sharp, sometimes unconsciously cruel or tactless. *It wasn't just me.* Sometimes she had no filter. I remember sitting with Sarah under the stars outside the house in Devon. We were looking down towards the sea below us and we learnt about each others' lives. We all spent time getting to know each other. We learnt by celebrating Jane's birthday with tea and cake and the kids running round the pool and jumping in and shivering with cold. We learnt by being with each other as women, as mothers, as daughters of a woman they all knew so much better than me. The kids played together as if they had always known each other. Sometimes one of us would say something and the others would all laugh. We sounded like

Julia and her sister Kate just after they met

Julia meets her sister Sarah

each other. They got irritated with each other and snappy and it was fascinating for me to see them as sisters together. I could see how they were loyal and loving and exasperated and different and the same. Our lives had been very different. They welcomed me into

Sisters-Julia, Jane, Kate and Sarah

their sisterhood for Mum's sake but we made it work for our own.

CHAPTER 14 DNA

I put a message on a UK social media group one Sunday in 2020 giving some details of my father and asking if anyone had any information. I didn't really expect much. On Monday I woke up to a series of replies from people who had done some research on a DNA website. One of them came up with a list of names and details which fitted and offered to email someone who had a family tree. Later that day I got an email from a cousin. Apparently my father was one of twelve or thirteen children, a new and surprising nugget. I knew that he had died in 2017 and most of his siblings had gone too. But that meant there were a lot of cousins somewhere. I didn't know if he had any further children after me.

I made some exploratory contacts. And waited. I checked my email every two minutes. The trail dried up. Nerves started to rumble in my stomach and I was getting headaches. I wrote an explanatory letter telling people who I am and giving some information about my life. Then I got scared. *Is there something wrong with me? Am I not good enough? It's ok if I'm a relative but not if I'm the discarded adopted daughter that nobody knew about?* Strange thoughts rattle through my head. I resent my email. Here it is:

Dear V

Well, I don't know very much but what I do know may be a surprise, I don't know.

I was born in 1958 and adopted in 1959 (I am 62 now) and David was my father. He had been engaged to my mother, Mary. I understand he had been in the Royal Navy and she nursed him in hospital in London. She was a Londoner.

They were together for a year or so but when she got pregnant with me they ended the engagement. And I was adopted.

There is a letter on my adoption file from David.

I know he was from Birmingham and the family lived in Hall Green. I knew he had brothers but not that there

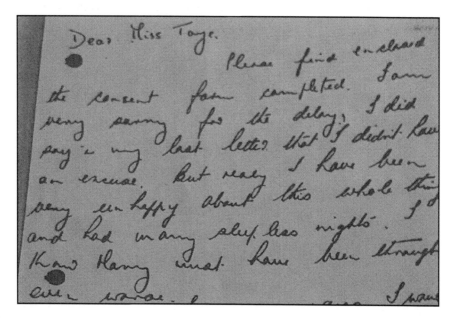

Letter from David, Julia's birth father

were so many siblings and I didn't have any names.

I know he went back to Birmingham and started a job in the Housing Department of the Council which is where he was working when I was adopted.

I contacted my birth mum many years ago and she died in December last year and I have ongoing relationships with my half sisters and family on her side. She never told me much about my father except to say he was a nice man.

I have one photo of him taken in 1957 I think but nothing else.

I had his mother's and father's names but not his mother's maiden name until someone found it for me through ancestry.

It is amazing to hear information. I didn't know if

people in his family knew about my birth or adoption and I certainly wouldn't want to upset anyone. But I would love to find more of my extended family.

I think sadly David died in 2017 in Stourport area. I don't know if he had any children or whether his wife knew about me.

I live in Staffordshire now. I am happy for people (family) to know about me and have my email or I can pass on my number. I am also on facebook if that helps

I will attach the photo I have so you can see. And one of me too.

It looks like we are family!

Julia

I got this email back straight away:

"Wow, Your Dad is definitely a Perks, (family name). He's even got the nose!"

She told me that my birth father was her first cousin on her father's side. And gave me the names of all his brothers and sisters, twelve of them and that most of the boys in the family had been in the police force.

Letter from my birth father to the social worker

Dear Miss T

Please find enclosed the consent form completed. I am very sorry for the delays, I did say in my last letter that I didn't have an excuse. But really I have been very unhappy about the whole thing and had many sleepless nights. I know Mary must have been through worse.

In many ways I would have liked to have Mary and baby back, all of us together.

Perhaps I was being selfish. I don't know.

I have signed the form now and I shall pray that Julia is very happy and her parents very good to her. And for Mary too. I hope time will ease the pain a little and that she will be very happy with someone one day.

I will send the money outstanding as soon as possible. I know its been a long time but I really haven't had a lot of money. Everything is all right now though.

Once again I would like to thank you for all you have done for Mary and baby.

Yours faithfully, David.

Dear David

I wish I had been able to meet you. I love this letter from you, it touched my heart the first time I read it. You seem so sensitive and caring and that you feel deeply. I have often wished that you and Mary had stayed together and had me. It makes me sad that we didn't have that. I am sorry I didn't find you before you died. I was too scared and now it's too late. I wish we could have sat together even just once and drunk coffee and got to know each other. I wonder if we would have got on? I think we would. You sound like such a nice person. I am sending you love. From your daughter

Julia xxx

Doing it by myself

My brain fizzes. Some days it's hard to settle. I find yoga helps. It calms me most days and then there are days when my body doesn't want to co-operate and my mind is off running somewhere. But I need the stillness.

I am in a period of transition again. I have made contact with my birth father's family, some tentative connections made over email to fairly distant relatives. But this is new territory and I am afraid of what it will mean. I have a sense of shaking inside. And the fear of annihilation. There is excitement and obsessive thinking.

I am not doing any of this alone. Not the search for my father's family. Not the writing. Not the becoming. That was my old pattern. Do it yourself. But it isn't good for me. I'm not sure it's good for anybody. I believe we are meant to be connected. We are meant to be in relationship with each other. We don't heal on our own, we heal by connection. I am asking for help, for support, looking for encouragement. I have asked someone to coach me with my writing.

I am asking my wife to help with some searching. I am trying to keep my parts connected, not separating them off into boxes. My writing creative self, my searching self, my adoptee self, my mother and wife selves. I am so used to keeping each part of me separate it feels risky to let them touch each other. I am opening up doors I have kept shut. Being vulnerable is scary but it also connects us. I know that when I tell my story people engage. When I share my real self, people respond. When I tell a story of struggle and hope I hear one back. I have learnt this through difficult times. When family situations have been such that I have felt despair or fear. When I have felt that I must have been the worst mother, the worst daughter, the worst wife and I have shared my shame and my willingness to grow then I have heard from other brave and compassionate souls who know. They know because they have been there too.

When my kids have had struggles and I have felt alone. When my relationships have felt like they were over and I know that I did it all

Julia with Toby and Jonathan 1988

Grandpa Stephen and Toby

4 sons and a father
Joe, Ben, Toby, Jon (L-R)

wrong. When I am sad but I don't know why. When I am grieving but I don't know how. I have learnt to reach out. Tell someone who I trust. There is comfort there. When I stopped using substances to cover up my feelings, when I stopped stuffing my fear and anger down with food, when I couldn't drink enough to make it all go away, then I learnt that being clean and sober and free from addiction also meant beginning a new way of living. Being present. Being here, right now, in this moment. And this one. And this one.

One of my friends says that recovery from addiction is like being a peeled prawn and then being squeezed with lemon juice. We are naked and it hurts. But it is real and we know why we hurt. It's the freaking lemon juice.

Dreaming
This morning on the yoga mat I allowed myself to dream of new

creative projects that connect the parts. It will be fragmented because that is how it is. But it will be beautiful. I want this to be collaborative and about connection. My instincts are pulling in two opposing directions. The instinct to be alone, not to trust, to remember that I only have myself. And the other instinct, the healing path that says connection and love and art and sharing are the way forward. My life is lived on the edge of both of these. It is more than an introvert and extrovert leaning towards personality type. It is based on my experience.

I have a very strong reaction to lies and betrayal. I know them and feel them in my body. My guts literally clench up and I feel like I might throw up. I have the same reaction to hearing of people who are going to adopt. I want to stand in the street and scream, *"Don't do it. You have no idea what you are doing. Please stop"*. My whole body reacts. I hate being lied to. But I understand it because I learnt to be very good at it myself. I try not to do that anymore. I try to live in my own truth and that is where my body knows. I would rather have the truth and it be hard.

The searching process is hard. Every road I go down seems to lead to a dead end or to another path that I have to follow. There is no guarantee that the trail I am painstakingly following will result in a connection to someone who is related to me and it's very hard to tell. It takes a lot of emotional energy and there is always the spectre of rejection hanging around. Along with that is the possibility, which may be strong, that people in my extended birth family know nothing about me. So I walk a tightrope of trying to be sensitive to other people's feelings and not bringing a giant scary white rabbit out of the bag at the family party.

In December 2020 I had an email from someone who might be a relative on my birth father's side. I picked up the crumbs and followed the trail

I get tired of putting my big girl pants on. I want someone to do it for me. Someone to look after me. Someone to wrap me up in a blanket and soothe me. But I am not good at being looked after. I am someone who always answers 'I'm fine'. But I am learning.

I am learning that it is ok to have feelings. It is ok to have big feelings. It is ok to be confused, frightened, excited, brave, happy or sad. I don't know when it is appropriate for me to feel these things sometimes and I worry that I don't seem able to have the feelings when I think I 'should' have them.

CHAPTER 15 THIN ICE

I find a wooden picture frame in a charity shop and take it home. It will look nice, I think, with one of the picture cards I bought in Norfolk on holiday recently. Maybe the one of the boat. I discovered that coastline because my birth Mum Mary lived there when I found her. We ate crab sandwiches on brown bread and sat and watched the boats and the birds. She pointed out a white egret. We ate ice creams. I remember her sitting in a camping chair from the back of our car. She was wearing a pink jacket to keep off the wind although it was a sunny day. She couldn't walk far because her legs wouldn't carry her well any more. We went to Burnham market and bumped into two friends of mine from home. I said, 'This is my Mum'. They are the only people, apart from my immediate family, to whom I ever said that. She never met my parents or my friends. We lived too far apart and she only visited me once at my home.

Our relationship was strained at times and as she got older the journey was too much. But as I say that I wonder if it is really true. She never saw my second son after she visited us as a family when he was about 10 years old. The rest of her life I visited her. The younger two boys came with me sometimes and my oldest son got to know her a little again much later. Second son didn't come. I think he felt resentful that I was giving time and attention to this mother who had given me away. He said to me 'Sometimes the way you spoke to Nana was horrible' and he was right. It makes me sad. I think it made her sad too.

I used to be angry that my mum Mary wouldn't be a Granny to my children. She just wouldn't take on that role. She didn't mark their birthdays or Christmas. She was, I think, tentative about her connection to them just as she was with me. She didn't want to impose or intrude. I often experienced this tentativeness as a lack of interest. I thought she should make more of an effort. I felt like she was the 'adult' in the relationship as the parent and it was her responsibility. Now I understand her better. I think she grieved the loss. It was one of the things we talked about in our last conversations when she was in hospital with pancreatic cancer. As a qualified, experienced nurse she knew that she didn't have long left to live. She said to me, 'I am sorry I wasn't a very good mother or Grandmother'. I said, 'It is all OK, there is no need to feel bad now, we found each other and your grandchildren all love you' — I meant my sister's children, but she misunderstood me and thought I was talking about my boys. — and she got teary eyed and emotional and said, 'Oh, that means a lot'. In the end I just wanted her to have peace. When she died I knew that we had loved each other the best we could. It might not have been the mother and daughter fantasy in my head but what would I have done with that? Probably run a mile. Our relationship was what we had made. My grief over losing her began the day we were first separated so her death was only a physical manifestation of a familiar vacuum. I don't regret our reunion, it has been a defining thread of my life. Knowing my Mum Mary was literally a lot better than nothing.

Mary and her two sisters were separated from their parents by the mass evacuation of British children during World War II. The family's home was in London, but their father, Alan, was taken Prisoner of War by the Japanese and her mother, Hilda, had to send the girls into Kent to the countryside. It was several years before the family all saw each other again. Mum Mary talked about the evacuation as a happy time although she missed her older sister who was billeted separately and her mother and father. For several years the family did not know if they would ever see their father and husband again or if he was alive or dead. I wish we'd talked about the possible parallels in our emotional landscape. My experience of multiple separations from my parents in my early weeks, months and years and hers from the evacuation may have left us with similar feelings of insecurity and abandonment. I know that we both reacted similarly in many situations. We were both shy but able to behave as if we were extroverts. We both believed we had to deal with things by ourselves. Our mantras would have been, 'Just get on with it'. We were both prone to depression and introspection and self criticism. For years I had no idea that we were similar. My wife, Teresa, was able to show me our likenesses. She helped me to understand and she held me up through the terror I used to feel when we went to visit my Mum Mary. My inability to just pick up the phone and call Mary. It usually took me several weeks or even months to pluck up the courage to ring her. Often Teresa and I had arranged and booked a trip to Norfolk where Mary lived and I still had not picked up the phone, wanting to phone to arrange a visit and then only be able to do it a couple of days before we were due to set off. The shaking and shutting down. The panic that would well up after a certain amount of time in her company when my need for connection and my perception of her withdrawal and rejection felt too great for me to encompass. The terrible urge to run and leave, to get away, now, now, right this minute. My eyes saying, *'Get me out of here now! Before I start to scream and break down.'* My inability to ask for what I needed. Mary's inability to be honest.

I could count on two fingers the number of times she rang me in twenty years. She just couldn't do it. I thought she wouldn't. In the early years after our initial reunion I got angrier and angrier and more and more hurt. I thought she would never contact me if I didn't contact her first. To me that meant she didn't want me. Part of me believed that she had given me away to be convenient for her. I had a fantasy that she broke off the relationship with my father because she had met someone else, maybe my sisters' father, and so the pregnancy was an inconvenience. I was inconvenient. I had a huge hidden resentment that she didn't keep me because I just wanted to belong.

I wondered why she hadn't just married my father and got on with it especially as she found herself pregnant with me. After all, he seemed to be willing to. I never said that to her. I knew it sounded mean and anti-feminist and childish and selfish. But that was the truth. I wanted to be wanted. I needed to be loved, not to be given away. This is the curse of adoption. At a cellular level I believed I somehow wasn't enough. Something about me as a baby was wrong. Even when I was told the fairy story by my loving adoptive parents, 'We came and saw you in a roomful of babies. And we chose you. You smiled at us and we knew we had to have you'. Being chosen feels risky. *Maybe they can un-choose. I wasn't theirs to start with. It relied on some characteristic they saw in me or my behaviour. My smile. My perceived sunny nature. Maybe being chosen means Being good, Being nice. Being grateful. Not being difficult, or mouthy or rebellious.* I became oppositional on the inside years before it translated into my outsides.

One year my birth mother Mary came to stay with us, me, my husband and four children. She drove over for a weekend and I spent hours trying to get the house tidy and spotless. I was still vacuuming ineffectively when she arrived. I'm quite sure it didn't meet her exacting standards anyway. The beds were certainly not up to standard. Mary would make all the beds with strict hospital corners. When I stayed with her she would remake my bed because it wasn't done properly. She did the same with my sisters. She liked things done properly and we all had to hear her tales of Matron on the ward making the student nurses re-make beds time after time.

The boys were young. My husband cooked and made us nice meals. Mary kept talking about her marriage which had ended in divorce several years before. After she had me she went back to nursing and got posted abroad where she met her husband. They were married quite quickly the year after I was born and my next sister came along quite soon. Mary was talking about the island where they were living and she said, "It's a difficult time to talk about because it makes me sad". I thought she meant because it was not long after my adoption. *It must have been such a hard time. I can't imagine what you went through, being pregnant then giving up a baby. I don't know how you ever get over that or through it. You must have been grieving terribly.* I said, "It must have been a hard time". She looked confused and said, "Oh no, it's hard to talk about because I was so happy then with him there. I have such happy memories and that makes me sad because it all went to horribly wrong in the end".

What? Wait? What? You are sad because you miss the happy romantic time with your husband? The man who treated you so badly? You are sad to remember happy times with him but you aren't sad because that time is when I was being adopted? Not sad that just a year before, you had given birth to me in a nursing home and then given me away? Were you not thinking about me then at all? Was I so unimportant that you had just brushed me off and left me behind?

I felt shocked and couldn't say so. That moment was typical of Mary. She could say things carelessly that cut like a knife but she was oblivious. I thought it was just me until my sisters told me that she was the same with them. One of them told me that my Grandma was the same way and Mary's sisters. It helped to know it wasn't just me.

Our reunion was not bad. I am glad and grateful that I found her. I am glad and grateful that I found my sisters and nieces and nephews and cousins. I am glad and grateful that I now have this amazing extended family. I feel a part of it. They are my family and I love them. I don't regret searching or finding. Maybe you are thinking, 'Well of course it won't be easy!' The hard part is that it's never the parts that you expect to be hard that are. I thought she might not want to meet me at all. I thought I was comfortable with my adoption and that I had had a happy childhood. I didn't see how being adopted had caused me to have any problems at all. I thought I was well prepared because I had studied attachment and adoption and children's development. I had read anything I could find about adoption and birth mothers and reunion, not that there was much. But I didn't know just how hard it would be. I didn't realise what my own expectations and fantasies were for the relationship. And I had no idea what she would be struggling with. The truth is we were both traumatised and damaged. And we couldn't heal each other, not by ourselves.

There were a few years where my relationship with my birth Mum was on thin ice. We never entirely lost touch although we must have come close. My sisters kept us connected. They didn't let us go. They kept us both informed about the other and tried to interpret for us across a sea of mixed messages. Some years she missed my birthday. One year she sent me a cheque. I was so angry that I refused to put it in the bank. I didn't say anything or send it back. I just ripped it up. Months later she wrote to me asking if I had received it because it hadn't shown up on her bank statements. I just said, 'yes, thank you'. But I never used the money. I was still a child wanting my Mummy to notice me. I wanted to be seen by her. And we were both getting on with all the other stuff that makes up a life.

Now I know we did well. We kept going. We were both stubborn and kind and we wanted to have a relationship, we just didn't know where to start. We had to unlearn all our beliefs and expectations about ourselves and each other. We had to start again. I had to decide to accept her just as she was. That was the key. I had to stop wanting to try to change her. I had to stop wanting her to be the Mum I'd never had and just get to know her now. For a long time I called her 'Mary' when really I wanted to call her 'Mum'. But she never asked me to so I felt that I couldn't. It seemed like I would be crossing a line. It's hard to have a Mum that you don't call 'Mum'. It feels like the relationship is hidden again.

I wanted to belong but I kept trying to just fit in. I assessed and observed and changed my behaviour to try to fit with what I thought she wanted and then that got too hard to do and it didn't get me what I needed either. So I got angry and resentful and sulky but I kept that away from her too because I was too scared to have any conflict with her in case that meant I lost her again. It felt as if I had found her but didn't belong but losing her would mean being abandoned again. Brené Brown says, 'True belonging requires you to be who you are'. I still only had glimpses of who I was and Mum Mary didn't like herself. It took me a long time to recognise how deep her self hatred went. She had no good things to say about herself. She believed she was a bad person. And she felt like she was a bad mother. She was genuinely surprised to realise in her last few months that she was loved. I am so grateful that she did understand that then. She was a complicated woman, not always easy. She could be harsh and tactless. But she was also funny and clever and kind. She loved her family and she was so proud of them. She could talk to anyone, and would. Often it seemed as if she loved our partners more than us. They got all the attention. She would always ask what they thought about anything we might be up to. She had old-fashioned views about men and women and roles but when I told her I was a lesbian she never batted an eyelid and she supported me and loved Teresa from the moment she met her.

When I met Teresa I told her I was adopted and about my reunion with my birth family. It was part of the deal of being me. I come as a package with four children and my adopted child-self.

I was barely in contact with Mary, we were hanging on by a thread. But I wanted my love to meet my mother. I wanted Teresa to see me with the woman who had given birth to me. I hoped she would see similarities that I couldn't yet see. I was looking for someone to hold up a mirror for us. And I wanted my mother to see me with Teresa. I wanted her to know me as I was becoming. I suppose I wanted her blessing. Teresa and I stayed nearby at a Bed and Breakfast. That worked better for me. So did having a buffer. I have had mother-buffers all my life to protect me from the intimacy. Intimacy brings up the fear of being overwhelmed. Teresa did for me what my sisters tried to do, she interpreted for us. She told me how alike we are and explained how. She recognised my insane level of anxiety and she knew about attachment and trauma. She explained it to me in words of one syllable so that I could relate. She made sense of what I was experiencing and how I was and she didn't judge me or expect me to

171

be a certain way. She loved me and she loved my mum and she kept bringing us back together. One summer we took the two youngest boys, Ben and Joe, and went camping for two weeks in Norfolk. The weather was perfect. The sun shone and even the cold North Sea was just about warm enough to swim in. Every week before we set off on the trip I intended to ring my birth mum and tell her we were coming to Norfolk and could we visit. For the whole two weeks we were there I prevaricated. On our next to last day Teresa said to me gently, 'Are you going to phone Mary today? We can go and see her on the way home?". I said, 'I'll phone her later". That evening I still hadn't phoned. I said I would go to the supermarket to buy treats for dinner and after. I spent recklessly on bags of sugary sweet stuff and pastries. Teresa just looked at me, 'Now are you going to phone her?" I took out my phone and started to dial. I felt sick. As the number rang out I thrust the phone at Teresa and said, 'You do it. I just can't. I can't speak to her". I was too scared of rejection.

We met up the next day at a pub for lunch. Teresa and I and my little Mum Mary and Ben and Joe. I have so many photos of us from that day. We are wearing the same colour turquoise and we are all smiling. It was the best time I had had with her until then. That day changed how we were together. She understood something she hadn't known about me because I was too scared to make the call. And she wanted me to be ok. I realised she was pleased to see me and there was a spark of hope and trust we might kindle.

Being sick and telling the truth anyway.
Even as an adult adoptee I have lived with the knowledge that I was abandoned. The language matters. There are other words I could use. Relinquished. Displaced. That was my internal reality and it hurt. It is a fact of my existence. Now I choose to tell myself a new story. I am loved. It doesn't take away the truth of the original version but it reminds me who I am now. As a baby I learnt that someone would feed me and clothe me and change me. I was kept safe physically and

no-one hurt me or abused me. But something wasn't right and I knew it although I couldn't have told you what it was.

When life has got too hard my body shuts down. I get sick or I fall over and injure myself. My safe place was always bed or my car. Somewhere I could make a nest and snuggle down. Often I would take things to my nest that made me feel safe, blankets and food and books that are easy to read like childhood favourites. I regress into someone I've never really been able to be, the child who is safe. For me to do that I've used addiction to provide the warm fuzzy feeling.

Addiction got me here. But so did so many other things like hope and determination and courage. Like friends and love and family in all its many colours. Right here to this place where I am sitting staring at a page and realising I am writing a book about my life. But not just for my life. I am writing this for my teenage self. For the girl in the mirror who doesn't like what she sees. For the angry, scared girl who just wants some answers and to be heard. She wants to be able to ask all the questions she has kept inside her. To say, "Who am I and where did I come from?" "Tell me about my mother". She doesn't want to have to pick her time and her words with extreme caution. To wonder when it might possibly crack open a door that will let her see in. I want to tell her it is OK to ask.

And I want her to know that she can trust herself. She has a deep and powerful intuition about people and about what is true. She can trust that guide if she learns to recognise it and practice using it. I want to tell her that when her intuition calls her name, when that nudging is strong like a flutter in her stomach, like a voice in her ear she should stop and be quiet and find somewhere to sit and close her eyes and breathe. She should listen to what the guide is saying. Write it down. When those thoughts come try and hear them. They will lead you to your next step.

It is good to ask for help. It is good to say the actual words, "I need help." She doesn't have to know what the help is she needs. Sometimes just saying out loud "I need help" will bring an angel in disguise. And I want her to know that she will find her people. We are

173

here waiting. Other adoptees, other people who have lived through trauma, people of diversity and integrity and sensitivity. She will learn to recognise them.

I need people. Even though I might want to hide away, even though I am terrified of loving because it means losing, I can make a decision to say, 'Yes.' I needed to find the people who were mine. Some were mine for a while. Not everyone is with us for a lifetime. Friends, lovers, parents, partners and even children may come and go. But my real people stay because I take them inside deep down and they live inside my heart and mind for ever. Sometimes the ones who have gone may pop up again and tell me what they think or I will feel their presence in a place. It may be a memory that makes me smile or a phrase they used to use, but I know they haven't really gone.

And then there are the people and situations I have had to let go.

The social work machine is both good and bad. In my work life I used my skills of empathy and an appreciation of difference, and understanding of trauma from the inside and an awareness on a visceral level of identity and meaning. So why now? What has been the trigger or the reason to embark on a lifetime journey in words? Well, there are few stories in the world that have been heard less than those of adoptees. Our voices have been silenced by the expectations and agendas of all the adults involved. Adoption was designed for and by adults and the legal system perpetuates that. We have few rights to knowledge and information about our roots and origins and that leaves us with a distorted sense of self. We have been a hidden generation. Some truly awful and headline grabbing stories have been rightly told. Some have been made into films. I am thinking of 'Philomena,' 'The Magdalene Laundry,' 'The Rabbit Proof Fence" and 'Oranges and Sunshine' to name a few. 'Secrets and Lies,' by Mike Leigh also reflects a British transracial adoption experience.

A quick trawl through Twitter reveals a world of pain still being experienced by adult adoptees. People have talked for us or over us. Not least the Adopters. For a long time I was resentful and wary of all adopters, I didn't trust them. I believed they all had their own agenda which was confirmed by adoption workers and adoption agencies — that they were saints 'rescuing' children from poverty and despair and the sins of illegitimacy. There seemed to be a biased and judgmental attitude towards birth mothers who were seen as dangerous in their wantonness. The true Mary Magdalenes of our age.

The adoption triangle seemed to me like a Grimm's Fairy Tale of monsters and witches where babies were snatched and hidden away in Gingerbread cottages whilst on the inside was a dark miasma of shame.

I have been angry. I have had moments of rage but they usually seemed unconnected to my adoption experience. I had little understanding of my own emotions. Rage seemed to spiral up from a place deep inside and explode in relationships. I wanted to smash and burn. It was sometimes the only way to feel. The red hot anger would spill out in screaming and then the tears would come. I slammed a lot of doors and left a lot of houses in the height of my turbulence especially in my twenties and thirties. My adolescence raged on into my adult relationships as I tried to form roots and make deep intimate relations and whilst I left scorched earth behind me. But rage was not allowed in my childhood. Anger was not nice. I was dangerous, 'too strong willed' and I could see that my big feelings were impossible for my adoptive mother to manage. I was too much for her.

When I read this from author and adoptive parent Nancy Verrier I got goosebumps: "In my eyes adoption is a problem of unaddressed rage, and under that, unaddressed heartbreak".

In fact rage is an appropriate response to our experience.

Over and over again adult adoptees reflect back to the world their experience, "I was abandoned", 'She didn't want me", " I didn't fit in my family", "They didn't understand me", "I never felt safe", "My family didn't mirror me", "I must be bad or wrong because I was given away".

Crying a river

Crying didn't work either. Except to get me fed. My adoptive mother was a feeder. She soothed herself and me with food. Once when she was old I was visiting her and my Dad early in the mornings to make sure they were well. I would let myself into their bungalow and tiptoe into the bedroom with cups of tea. One morning I arrived as usual and called out 'Hello' quietly as I pushed open the bedroom door. The light was dim through the curtains and I could just make out their heads on the pillows. My Dad was snoring and the dog was in his basket next to the bed as usual. Mum was nearest to the door and I could see a dark stain from her mouth and down onto her chin. In the half light it looked like dried blood. My heart stopped. "Mum, are you OK?" I whispered. She sat up slowly, "Oh Love, it's good to see you" she said, sounding her usual self. "You have something on your face Mum". She reached up and wiped it on a tissue. "Oh it's just chocolate," she said. "I couldn't sleep so I got up and put a piece of chocolate in my mouth and then I must have fallen asleep as it melted". Soothed to sleep by chocolate. Both my mothers could have done that. So could I. The matching process may not have been perfect but the sugar addiction matching was spot on.

I hid my feelings because I wanted to protect other people as well as myself. My feelings were too big for them but they were also too big for me. I didn't know what they were and they were big enough for me to feel that if I let them out they might kill me. I knew it was my job to keep the peace. To close doors quietly and speak in a soft voice. My stomach aches and constant earaches may have been a function of my constant anxiety.

Writing about my adoption experience feels like crossing a line. It is a coming out all over again. It is shining a light on it all. It is writing the unvarnished truth from my perspective. Not trying to edit or play nice. Not having to worry about how my mothers or fathers would feel about what I have to say. It is being able to say all the things I have never been able to say out loud, even the things I didn't know I felt until they came out on the page.

It means telling the truth in a way that is scary and liberating. Setting myself free from the slavery of other peoples' narratives. It means that I am setting myself up potentially for questions and challenges, for criticism and disapproval. All the things my adoptee soul trembles at. But it is liberation because I am acknowledging my own reality as important and true. I recognise that my knowledge, my learning, my life and my experience is valid and that I have a right to them. They are mine. None of it is good or bad.

I wrote this after a Flourish class with a wonderful group of adoptees. The class was facilitated by Anne Heffron and Pam Cordano, both adoptees themselves, writers and truth seekers. We were talking about what Anne and Pam have called the 'Megaphone voice'.

The voice that pops up in our heads but doesn't come out of our mouths. The voice that is so loud we are scared to let it out. Our 'megaphone voices' were sad and angry and so funny. We laughed and cried and laughed again at the truth being spoken. Anne asked us to write one sentence that we would say if we were to make one statement out loud that we wanted everyone to hear about us. We are so good at being good. This is what came out for me.

I AM NOT GOING TO BE NICE
I AM NOT GOING TO SAY YES
NO I WON'T
I DON'T WANT TO BE NICE
I WANT YOU TO LISTEN TO ME

This was so hard. My mind went completely blank when I was asked to write just one sentence about what the best thing I could say would be. I can't even remember exactly what it was Anne asked us to do. Pam said that its trauma makes our mind goes blank. My heart hurt when I heard all the other adoptees try to say their truth out loud in big strong voices and I saw how we shook and my eyes slid sideways and Pam asked me to say it again and again until I could almost look them all in the eye as I said it. I am writing and writing and trying so hard to tell my truth and still it makes me shake because I am scared that people will think I am being over dramatic or whiny and that I should be grateful for what I have. I wrote down a few lines because I couldn't make my mind up which one I wanted to say most and then I wondered if they were true anyway. I don't want to be nice ALL THE TIME is what I mean. I don't want to always have to be understanding and polite and to let you tell me how I feel. I am still the good girl inside even though sometimes I just want to be able to be my bad self and not be on mute. I want to be able to dance wildly and scream and sing really loud. And I don't want to have to use drink or drugs to take the edge off my inhibitions or food to make me quiet and sleepy and compliant again. I just want to be ME. Nice. Not nice. Loud. Quiet. Yes and No. Me.

CHAPTER 16 LASHING OUT

The breakdown and burnout of 2010 changed me. Something had happened to my brain and my body, I had less resilience so I just had to stop when I was tired. I was forced to say, 'No'. I began to recognise what self care might mean. Life was complicated. My kids were struggling in various ways. We have all had experience of depression and anxiety and found ways to self medicate. It was hard sometimes being a parent of kids who were finding life hard. There were times when I held my breath every day and prayed we would get through and that they would make it. Sometimes life for them got dark too and I knew that they were holding on by a thread. My wife was working full time in a stressful job that took every bit of her energy and attention and I felt like she had left me for work.

Mummy was now in a care home and had dementia and I was worried about her all the time. I was feeling very stressed at work too, there was too much negativity and although I loved some of the work I did it was getting harder and harder every day to go in and be there. And I was getting bigger and bigger. The food that I was shoving into my body to try to calm the raging anxiety was only effective in the moment of eating it. I hated how I looked and how I felt. I had physical health issues and I was falling over and hurting myself frequently because I couldn't get my balance and I had trouble literally feeling my feet. It was all too much.

On top of all that was the relationships with my birth family. Mum Mary and I still struggled to make contact with each other. She never rang me and I couldn't bring myself to ring her very often. It was hard to keep all the balls in the air and my juggling skills were not very good.

Several times when I was driving somewhere that I knew well I would completely forget the route.

I was scared that I was losing my mind.

I didn't know how to get heard.

One morning I snapped. Teresa was going to work. We had eaten breakfast and were in the kitchen and it was nearly time for her to go. I was at home. I had been trying for months to contain my anxiety. I kept telling myself, "Don't be selfish, she is really busy." I tried to remember all the calming soothing words like "This too will pass" but they weren't really helping any more. I would ask constantly, 'Are you OK? Is everything all right? Is it me?'

I tried to remember that she was in the middle of a big project and an inspection and that all her energy and focus was there. I told myself it didn't mean she didn't love me. It didn't mean she wasn't available. But when she came in from work and didn't want to talk, ate dinner and then worked or fell asleep on the sofa I felt abandoned. My attachment style is so insecure that I felt her emotional absence as rejection and it was starting to eat away at me. That morning as we sat at the kitchen table I tried to say something. Tears came into my eyes and I did a lot of sighing. I was playing out a pattern from my childhood.

The pattern goes like this, "Don't say what is the matter, don't be direct and ask for help. Cry and sigh until 'she' notices". I used it with my Mum and sometimes it worked, sometimes it didn't. The same is true today. I was waiting for her to realise that something was wrong and to fix it. Part of me knew this wasn't a grown up way to behave, it felt childish and passive aggressive but I didn't have the skills to change. When I am stressed it seems I regress back into early patterns. I felt caught in a web of wanting to be a supportive partner and just wait it out and the growing terror that was starting to overwhelm me. I was not functioning very well anywhere but on the outside it all looked OK. I am good at that. It is another part of the pattern. Perform and pretend.

Being left by my mothers was a repeated pattern. There was the first abandonment when my mother walked away, my second mother figure was the foster mother who cared for me for three months before I was given to Mum and Dad. Then Mum had to go away too. It didn't matter to my baby self that there were good reasons for the separation. Being left meant there was no place to call home. It meant I didn't know how to get back. I was powerless. Powerlessness and fear took me into a child state. My safe person had left me before and it felt like I would die. As a baby, abandonment is life threatening. My nervous system knows how to cope with the threat of abandonment. I go on high alert. I get very watchful. Every breath and look, every turning away and blink of an eye, every moment of feeling disconnected is torture. And stress ramps my response up. I didn't know why I responded that way. I suspected that my history was involved but I couldn't separate out what was real 'now' and what came from the past. Post traumatic stress disorder was triggering my fight or flight response

Breakfast was done and it was time for Teresa to leave for work. I started to cry. *I bet she's sick of my tears. Please don't go, please don't go. I need you here. Please look at me. Please listen to me. Don't go. Im scared. I don't know what to do.* I said vaguely, 'I need to talk to you, I'm really not doing OK". She said, "I know that, but I need to get to work now, we will have to talk later." She turned away and started to walk away. *No, no, no I can't do this, don't go, don't go. I need you here. Don't leave me alone. Help me. See me, I'm drowning.* Terror overwhelmed me as I screamed, 'Don't you dare turn your back on me, don't you dare". I could have added 'Mummy' and it would have all been clear. I just knew I had to make her stop.

I flew across the room at her and thumped her hard on her arm three or four times. I was crying in rage and terror and then we looked at each other and everything stopped. She looked at me and her eyes were filled with tears. I'd hit her hard enough to leave bruises for days.

I said, "I'm sorry, I'm sorry, I'm sorry" and she replied, "We'll talk about this later, I've got to go, I have to be at work" and she left. I stood there and watched her walk away. *I can't do this. What have I done.*

I've ruined everything. She'll leave. Why can't she listen to me? Why can't she see what's going on? I am a terrible person. She will never forgive me. What will people say? I can't tell anyone what I've done they will think I am disgusting. I have lost everything.

I went numb. I went to work. My friend at work knew something was wrong but I couldn't tell them what. I was near to tears all day but I carried on. The next day I couldn't go in. Teresa told me she was going away for a few days. I didn't know if our relationship was over. I felt my life fall apart.

This is all my fault. You've finally done it. You have driven her away. You have proved to everyone that you are bad. You have crossed the line. You are unforgivable. You deserve to be left. No wonder they left you.

It all fell into place and smashed into pieces. And so did I. She talked about domestic violence in the same breath as talking about me. I felt judged and condemned, most of all by myself.

The next few months were hard for both of us. Teresa went away for a few days and I thought she wouldn't come back. I wanted to die. I sat drinking coffee one day at a Motorway service station because waiting at home was too excruciating. I felt like the walls were closing in on me. I was so ashamed and I had no idea how to make it right. I was scared that I couldn't. I talked to a couple of trusted friends and so did she. I looked for help. I arranged to see a therapist and this time I decided I would tell them everything. I would talk about adoption. I would stop pretending it hadn't affected me. I started going to a group for people in co-dependent relationships. I drove for over an hour twice a week for months for therapy and for the group. I started to explore the broken parts of me that were so scared of being abandoned that they had jumped right out of my skin and attacked the woman I loved. I had got my lover and my mothers jumbled up because I had never known the depth of the trauma I had experienced as a baby and child. I had to go deep to begin to understand myself and the impact on my relationships and I couldn't have done it alone.

I realised that this had happened before. I had raged at my kids, I had broken doors and smashed and screamed and exploded. I could be scary. I had scared the people I loved the most and if I didn't do something about it now I risked losing everything again. I had smacked all my kids. Not often but I had crossed a line there too. I had behaved in ways that I was so ashamed of that I couldn't bear to acknowledge them or bring them into the light of day. But now I knew I had to. I had to get down and dirty with myself, clean up and find out what was really going on. I couldn't go on living my life in a fog of resentment about my adoption and abandonment and attachment issues. They were poisoning my whole life.

Teresa and I stayed together. We are stronger and braver now than we ever were before. And we know each other better too. For her it felt like the worst thing I could have done then. The worst thing for me is being left and being betrayed and lied to. That kills me. I cannot bear betrayal. For me that means saying one thing and doing another. Making promises and breaking them. Telling me what you think I want to hear. I need the truth.

I did the worst thing for her and she didn't leave me. But I had to take responsibility and change. We both made changes to listen to each other on a deeper level. We learnt to understand each others patterns and what triggers our deepest fears. I had never consciously thought of her as my mother but in that moment of the terror of abandonment I reacted to her as if she was. Occasionally in a loving moment she would say, "You're my baby" as if that was a good thing. I hated it. "I'm not your baby, don't call me that, I'm not a baby" . Being a baby felt like a dangerous place for me to be. It was so messy and complicated that I could hardly bear to look at it in retrospect but I had to if I was going to have the life I actually wanted. I had to grow up and come out of the adoption fog.

The FOG.

This is a term I didn't know until relatively recently. It is part of the reclaiming of our experience by adoptees. In the fog we tend to not be able to name how we feel. The FOG is an acronym for Fear, Obligation and Guilt. I used to say things like, 'Yes I was adopted but I had a happy childhood, it didn't make any difference to me' or 'I was lucky'' or 'I am fine'. The adoption fog can manifest in gratitude to birth mothers and telling them that 'they did the right thing'. It can show up in denial and numbing out. The fog was acted out in my addictive relationship with food, alcohol and nicotine and in depression and anxiety. Coming out of the fog meant feeling the feelings that I had carried in my body for a lifetime and that had gone unrecognised. There was grief, anger and rage and bone-deep fear. I have learned that there is an emotion called 'Panic/grief'. It is a feeling that people who have experienced trauma will understand. It is what an adoptee who is coming out of the fog feels. Panic/Grief is what triggered my lashing out that day. I had no idea that it had a name but I recognised that it came from a primal place where I didn't have the words to express my emotions. Panic/grief or Primary-Process Separation-Distress is what happens when a baby is severed from it's mother or primary care-giver. Pam Cordano says that the bridge out of this experience is curiosity or the 'Seeking System'. 'Curiosity is a bridge to a new possibility; it is the way out of "Panic/grief", despair and depression.' (Cordano 2020). Getting curious and putting all my attention on learning to live in the present moment whilst acknowledging and feeling the feelings from the past is what catapulted me out of the fog. It took a specific moment where the perfect storm of events and experiences collided for me to be able to see that I needed help. Many adult adoptees find themselves in similar situations or in therapy (again) where an adoption competent therapist recognises PTSD. Coming out of the fog was tough. Being in the fog was like living underwater and trying to knit.

Teresa and I have had a lot of issues arising from my adoption trauma. On the surface it all looks great but it has been challenging. I have a very anxious attachment, anxiety and being unsettled are my default setting. I want to keep everyone happy so I will tie myself in knots to be in the middle of all the family relationships. I want to be held and I want to push her away.

Teresa and Julia 2020

Touching Base

Teresa says to me 'I love you' all the time. She is a physical person, she loves to touch and cwtch (that's Welsh for cuddles) and kiss and cuddle. She likes to be in contact. Sometimes we get what we need even when we don't know it. She has taught me to be comfortable with my body in a way I had never been. She loves my body and she always tells me I am beautiful. No-one ever told me I was beautiful before or maybe I didn't hear them. Teresa has told me so many times that I believe her. It's not just the words., my whole self knows she is telling me her truth. And I know when she isn't. I know I am not very good at giving compliments back. I hesitate to commit to words and touch that seem to take me over a line. The line is saying that I am all in. I try to show it in different ways. She doesn't let me off the hook though and that is good for me. When we first got together she told me that I couldn't hold back, I had to make the leap or it wouldn't work. She saw something in me that other people hadn't. She saw that I could appear to be all in but still hold myself apart. She didn't want to be in a relationship with me where I kept a part of myself back. It was all or nothing. She would tell me that she loved me for ever, that she loved me unconditionally, that there was nothing I could do that would stop her loving me. She said we would be together for ever. I half believed her but the 'unconditional' word freaked me out. I always had a little part of my mind running a commentary. The commentary went something like this, "This is all very well now. She says this because she wants you now but no-one loves unconditionally, there are always conditions. She might leave. Everyone leaves." I would watch for any sign that she was cross or distracted or not present. Any time she appears withdrawn or irritated with me especially if it would go on for days or weeks or times when I 'just knew' she was thinking bad things about me and I would add them all up in my bed and say to myself, "*See. There. And there. She doesn't like that about you, or that, or that. She is angry with you. That means she doesn't really love you unconditionally. She says she does but it isn't true. She's lying.* I was confused about what love was. I believed that to be loved meant no-one ever got cross with me. That they would think I was perfect. That I could do no wrong. When I write it down and say it out loud I know that it is a lie and a childish belief. But somewhere it is what I had absorbed. Love means never getting upset with people, never getting cross with them.

I don't know where I got this skewed belief from. I know that I can be cross with my kids and still love them. I know that there are times I can be upset or hurt deeply and still love someone. Love is not so fragile that it can be wiped out by momentary irritations. But somehow I believed one thing for me and another for other people. I knew my love for my children was strong enough to withstand anything. Could the same be true when someone loved me?

Physical touch can be a big deal for an adoptee, because it is the most primal form of communication for us as babies. I both crave it and fear it.

I used to get physical attention by being sick. When I was sick my Mummy came into her own. She liked caring for me then, she was able to be practical and would make me stay in bed and bring me soup or drinks like Ribena or Lucozade, that orange fizzy sugar concoction which only came out when I was ill. Comfort was a a hot water bottle for my tummy-ache or constant ear-aches or cold Ribena. I felt nurtured and when I was sick I could accept that because I couldn't look after myself. Often when I'm sick it is a way I can cry, I become babyish and I want someone to make me soup and just be nice to me. I want my mummy.

When I was little and something upset me I would sit in my room and cry until Mummy came to find out what was wrong. If I had a nightmare I would go into my parents bedroom and get into bed between them. I liked that. For years I wanted my Mummy when I was sick. I wanted to have that care she gave me then. She would often buy me a treat like a colouring book or a small puzzle to keep me occupied. It made me feel loved to be physically cared for. Being sick was a time I could stop having to be anything other than myself. I could be needy and let someone else take care of me. I didn't have to do it all by myself. Mum would look after me when I was sick because she knew how to do that. She found it easier to help me when she could bring me nice food or drink or a toy or new book. I would let her touch me when I was sick without having to push her away. She could brush the hair off my forehead and tuck me in to bed. I have always found it hard to be taken care of.

I have learnt to be more of a hugger. I have always been physically affectionate with my children because I learnt that from my friends who were mothers before me We hug and say, "I love you" whenever we speak or get together. Not hugging in 2020-21 has been hard for us just as it has for the rest of the world. The children are awesome at hugging. They are men who can hug and say 'I love you". I love that about them.

In intimate relationships I find initiating physical touch scary. I will reach out with a toe or finger rather than go straight in for a cuddle. Teresa and I have a super king size bed. When we were both a lot bigger and we had dogs who also slept on the bed it was great. We had loads of room. We spent a lot of money on it and got one with a memory-foam mattress. Because we were both several stone heavier for many years the bed has become flat on either side where we lie and has a huge hump down the middle. If we want to get close one of us has to make the ascent over the hump. It makes cuddling up close quite a feat. We should probably get a new mattress. I scoot across the bed with my toes and touch her leg or I stretch across the Great Divide until my fingers just touch her back. Sometimes I pretend it is accidental or that I am just seeing if she is still there. I don't commit to the physical contact. I always wait to see if she is interested first. This isn't a very successful romantic strategy.

I always leave the door open for rejection.

CHAPTER 17 CAKE AND A PARTY

My Mum Margaret's world was getting smaller. Where once, heaven for her would be an afternoon of sitting at a pavement cafe, chatting and watching the world go by, by 2011 it was all about the ice cream. Every weekend Teresa and I took Mum out from her care home. We visited garden centres and cafes and parks. In her final year Mum needed a wheelchair for trips outside but she still loved to sit in the sunshine and watch people and their dogs. As we drove to the park every week we would pass the fish and chip shop at the end of the road. 'Oh I love those fish and chips' she would say. Often on a Sunday we would hear the church bells ringing from St Giles's church. When she died and they took her body away the bells were ringing as she left. Mum noticed everything that year. She noticed the spring lambs in the fields and crocuses blooming on the verges. Her memories were in the past but her childlike appreciation of the world about her lived on. Shopping for clothes and hats and jewellery still raised her spirits and I was the perfect accomplice in that arena. One Sunday at 'Cadwaladers' ice cream parlour I bought Mum a small tub of chocolate and Welsh cake flavour ice cream which came with a plastic green scoop for a spoon. Welsh cakes are like flat scones with currants in and are made on a griddle. My Welsh wife Teresa calls them 'bakestones.' I bonded best with my mothers over sugar and shopping. It was a source of connection and conflict. We all loved sweet food. I came by my food addiction honestly. Nature or nurture, I had a double whammy.

Mum looked at the ice cream tub in her hand and sighed. She said plaintively "I'm not getting any". I saw that she was sucking on the green scoop as if it were a straw. Using cutlery was becoming too much of a challenge. Finger food was what she needed. Mum's decline into dementia had elements of tragedy as well as comedy, a relentless journey towards the ending of this life. I saw changes in her every week. Mum needed reminding of the boys' names and who was who on the photos she had around her room, but she always knew that she adored them when they visited. She still loved to laugh and seeing her grandsons was the highlight of any day. Her other love was Geordie, the black rescue poodle she and Dad had adopted a few years before. Now Geordie lived with Teresa and I and the boys and we would take him to visit Mum. Geordie had got fat as Mum forgot when she had fed him so he was constantly topped up with doggie and non-doggie treats. We had him on a strict regimen of weighed and measured food and walks. I used to joke that I should do the same. It wasn't a joke. I just couldn't do it then. Geordie would willingly sit all day on a comfortable knee and Mum would stroke his curly coat and rub his ears. Dogs are the best comfort. Geordie came on all our outings together with Mum and he would happily visit the other residents at the care home.

That day when we took her back to the home Mum didn't remember which room was hers. She seemed to be diminishing. I wondered how long we had left. I had the sense that it wasn't going to be long. I didn't want her to go, but I hoped she could go easily when the time came. On the way back Mum said, 'I was talking to a nice lady and she is 87'/ She sounded astonished at this grand age.

I said, "That's like you Mum, you're 87 now aren't you?"

"How can that be?" she said, "How can we be the same age? I don't feel like she is my sister. If we were born at the same time we would be sisters.'

Sometimes the cognitive dips and signs of another spark in her brain that has fizzled out took me aback and I would find it hard to speak.

At Mum's 87th birthday the week before we threw a small family party. One or two friends popped in to see her during the day with gifts of flowers and chocolate. Teresa and I brought party food from Marks and Spencer's and we laid it all out on a table with flowers and a big birthday balloon. I joked that 'It wasn't just any food, It was M and S food'. It made Mum laugh because she remembered the TV advertisement and she had always had a soft spot for M and S, the

British middle classes' foodie heaven.

Phyllis, another resident who had just moved in to the home and was also quite confused, wandered in and out of the lounge where we were. She joined us for a little while and drank sparkling grape juice and ate cake..

"Is it someone's birthday?" asked Phyllis.

"Yes, it is Margaret's. This is Margaret. Mum this is Phyllis".

"How old is she?" said Phyllis.

"Margaret is 87".

" Oh, not as old as me then I'm 84".

Numbers are confusing.

Mum Margaret and the new hat

One weekend on our regular outing Mum seemed sad. She kept repeating "I just want to cry".

At lunchtime Mum didn't want to eat. She said, "I just want to cry and I don't know why".

I said, "You sound sad, Mum".

'Yes, I think I am. But I don't know why. I am lucky'.

I said. 'It's okay Mum, we all feel sad sometimes'.

She perked up a bit at the thought of some cake. I felt slightly guilty for comforting her with food.

Mum seemed sad all afternoon. She was quieter than usual and it was harder to distract her. It was exhausting when she was like that because nothing seemed to help. I found it hard to not become irritated with her. I practiced patience imperfectly. She said, "I just want to cry and I don't know why. I have everything I need and everyone I want with me." Teresa said, "It's okay Margaret, everyone has sad days". Sometimes it seemed as if everyone else got on better with Mum than I did. Nothing we said seemed to help that day and even cake didn't make it all better.

When we took her home I asked the staff if anything different had happened. Lily, Mum's next door house-mate had died the day before. Mum didn't remember Lily, but she knew she was sad. I felt sad too.

Another sunny afternoon in April, another shopping trip with Mum. Two pairs of cotton pull-on trousers for summer with two pretty blouses in the Edinburgh Woollen Mill and two beaded necklaces that would easily slip over her head. Mum spotted a turquoise sun hat and had to try it on. That went in the bag too. Mum couldn't manage fastenings any more but she always liked to look pretty. We talked about how she could be all dressed up for the Royal Wedding.

Mum Margaret, Geordie on her knee and the new blue hat
2011

Prince William was getting married to Catherine Middleton and there would be a party at the home to celebrate. Mum smiled.

We sat in the glorious Easter sunshine. I drank an iced latte, Mum ate a Cornetto. More sugar.

Mum and Julia in 2011

I took photos of Mum wearing the new turquoise sun-hat and looking beautiful. I look tired, depressed and I am at my heaviest ever. I am bang slap in the middle of my food addiction. Mum was happy that day. That year I ate my feelings away more than I had ever done before. Looking after Mum was complicated like our relationship. My eating disorder was out of control. When we got back to the home after our outing I put the new hat on a shelf in her wardrobe. I thought, next time it is sunny it will be a new hat all over again. That was one of our last outings. Mum died on August 12th 2011.

Dying to be noticed

Mum Margaret, my boys' Nana, died on August 12th 2011. There had been cards and messages and flowers, hugs and kind words. Our son Ben was waiting for his A Level results the next day. It would be the first family moment that Mum was not there for. I would catch myself thinking of telling her things and noticing little moments of loss. Colleagues gave me an orchid. Mum always managed to keep them growing beautifully. She gave me several. I killed all of them. I wondered if she would help me keep this one. It is still flowering so maybe she did. I wrote some words and tried to say something about her life, remembering moments, telling stories, collecting memories. My mind kept going completely blank. I told myself that I had been writing about Mum for months, sharing everyday gems and the joys and sorrows in a blog. But still it was hard to do. I kept starting again and the boys wrote their own words. Son Jon wrote a beautiful poem.

My half-sister Kate told me she had written a letter to her Dad when he passed away, that helped to think of how to write. I felt numb a lot of the time. I wrote in my journal *"I don't know that I am feeling what I am supposed to feel. I feel caught in a limbo and in other people's expectations. I will do the right thing and that will help. I have been searching for a quote, a few pithy words, a poem, a line or somebody else's words to express the feelings I don't know how to share"*. I still don't know if I feel what I am 'supposed' to with grief. Everything about being adopted is complicated. I don't have the words to explain why the loss of my mothers is hard but not hard at the same time. I have feelings but I don't think they are the feelings 'normal' people have when their mothers die. I feel like a fraud, a Cabbage Patch doll of a daughter. And yet in the end I behave like a daughter in all the ways I am expected to. Maybe that in itself is an act of love

Do you have children, Margaret?

Mum Margaret was an only child. She was a passionate teacher and very proud of her profession. In her eighties and in hospital after a fall a nurse asked Mum, "Have you got children Margaret?" Mum looked puzzled and smiled hesitantly at the nurse and looked at me, "I don't know, I don't think so" she said, "But I think I must have had because I always loved children". She looked at me quizzically trying to place me. I smiled and said, "Well I'm your daughter Mum aren't I?" And she relaxed and said, "Oh yes, of course you are" and smiled but she still looked puzzled. I didn't say, 'You adopted me'. I was so used to not telling the truth about it that it didn't occur to me. My discomfort with her confusion made me try to rescue her but she had told her own instinctive truth and I unwittingly perpetuated the lie. White lies can hurt too. I got caught up in the story that we had lived with for so long that I didn't know how to break out of it. I kept quiet. She hadn't had children until she adopted me. I was hers and not hers. That is the paradox of adoption. You are mine but you come from another mother. It was still too hard to acknowledge it between us. Words and our shared narrative failed me. I didn't have the language for the sadness, and neither did she.

Mum and I loved each other, but we didn't think the same. She was a kind and essentially gentle person, full of self doubt and anxiety except in her professional identity where she was confident and sure of herself. I found her often controlling and needy, so desperate to be in my life that she would try to shoe-horn her way into every relationship and any situation to be a part of it. I held her at arm's length because of my terror that she would overwhelm me with her neediness and she kept trying to get in. We struggled to meet in the middle and relied on other people to broker our discordance. Mum copied me to an extent that drove me crazy. I felt like I had a stalker. If I bought something she would have to have one like it. It didn't matter if it was a new dining room table or a jacket, I could guarantee the same would appear in her house or over her arm.

We rediscovered each other in the last part of her life. I learnt to be kinder and more patient and not to argue with everything she said. After my Dad died I expected Mum to fall apart but she didn't. I underestimated her strength and her instinctive joy in life. I saw a different person for a while. Both my Mums were strong and neither of them appreciated their own strength. Mum Margaret seized onto life in widowhood with renewed enthusiasm. A few weeks after Dad died, I rang her to ask her of she would like to come to an event at the children's school. She said, "I am just going to say 'Yes' if anyone asks me to go anywhere." Mum started to have fun again. Her social life took off with a vengeance. She found a new friend called George and they developed a romance with Valentine's Day dinners and trips to the theatre. He paid her compliments and bought her gifts like jewellery and flowers and she blossomed. He bought her a ring and I was so jealous I found it excruciating. I managed to smile and be polite through gritted teeth. I felt excluded and I felt ashamed of my feelings, they seemed so childish I thought. And they were. I told myself I was being stupid.. There is a saying in twelve step rooms, 'Hysterical is Historical'. My 'hysteria' or strong emotion was definitely triggered by the past.

I tried to be glad for Mum and happy that George being around meant I didn't have to 'Mum-sit' every day. I wasn't angry on behalf of my Dad. It was for me. As Mum got older and the dementia started to appear she also developed friendships with people who took advantage of her. As she started to rely on other people she seemed to stopped trusting me. It felt like the ultimate betrayal. I started to believe that she hated me. Sometimes I would look in her eyes and what I saw was hate. Now I know it was fear and her delusions. Mum's hostility scared me. I started to believe that I was seeing the 'real' Mum. I told myself that this is how she really felt. *She hates me. I have made her hate me because I was am such a horrible person. I deserved this, it's my punishment for being so mean to her and always arguing with her. She doesn't love me. I am scared. She scares me. She has always scared me. What am I scared of? I am being ridiculous? She is a kind person. Everybody loves her and thinks she is nice. Why can't I be the daughter that she deserves?*

One day Mum said she that didn't want to see me again because I was "making her stay in the home". I had made her room beautiful with her favourite pictures and a blanket and photographs but it wasn't home. She said, "You had no right to take my things out of my house. You are stealing them". That day when I left her I felt like I had lost her all over again. I thought *'This is the way it is all going to end. She will cut me out of her life and her Will and if I see her she will just keep looking at me like that, as if I am the devil and she doesn't know me at all.'*

Mum was developing delusions and her anxiety tipped her over into paranoia and occasional delirium.

Mum started behaving more strangely. She hid her jewellery outside on the window ledge of her room. She kicked and hit one of the female staff because they wouldn't let her go into the garden because the tree surgeon was cutting down some branches. Mum thought she was being kept prisoner. She started to make secret arrangements to meet a woman she knew who had promised to 'sort out her money' for her and one day the carers found Mum in a 'compromising' position with a male visitor in her bathroom. The staff were concerned for her welfare and that he was taking advantage of her. The social workers, a psychiatric nurses and the psychiatrist who had done an assessment all agreed it wasn't safe for Mum to go home. A protection plan for Mum was initiated to keep her safe. I felt as if I was failing her because I couldn't make it all better.

My phone rang one day in the centre of the Welsh city of St. David's where Teresa and I were staying for a short break. The manager of Mum's home said that a woman who mum knew was visiting and appeared to be trying to get Mum to sign legal papers so that Power of Attorney over her finances could be transferred. I stood in the centre of that beautiful city with tears pouring down my face as I tried to talk to Mum on the phone. The next few weeks and months were hard. I felt as if the foundations of my world had been built on quicksand and I was going under. What saved us both was support. Unlike childhood where we muddled through in splendid isolation, this time we had a team of helpers. Family and friends and professionals rallied round us. I didn't have to do it all by myself and by now I was learning that asking for help and letting myself be cared for was easier than being stubbornly independent. My boys could chat with their Nana and she was distracted by them and happy. One day she had a fall at the home and needed an X-Ray at the hospital. Toby the eldest grandson at twenty-seven, stayed with his Nana whilst she waited to be assessed. The next day when I visited Mum, she was happier than I had seen her for a while. 'Oh I had such a lovely night' she enthused. 'Toby came and he brought me a Kit-Kat and some Maltesers and we had a lovely chat.' No bones were broken and a grandson and chocolate could make most things better..

My childhood friend Iain drove up to Staffordshire from Dorset on the South West coast specifically to visit Mum with me. He said, "You have found her a good place and you are a good person. You are doing okay. And your Mum is doing as well as she can". Mum started to have anti-psychotic medication for her delusions and para-noia and that made all the difference. She became calmer and more contented. Her constant anxiety melted away.. She was so much easier to be with when her mental health was treated. My fear of abandon-ment and rejection settled down in equal measure to her diminishing anxiety. We were often enmeshed in each others fear but the last year of her life we found a new way to be together. I am so grateful that we had that year. When she died I knew that I had loved her and Mum and I had both done our best. The memories I have of Mum's last year are good ones. I was able to massage her dry hands them with cream and paint her nails. I would kiss her and give her a hug when we visited. I still found physical contact with her difficult but I tried to find ways to make her happy. Her dementia taught me that arguing with her just made us both unhappy. I learnt to tell her sto-ries and treat her as if she was special. Most of all I didn't do it alone. I used a lot of sugar that year.

I wrote something for the funerals of three of my parents. Two Mums and my Dad. I wish I had known my other father, my first one. There is a space inside me that misses him.

I wrote for my birth Mum but it could apply to either of my mothers.

"Sometimes Mum's version of events of the past was tidied up and we could find ourselves down a rabbit hole of questions and memories that we had to put aside."

How Not to Cry
When my adoptive father and then my adoptive mother and then

my birth mother died, I couldn't cry. I don't know how to cry at the right time. Sometimes other people cry for me. In the Middle Ages there used to be a 'sin eater', an exile from the village, who lived outside the parish boundaries. He was feared and despised and yet he was useful. When someone died he would be given bread to eat and wine or beer to drink and by eating the food ceremonially over the corpse of the person who had died, he would 'eat' their sins, leaving them cleansed.

When my adoptive mother died, Teresa cried buckets. She drank quite a lot of wine too and that increased her emotional lability quite a bit. Teresa is Welsh and in times of high emotion her inner Celt comes out. I love that about her and it drives me crazy. That night I sat and watched her cry and eventually sent her to bed to sleep it all off. When she cried all those tears it felt like she was crying my grief. And it made me angry because my eyes were dry. I wondered what had happened to my tears. I felt numb. I couldn't sleep. I knew I was sad and I was exhausted and wired so that my brain wouldn't shut down. I couldn't sleep. I sent out notices to let people know and stayed awake on the sofa just waiting for the next day to start. The day that would be after the day that my mother died. I needed to be alone or I needed to be held. I'm not sure which.

I envy the way that tears spring easily to other people's eyes. Conflict makes me cry and feel shame. Pain makes me cry, and illness. Sometimes the tears come out of nowhere and it is like a tap has been turned on inside me and I can't stop.

One day a few weeks after I had separated from my second husband, Mum announced that she wanted her and Dad to go into a home. I felt as if I had been knocked sideways. Mum had been ill physically and mentally and in hospital again and we had discovered that she had been mixing up her medication and poisoning herself in the process. She had days where she seemed quite rational and other days when I knew that Mum had left the building, leaving some sort of crazy person behind who was angry and hostile, especially to me.

Dad and I set off in my car to inspect one of the places Mum had shortlisted. I knew she wasn't rational but I seemed to be the only person who thought that way. I started to drive and the tears just welled up from my chest and leaked out through my eyes and nose and mouth. I couldn't say why I was so upset but I felt bereft. Dad said, "You and your Mum, I don't know what to do. You just have to let her work this out for herself.". Dad knew that Mum wasn't well but he would never disagree with her once she had set her mind on something. That episode passed and Mum and Dad stayed in their own home for the rest of Dad's life.

When Mum and Dad died their house was full to the rafters. I joked that my dad seemed to have kept every piece of paper he had ever received. His filed payslips went back to his first job in 1938. All his records were in alphabetical order.. There were files with my old school reports. Mum had kept my baby clothes and toys. It took Teresa and I and the four boys weeks to clear their house. There were clothes belonging to my grandparents, old fur coats and costume jewellery, thousands of photographs and pairs of soft leather gloves wrapped in old tissue paper. In the wardrobes and chests of drawers were clothes that hadn't been worn for decades. Mum's wedding dress, once white and now royal blue, was hanging under a cover. The relics of their lives and those of their ancestors. There were boxes full of pristine linen sheets, tied up with ribbon and folded into stiff creases from thirty years of storage. Boxes of photographic slides from forty years of holidays, hundreds of faces of people whose names were lost in time. Greeting cards from Christmases, birthdays, weddings and funerals. Postcards and drawings from the grandchildren. Mum and Dad had a puppet and marionette collection which I boxed up and sent to a puppetry friend of theirs in Edinburgh. I sold things on e-Bay and at auction for tiny amounts that would have made my mother cry. I gave hundreds of books and bags of clothes to charity. The boys chose things they wanted and that had special meaning but there was so much that sentiment fatigue was very real. In all that squirrelled lifetimes hoard there was not one piece of paper that related to my adoption. My history and our conjunction was erased from view. No certificate, no dates, no names, no papers, no notes, no history. I sat on my parents old bed with the bitter taste of a final disappointment in my mouth. That feeling was hard to stomach.

Mum Margaret

You are old and frail
Now my mother
Ties bind us
Into knots of conflict
And love

Sweet mother and daughter
Never came our way
Although you yearned for it
But I was always running
Running away

Now time flies
From day to day you change
Fading in and out
I am angry at the loss
Of possibility of connecting

I see your handwriting
And it breaks me open
With its trembling incomprehension
Of a tired mind
You still kiss me when I leave
I feel the breath leaving you.

CHAPTER 18 KEEP TAKING THE TABLETS

Depression

Depression has tracked me down and laid me low too many times to count. I can see the timeline when I draw it out on paper but I can't count the episodes. It has been a dark thread since I was seven or eight. It has often felt like an enemy but really I have learnt it is the warning sign that self-care is missing. It is the canary who stopped singing in the mine. When the canary stopped singing it had died giving the miners a chance to escape the poisonous gas in the pit. Depression seems to stop the singing. It pulls down the covers and muffles the sounds of joy. It is a foreboding of disaster that means 'This may be an emergency, take action now'.

My family didn't believe in mental health problems unless you were having 'a nervous breakdown'. We didn't have those in our family. We got on with it. We didn't talk about feelings. I had glandular fever when I was fifteen. I was poorly for a few weeks with the physical symptoms and then I developed chronic fatigue and depression. I had no energy, all I wanted to do was sleep. I hated school and being in that huge concrete box with so many people. I never felt like I fitted in and I just wanted to stay at home and do my work there. I hung on to academic success as a way out of the box I felt trapped inside. I had become adept at truanting under cover of 'missing the bus' and spending the morning or day in the next town with one of my friends. We would go to the Italian coffee shop. It felt sophisticated and a heady taste of freedom and pretend adult life. We drank milky coffee from glass cups and saucers and talked and smoked cigarettes. We used to spend our dinner money on cigarettes and bus fare and take an orange from home for our lunch. Sometimes my friend's little sister would come with us because she stayed at home to babysit when her Mum wasn't well. The baby would sit in her buggy by the table and I expect people thought that one of us was her Mum. Nobody ever asked us why we weren't at school. I forged notes from my Mum to say I was ill and nobody ever checked until one day I got caught smoking in the girls toilets at school. The teacher rang home and brought up my absences and Mum covered for me on the phone before she told me off afterwards. I remember being proud of her for standing up for me. I was surprised that she was willing to cover for me and it made me feel safe that she was prepared to have my back. I think she didn't want to admit to not knowing what I was up to, her pride was at stake. When push came to shove she was always there for me. She bailed me out of debt and overdrafts and paid for family holidays that I had booked then couldn't afford because of my spending. I knew if I rang and was upset she would rescue me. I'm not proud of that.

Once I'd had glandular fever Mum let me stay at home if I said I wasn't feeling well. She took me to a private doctor who prescribed some tablets and told her that my fatigue and low mood could last for months. Years later I realised he had given me amitriptyline which is an anti-depressant. That doctor gave me permission to escape. I could sleep until I woke up. I didn't have to 'pull myself together'. He gave me permission to rest. Permission take time off school. I more or less had a year off. I think that doctor saved me. The depression didn't go away all together but he taught me it was possible to survive. I thought about death and dying and I felt like I hated everyone and everything. I didn't know that this was depression I just thought it was me. The adoption mask was starting to crack. I wanted answers and I couldn't get them.

I felt trapped in an existence that didn't feel like me. I wanted escape, I wanted to be somewhere else. I wanted a geographic solution. I thought it was being a teenager. But I needed connection with people who understood.

The suicidal thoughts got darker when I went back to school and exams. I was walking home with one of my best friends and I said to her, "I just want to die. I hate school. I hate everything. I hate Mum and Dad, I wish they were dead. It all feels pointless'. She laughed and said, 'Don't say that, you don't mean that". But I did.

My parents were worried enough that they asked me if I needed a break. For a few months over that summer I volunteered at a Christian retreat centre on an island off the North East coast of England. I wanted to get away but I was lonely. I made some friends and I found a sense of peace and stillness in the wild beauty of the island harbour at dawn as I watched the fishing boats come in or as I walked for miles around the rugged coastline. I sat on empty windswept beaches and watched seabirds swoop down and waves break on the shore. I found a part of myself there that gave me a sense of peace and a feeling of connection. I have never lost that sense of a sacred thread between me and the sea and sand and swaying marram grass. God meets me where the world ends and the sea begins. She is the wind and the waves and the sky. I didn't want to go home but eventually when the summer ended I had to.

We adoptees have been treated as a commodity. Loved and wanted, yes that is certainly true for many of us but not all. But we are all fantasy children, changelings, a dream that may turn into a nightmare on either side. We are the stolen child and the replacement. We are always somewhat in the wrong place. Always somewhat in the wrong. We feel it in our bodies and our souls. When that umbilical cord is cut there is no sticking it back together with some sort of familial super-glue. Often there is a period of separation before the adoption so we float in a soupy limbo where other hands and voices care for us but we don't belong there, we aren't loved or known. An institution is no place for babies.

When I was a young social worker I used to visit Local Authority nurseries. Children whose families I worked with would be placed there for day care. The babies used to be 'put down' for a nap in prams or on camp bed cots at the same time every day. There was a row of babies and toddlers all having a sleep at the same time. Everything was regimented. It used to make my blood run cold. I can still see it and feel the fear it instilled in me. Something in me abhorred the routine but I think it was much deeper than that, it was a visceral terror of the institutionalisation of care.

In June 2010 I wrote:

"Today is a duvet day, an 'I can't be bothered to shower, turn off the phone, don't want to talk, where's the chocolate sort of day.' Two steps forward and three back is how it feels. I can get knocked back into anxiety and low mood with a difficult phone call, someone else's expectations or a meeting about work that brings me down. I know I'm wobbly when walking round the supermarket is a challenge, when I'd like to hide behind my sunglasses and when getting dressed is too much effort. I've learnt that making the effort, putting on the face and the earrings helps. I might skip the shower but iron my trousers, put on a cheerful top and stick the earrings in. The house is quiet and the silence is soothing. I'm trying to separate could from should. Should, is guilt filled expectation, my inner critical parent voice who nags and undermines, constantly telling me I'm just not good enough. There is a sort of rhythm to listen to in this, a pattern underneath, a whisper of knowing"

I had come to a crashing halt after experiencing burn-out and I went through some dark days. I was sad, angry, irrational and exhausted and I had the worst anxiety I have ever had. Recovery took time. I had to change my job, take medication and I started on another round of therapy. I still never mentioned adoption and I was so scared of the feelings that wanted to come out of me that I would eat chocolate all the way to therapy and then all the way back again after. Being tucked inside a sugar coma meant I could just about take on board some gentle support but I didn't cry and I never talked about what was really going on because I didn't know myself. I will say that again and breathe. I didn't know myself.

Like the swan my feet kept flapping away underneath. Sometimes

I got stuck in the weeds. My stubbornness kept me pushing through, pushing on, fighting against the tide and the current and the sticky green tangle of being that wrapped around my legs and pulled me further beneath the surface. Burn out was just like drowning. Not waving.

I wrote:

"It has been two years of hard. Not all the time, but a lot of it. I've hidden in my bed. Forgotten to shower and had to make myself lists of what's important to get me through the day. They are on my phone as daily check lists and this time last summer I was still working through them every day to get myself going. Some days it worked."

Julia (Fiona) at 18

Dear Julia

I know it's tough now, but it will get better I promise you. Searching for your identity and where you come from is a journey of discovery that you will make. You are brave and strong and funny and kind and beautiful although you don't know it and you are loved. Being adopted isn't perfect. It's not you. You aren't bad. And you have a right to know your own story. You are a young woman with a life to live, full of possibility and change. I want to tell you that your feelings and questions are normal. Don't be discouraged.

You will learn to live with depression and you will find a way through all of this. There is light at the end of the tunnel. There is always light. You will be happy and you are loved. Your life is worth living. You have so much to offer. I love you. Love always, me xxxx

In July 2020 I was feeling sad and tired. I was missing Mum Mary because we were on holiday in Norfolk near where she lived for years. It is not just the memories and her presence which feels very real, but my fear that I didn't properly belong to her anyway. I often thought of myself as the tagged-on daughter in events. Her three 'real' daughters and then there was me. I didn't really challenge anything she said because I couldn't bear the conflict or the loss. Depression creeping back exacerbated my negative thoughts so that I was an insipid copy of myself like a prologue of winter. It was a warning. I missed using food or alcohol or a sneaky cigarette to numb out. There was a sort of crawling, nagging unsatisfied feeling of grey lowness and the constancy and consistency of it like watery porridge.

My mood was going up and down. I had been trying to come off antidepressant medication. It felt like giving up smoking, or alcohol or sugar. There was nagging feeling of something not being quite right. Other people noticed that I was avoiding contact and becoming more reactive. For a while I tried to convince myself that I was doing just fine.

I tried all the usual things which could be useful. Sunlight and self care. Doing yoga and meditation, going out for walks and being in nature. Trying to keep connections to other people. These things were getting harder. Depression is sneaky and it tells me lies. Depression has a mean voice. It doesn't like me because I'm lazy or stupid or fat or just wrong inside. And it says I'm going to die soon or everyone will leave. It tells me nobody would care that much if I wasn't here. It tells me I should run away.

Depression makes my world a darker place. One where gratitude is remote and isolation is necessary for self protection. It wants me to sleep, maybe forever, or at least until the sun returns.

Knowing that my life was mostly wonderful and I had so much to be grateful for wasn't helping enough. I had to have stop trying to hide how I was feeling and take some action. I committed to not be silenced or shamed, even by myself. I recognised that I might always need the medication because it keeps my brain this side of the abyss. And that is just perfect. I wrote a poem called "I Fucking Hate Depression". And it was true and not true at the same time. Depression is a curse and a gift.

Anxiety 2020

Why is writing this making me feel so bad? I can only manage short chunks at a time and the deeper I get the harder it becomes. As I write it is August and sunny. My type of weather. Sunshine makes me happy. My mood usually perks right up. Not this year. Covid and a deep dive into writing and re-experiencing the trauma of adoption seem to be taking their toll. Everything else is going well. My life is great. But my sadness and grieving are pervasive. It is there when I wake up in the morning. I carry it round like a stone in my chest. It is hard to reach out to friends. I can't manage anything too stressful or complicated. Don't ask me to rescue you this week. I just want to hide under the covers and wait for this to pass.

But I know I have to keep going. It matters to me. At the moment it is a hotchpotch of words and memories and reflections. It doesn't hang together. Will it eventually? I hope so. I'm not going to let myself get overtaken by self doubt or destroyed by the pain of going through it. A wise friend who is a memoirist told me that writing this way is hard. We have to re-feel and re-live the experience to get it down on paper. I can do so much and then I need a break, it is teaching me so much about myself as a writer, a person. I am learning to give myself what I need. Rest, meditation, walks, hugs, yoga, sleep, connection.

I Fucking Hate Depression

I fucking hate depression
It's not really a secret
Although I wish it was

My brain just doesn't work right
It needs a chemical solution
I stay on the medication

For months and years
Suffering the side effects
Instead of the alternative
The numbing out
The lack of connection and
Failure of intimacy and spiritual
Destruction

I fucking hate depression
Because it makes me sad
The greyness like a murky veil

The heaviness
The light goes out
There is no sunshine
And everything is weighted

I can't get out of bed
Because I want to sleep the day away

I fucking hate depression
Because it makes me feel bad
That I am bad inside
I think there's something wrong with me
Something I can't fix
I must be broken
Sensory overload is
Excruciating

I fucking hate depression
I've lived with it too long
I hate the drugs
The chemical cosh
I want to be free to feel

And then I can't bear it
Because it's too much pain

I fucking hate depression
Because it kills
Friends are gone seeking peace
With pills and ropes and jumping off bridges
With car crashes and addiction

Drugs and booze and food
Seeking oblivion and dark silence
Where there is no more pain

It makes me think of death and dying
I fucking hate depression

CHAPTER 19 COMING HOME

Things that are a Thing when you are Adopted:

Number 1. Birthdays

Number 2. Family Trees

Number 3. Questions at the doctor's office

Number 4. Who do you look like?

Number 5. Where were you born?

Number 6. Seeing your birth certificate and it not looking like other people's

Number 7. Having to 'Come Out' in every new relationship

Number 8. Lying

Number 9. Being an expert in hyper-vigilance

Number 10. Having children of your own

Number 11. Feeling different and identifying with other people who seem different

Number 12. Don't bother leaving me I'll leave you first or How to Run Away

Number 13. Not being able to make a choice without knowing what you want first

Number 14. Terror at the root

Number 15. Not know what we feel until somebody tells us

Number 16. Addiction

Number 17. Mothers Day

Number 18. Touch?

Number 19 Emotional range - Fine to Crap with Suicidal

Number 20 Not knowing where we came from

Growing up, who am I?

I learnt to love being outdoors. Going caravanning, the freedom of the outdoors always soothed me. Boats and lochs and mountains, the sea and the sky. Nurture as well as nature gave me a lust for travel and the open road. There is a photograph of me with my Dad in a boat on the shores of a loch in Scotland. I am under one year old. Such a happy face with chubby cheeks, my teddy (I still have him) and I am in dungarees made by Mum. That photo makes me happy. I see myself in her. I grew up with tea parties in the garden with my godmother, donkey rides on the beach. Dressed up in party dresses or in jeans and a cardigan and dungarees. Laughter and play and fun. The photographs of the little me are happy. They show the outdoors version of me, playful, sometimes serious, sometimes laughing and posing for the camera, sometimes serious sitting on the beach in the sand. Safe and secure, loved and wanted, surrounded by love. I have always been loved. I have to remember that. Recently I took a DNA test via a well known site in the UK. The results were surprising. My results show that my DNA is 74% Scottish, 20% English and North Western European and 6% Irish. The Scottish connection is more specific in aligning my DNA to the islands of the Outer Hebrides also known as the Western Isles. The musical names of Lewis and Harris, North and South Uist, Barra and Benbecula and the long abandoned island of St. Kilda call to me. Islands have always felt like home. Seas and lochs and mountains and the wild reaches of Machair, the grassy land with white sand at the edge of the Atlantic Maybe there is something in this ancestry thing.

It matters because we are all connected, all a part of the greater whole. Life's rich tapestry is made up of friends and family and love and sometimes sadness and loss and tragedy.

I am good with an audience. I am hyper vigilant to looks, approval and criticism in a glance or a sniff. I can read a room in an instant and I know how to perform in a group or a crowd. But my inner and outer selves rarely matched up. I thought I was an extrovert. And then a series of mental health crises and breakdowns and episodes of depression taught me that I need time to myself. That where I recharge is on my own. I need quiet and nature and silence. I need sleep and reading and calm. Sensory overload kills me. Being an extrovert was someone else's story not mine. I learnt everybody's stories.

I've learnt that when I write it gives me space where I can tell the truth. It comes down onto the paper from the heart, unfettered, raw, bleeding and bruised or with joy and hope and laughter. I can speak through the words on a page and it speaks to other people. I have learnt that in there is my authentic voice. I can trust myself enough to know that when I say the hardest things, when I speak from that place of honesty and fear that my little bit of light can shine. I want to be useful. I want to be of service. It is an old fashioned word but I know that giving something back to the world matters. The best I can offer is my own experience and my self so I put it down on the page and hope it will help someone else.

When I was a young social worker. I collected a baby from the hospital and took him to his adoptive parents. I had visited them beforehand with the adoption social worker to tell them as much as I could about his birth mum and her family. I had got to know his mum well over a couple of years. She struggled to manage financially and emotionally. I had supported her and encouraged her and made plans with her and eventually she got pregnant again and decided that she just couldn't keep this baby and keep her head above water.

I remember how I felt I that day. He was a beautiful baby, dark haired and chubby cheeked. I felt heart broken that he would never know his mother and his siblings. I felt like I was betraying him by taking him away, that I was cutting his ties to his roots and sense of belonging. Everything in me felt sick. I was still emerging from my own fog about adoption but once again my body recognised what my mind struggled to accept. And it happened over and over again.

Eventually I reached a point where I knew that I could no longer be part of a system and a machine that took children away from their birth families and gave them to other families to raise. I had tried to believe it was for the best and the right thing to do, but more and more I knew it was wrong and I just couldn't be a part of it any more. Every time I had to do it a part of me was re-traumatised and died a little. That was how it felt. Now I know the process had started to crack me open. The varnished shell of the adoption story I had

215

been raised in was starting to crack. Little bits of the lacquer were falling off and crumbling on the floor underneath my feet. It would take a few more years before it all fell apart. And then I was able to start putting myself back together.

It's 2020 and I am watching a film about adoption, sitting listening to a young woman in a transracial adoption who had found her birth Mom in the USA. The birth Mom denied being her mother and all her family describe her as someone who is quiet, keeps herself to herself and 'doesn't do emotions'. The young woman is hurting so badly because she just wants to make a connection. I know when I had my own children how it made me feel. Having my eldest son started me on the path towards eventually meeting my birth mother and her side of my family. I knew I had to find out where I came from. At that point I knew nothing. It stirred up so many feelings. From the moment he was born and those first intense days and weeks I counted them. I left my birth mother when I was nearly six weeks old. That is such a long time when you have a new baby.

I watch episodes of adoption reunions and anything else connected to adoption. My wife cries her way through every episode. Not me. I never shed a tear. I get angry. It's all too easy. The part that makes me most angry is when the adoptee nearly always tells the birth mother that, 'You did the right thing'. Everyone sighs with relief. I have never felt that. Not once. I could never say it. It's not true. It's complicated. I love my parents. I grew to love my birth Mum. My birth Mum and I were strangers who had shared a birth. We had twenty years to get to know each other but we missed out on the previous forty. It's not that my adoption was bad. I was loved and cared for and wanted. But it wasn't LUCK. I am not lucky because I was adopted. I was traumatised. I had a loving family. I have a good life. But something was always missing, something inside me knew I wasn't in the right place. I missed the mother I didn't have as well as loving the one I did. Because of the trauma of adoption and repeated separations my bond with my Mum was fragile. I loved her but our relationship was fraught with struggle and heartache for both of us and what came out was anger and opposition and argument. We needed help.

"I always imagined taking this journey by myself because it's so personal. But now I can't imagine doing it without my family, I need them here"

"I feel like I deserve to know stuff …. Like she has an obligation to tell me some things" and it feels kinda weird to say that"

"I stare at her. How are we different? What sort of faces does she make?"

— Angela Burt Tucker, adoptee
from Closure: A Documentary About Adoption, 2013

Coming Out in baby steps

I feel like such a loser. As if everything I write about myself fills me with shame. I think I'm making myself out to be a person I would have no time for and I'm seriously worried about how my friends and family will feel reading any of this. It all seems such a disaster area. I seemed to be a disaster area through my twenties and then in my thirties I was just trying to be someone that I wasn't. I took on the role of wife and mother, social worker and friend. I had a busy life with a husband, house and four kids. Holidays were camping in France or in cottages in Devon or Northumberland. We spent weekends on family walks and picnics. My parents would babysit and we would go to the theatre with friends or for dinner with other couples. We drank a lot of wine. I ate chocolate and ice cream on a Saturday night and we settled into episodes of Twenty-Four after the kids were in bed. We moved house, bought a bigger car to accommodate four children and then they started to become teenagers. Testosterone started to rise all around me.

I was one woman in a house full of men and I tried to maintain some feminist standards. I challenged their language and jokes. I argued about having rap songs playing in my ear space with their misogynistic words. I challenged the mild porn that found its way

217

across the doorstep and under the beds. I started to try to explore a spiritual journey that I thought might help me feel better. I went out with women friends to keep a balance and I struggled with depression and my eating disorder. I started to read a lot of self-help books with a mystical spiritual theme and tried to meditate. I wrote poems and journaled. I went on diets and gained weight. I re-read Fat is a Feminist Issue from the seventies and The Women's Room by Marilyn French and The Female Eunuch by Germaine Greer. I felt confused and wondered intermittently if I was gay but I didn't know. My life was how I'd imagined it but something was wrong and I was pretty sure it was me. I was attracted to difference and to the people who were brave enough to challenge the status quo. My beliefs and values were often different to the family I had grown up in. I started to get to know more gay and lesbian friends and I would find myself feeling a pull towards them but I always stepped back from the edge. I drew a magic protective circle of being married and having kids round myself, psychically warding off the possibility of me getting too close.

Sometimes I came home with a woman's number or email address who wanted to stay in touch and I would daydream about picking up the phone and calling or just getting on a train and turning up on her doorstep. My thoughts turned more and more to escaping my life as it was but I couldn't imagine how that was possible. I wouldn't leave my children. I couldn't. I kept torturing myself with a push me pull you ride that I had to quieten down. Sex was the elephant in the room and it just kept getting bigger. I had fantasies that my husband would die, it seemed such a convenient answer to the riddle, but then I was so horrified with myself I'd pray for forgiveness and tell myself to stop being so stupid.

Coming out to my parents about finding my birth mother took my anxiety to another level. It took me a while. I waited to tell my parents until after I had met Mary for the first time as an adult. I was terrified. My Dad had been researching his family tree for years. Every time I would see him he would bring out papers and pho-

Dad Stephen

tographs tracing different parts of his family back through genera-tions. He would say, "This was your Grandpa" or "Your Great Grandpa" and I would cringe inside. Every time I wanted to say, "But they aren't really my family are they?" Instead I would roll my eyes and tut in adolescent disgust. It started to make me feel angry. "Why couldn't he understand how hurtful it was to have his family pushed in my face?" It highlighted for me that I was adopted. It was like seeing it in stark relief. "Here is my family" but yours aren't here because you don't belong. That isn't what he said and it is not what he meant. He wanted to show me that I DID belong, but he didn't understand that being adopted is not like that. Just because we have been grafted on doesn't mean that we are the same tree. And we know it. There was no connection there for me. I hoped that my Dad would understand the need to know my roots, where I had come from. They handled it well on the surface but I knew that Mum was upset and found it hard. We couldn't really talk about it although I let her know about the family I found. I told them that nothing changed how I felt about them. They were my parents and I loved them and would always love them. I tried to keep them happy and soothe their feelings because that had always been my job. But this was something else. I had to know.

I had to come out of the adoption fog before I could see who I was.

I always had a dream growing up. It haunted me for years and years until I was nineteen or twenty. In the dream I was in an old house with hundreds of rooms like the classic haunted house in a 1940's film. I was walking through the hallways and then running. I was trying to escape from someone who was chasing me and if they caught up with me I would die. I would run and run in the dark, going from room to room, each moment of entry my heart was in my mouth and I was gasping with fear. Usually I would get to the end of what seemed to be the very last hallway at the top of the house and then there would be a door. I knew if I went through it I would die but I had to go on because it was both before me and after me. I would push open the door and then I would wake up gasping and sometimes crying. When I was younger I would cry in bed and sometimes my Mum would hear me and come in. I never told her what I was scared of just that I had a bad dream. When I was scared at night or upset about something that was always my pattern. I would stay in my bed and cry. I would hope she would hear me and come in. Sometimes I would try and cry louder but if I heard her coming I would stop. I never went to find her. I could never ask for help, I had to just make a noise and hope she would respond. It wasn't always successful as a strategy unsurprisingly. I think I couldn't risk any more. I didn't dare be that vulnerable again. I carry that on into my adult life. I have always found it really hard to say what I want. I don't know what I want. I want to know what you want and then I can work it out. The only things I have known I wanted were children of my own, a dog and sugar in any form I could get it.

When I was nineteen and in my second year at University the dream started again. I felt haunted by it. It started to really terrify me. The dream had got darker and more vivid. I would open that door at the end of the hallway and she would be there. She was a witch. Like the ugliest worst witch from a childhood scary film. And she was my mother. I saw her face and I knew she hated me and that I was going to die. One night I had a knife in my hand and I threw myself on her and stabbed her to death. I woke shaking and sickened and terrified by my own act of violence. I was so disturbed by it I talked to my then boyfriend about it and I said I felt like there must be something really wrong with me. Maybe I was possessed? I didn't really believe that but it felt so dark and everything in the dream went against everything I believed about myself. I was a pacifist, non-violent. How could I kill someone? We talked to his Vicar about it. I came away from that conversation feeling worse. He seemed to think I was just a teenage drama queen, a silly little girl making something out of a childish dream. He more or less patted me on the head and told me to pray and go away. I felt humiliated and ashamed.

I decided I was going to do something about it for myself. My pattern of self sufficiency was well honed. Don't trust anyone else, you are on your own, take care of it for yourself its the safest way. I decided that when I went to sleep I would have the dream again and I would end it differently. I have no idea how I thought I could do that. But I did. Some time later the dream re-occurred and a part of me stayed conscious watching the scene play out. She held my hand and walked me through. I was scared, so scared but I knew I had to end this once and for all. As I got to that end room I took a deep breath and told myself it was going to be OK. I pushed open the door and there she was. I walked over to her and I looked her in the face and I said," I'm going now". And I turned around and left the room. She wasn't dead. She wasn't lying on the floor bleeding. I wasn't scared of her any more because I knew I could stand and face her. I never had that dream again.

Recently I had a dream that reminded me of the Mummy dream. I was at a party and I was drinking, something I haven't done for a while. I wasn't drunk but I was slightly fuzzy. I got into a strange conversation about my wife and then I decided to leave the party and go home. I got into my car and started to drive and then realised I had been drinking and this wasn't perhaps the smartest thing to be doing. I was trying to drive up a steep passageway with cobbles on the floor and high walls. I couldn't get my car out at the end of the passageway because it was blocked by a big skip full of rubbish. I knew I would have to reverse all the way back down. Reversing is not my favourite thing but I told myself to just hold on tight to the wheel and keep it steady and I would be OK. I was thinking that I would put the car back in the car park and ring for a taxi or my wife to come and get me. It was quite late at night and pitch dark outside. No-one was around because they were all inside at the party with music blaring out. As I reversed my feet got stuck under the accelerator and I couldn't pull them free. I was hurtling backwards going faster and faster and then I was going silently over the carpark and then onto grass. I realised that after the grass was a deep lake. I knew that the car was going to go into the lake and I wouldn't be able to get out. Once again in my dream I was going to die. I thought, no-one will know what has happened because there is nobody around to see. My last thought before I woke up was, "They will think that I killed myself".

I am dreaming all the time as I am writing. My stomach is playing up again with pain and reflux issues. I am going to make a doctor's appointment but I am sure it is all related. My insides are showing up in sympathy with my feelings. Some days I am literally sick. I believe it is part of the process. Is this being out of the fog or am I still emerging? I lie on the floor. I do yoga. I try to breathe. When I am in distress or trauma or recovering from trauma it is hard to breathe. Sometimes it helps to just take a breath, meditate. I think this is why laughter helps too and crying and singing. Making noise makes me breathe deeply. The process of re-visiting my life literally made me sick. I believe my body had carried the trauma and toxicity for so long that letting it all out onto paper let the poison leak out.

I can smell vegetables roasting in the oven. Heritage carrots, Brussel sprouts, onions and tomatoes and red and yellow peppers with garlic and herbs. Cooking good healthy food feels nurturing to me now. Planning and preparing and having it ready so that I don't have to think about it.

Yesterday when I got home I had an official looking letter. I opened it thinking it was maybe from the tax office. It was my birth father's death certificate. It was a shock. I had requested it a couple of weeks ago, paid the money and sent off the form. I also requested his birth and marriage certificates. I felt sad when I read it. He died in 2017 and the death was notified by a nephew. I wonder if my father had any other children after me? It doesn't seem as if he did. That part of my history is still a blank. I had always imagined another set of half siblings somewhere, now it seems that was another fantasy. I wonder what he thought about that. Did he think of me? He was a widower when he died. Did they want children and were unable to have them or was it a choice? As I read it I wished I'd met him whilst he was alive. Being adopted means not knowing any information about the families we came from. It takes a huge amount of effort to find information and the emotional effort is enormous. I think adoptees are superheroes in disguise.

I feel like I was robbed of a mother. Instead of one, I had two halves but they didn't make a whole. I was split into pieces like Humpty Dumpty and no-one else could put me back together again. When my Mum died people sent cards and messages and I was responsible for the funeral and all the arrangements. I received love and sympathy and I was grateful for all the kindness. People said, "It's so hard when you lose your Mum" and "you only have one mum". They made assumptions of a shared experience if they had lost their mothers, and their perceptions of me. Those perceptions told them that I was a nice person. That I had loved my mum, which was true. And that my grief and loss would be like theirs, bone shaking, earth shattering, wrenching, desperate, hollowing. And mine wasn't. It made me feel like I was wrong again. I felt ashamed, inadequate and I couldn't share how I felt because I didn't have the words.

Mum Mary

When my birth mum died there was less of a response because fewer people knew. Not everyone knows that I was adopted. If they know me well they know but not if we had just met through work on a social basis. It is such a big conversation. It doesn't just go easily. I am much more 'out' about it now than I ever was. For many years it felt like something I had to build up to telling. I went onto high alert to try to evaluate and judge the reaction. I weeded out therapists by whether they were adoptive parents (a No) or religious (also a No). I tended to feel uncomfortable around other adoptees because I didn't want to be seen as damaged. I was full of self loathing.

People are full of questions or they say, "Oh how lovely" or something like that which is grating and awkward and sets up so many gritted teeth moments that I avoid it. So then there was the issue of my first Mum being ill and coming slowly to the end of her life and how do I say that? I couldn't just announce it on Facebook because it would mean having the whole adopted conversation. The day Mum Mary died my half sister rang me in the early hours of the morning to tell me. That morning I went to work. I didn't mention that my birth mum had died. I told them a few weeks later that I had had a bereavement and then when asked if it was someone close, that, "Yes it was my Mum." I didn't want to have that conversation. I wasn't alone. My wife and kids and my close friends and I had my sisters and cousins and their families and we all looked after each other. But I felt like I was the odd one out. Neither fish nor fowl maybe. My sisters talk about "Your Mum" meaning my adoptive Mum and I talked about 'Mum' meaning my first mum. They were both "Mum" and I loved them and they loved me and it wasn't enough in either because our connections were wrong. The wiring was faulty and we misfired and misconnected and had to be rebooted over and over again. I suppose we were all persistent. None of us gave up on each other even though there were times when that would have felt like the easiest thing to do. People said, "When my Mum died I was broken". "My mum was my best friend" and "Be gentle with yourself, you are going through a huge grief". They were trying to help me. They

Mum Margaret

wanted me to know that they understood how hard it was and how devastating the loss had been. They wanted to help me through the same. But that is not how it was.

Losing my mum's was hard both times. But I think it was differently hard. I miss them both. I think of them both every day. I have lots of good memories and some not so good. I talk about them both. I have pictures of them and objects that are full of meaning that remind me of them. But I don't think I feel what other people do when they lose their mother. And that makes me feel like there is something wrong with me. I think you will judge me. I'm sure that some people will. It scares me that my kids will read this and think I am a bad person. That they will be angry with me for not loving their Nana as much as they did. It makes me feel like I am damaged, broken, faulty. I don't think anyone will understand and maybe I should just keep quiet and not say this out loud to anyone. If I just keep quiet no-one need ever know and I can carry on pretending to be the perfect daughter that I never was. I wasn't the perfect daughter.

Adoptive Mum would tell you that I was perfect. She would say that I was everything she had ever wanted. But it wasn't true. I knew it and I'm sure that somewhere inside she knew it too but she could never say it because that would mean blowing apart the whole fantasy she had created about our perfect life. I wonder what would it have been like if we had had help? Would we have been able to go beyond the fairy tale fantasy and reached a real understanding and connection? Our relationship was spoilt by repeated separations and the effect of broken bonds which couldn't be repaired.

We made the most of a bad job.

Calling her Mum

I did my best and I know it wasn't good enough. My terror of rejection was so bone deep and the rage from my unheard three-year-old self was so powerful that I couldn't move on. Her shame over infertility and her desperate need to have a perfect family was so huge that she maintained secrecy and stone walling in relation to any curiosity on my part with an iron will and a fragile personality. I knew if I pushed her she would break but I kept her at arm's length for the rest of her life because I didn't dare let her back in. What a tragedy is made by the mess of it all for everyone concerned.

I was taken from my other half, the mother I had lived in and been evicted from, and stuck into a new family where this new mother was supposed to be a new half to make me, or maybe her, whole. Why would that work? Superglue might stick my fingers together when I am careless but it won't bond me to another person. And when I lost my Mum's it was like I lost a half-Mum. And I grieve the other half all the time.

Mummy, Mum, Mother, Birth or biological mother, first mother, adoptive mother, Margaret, Mary, Mum Margaret, Mum Mary all these names for the two primary people in my life. To my children they were Nana and Mary. To my sisters' children there was just Granny or Granny Mary.

Julia now. Heaven is sun and sea. It's in the genes.

I don't even know what to call them both here. Whatever I write or say feels like it will be confusing to someone. And I just want to call them both 'Mum'. It took me fifteen years from the reunion to call my birth mother, Mary, Mum. First she was 'Mary', then she was Mum Mary and then finally and tentatively she was 'Mum'. I always wanted to call her Mum but it felt too exposing, too much of a leap to make without the confidence of a warm welcome. The fear of rejection made it too hard for me to ask. The first time I said it was when I was leaving her house after a weekend visiting. I didn't stay with her when I went down because it was too much for both of us. As I left that day I said very quietly, "Goodbye Mum" and I rushed out of the door as quickly as possible. I felt like the world might collapse or like Chicken Little the sky would fall on my head. She didn't seem to react much but I didn't hang around to watch. Later that day my half sister rang me to ask how I had got on. She said, 'Mum said you called her 'Mum'. I was a bit embarrassed and scared, I wondered what she would think. Was I going too far? Stepping on my sister's toes? Crossing an invisible boundary? She said, "She was really pleased". 'Oh' I said and moved on swiftly.

When I was married to my second husband my parents-in-law wanted me to call them 'Mother' and 'Father'. The other daughters-in-law seems to find this easy. The names just stuck in my throat. I couldn't do it. And I couldn't explain. I couldn't get the words out. I felt as if I was being ungracious. I was still swimming through adoption fog but it kept clearing. I spent years not calling them anything at all. When we went to stay with them I always had a supply of my drug of choice in my bag and I would raid the cupboards for her chocolate fridge cake. I needed a lot of sugar to get me through the feelings of incongruence. They were nice people. Do I need to say that?

The Joy of Water

Water is my favourite element. I am a fish, Pisces, often swimming in two directions. Choosing a water image was hard, I have so many. All the best days are spent near water, the sea, a lake, rivers or streams. I dream of living near water. The constant movement, the way the wind ruffles the surface with a gentle breeze or creates huge waves, the sound of rushing and gurgling or the soothing shush, shush of water lapping the beach. Holidays and days at the sea. Playing with water with the children in the garden, the fun of paddling pools and water guns. Soaking wet and laughing. Swimming, paddling, bathing and floating. Water to drink and wash with. The start of life swimming in water. Water babies and mermaids, Marina in Thunderbirds swimming elegantly in her own silent world. Dolphins and whales in the Bay of Biscay on a crossing to Santander.

Mum Mary (L) and Aunty Margaret (R) cousin Mary's
mother

Loch Lomond at dawn, March 10, 2009, honeymoon. We woke as
dawn crept across the sky and watched as the colours brightened and
the loch shimmered and gleamed in the first rays. All was quiet and
still, the only movement a seagull landing on the post. Later a single

canoe was rowed across the centre, a tiny splish as the oars left the water, the boat moved effortlessly as if by magic. It was the perfect start to an unforgettable day. Teresa and I had just got married and this was the first day of our honeymoon.

Sitting on a beach. Brown knees. Big blue sky with wisps of white cloud. The sea rumbling over the pebbles as the tide comes in. Today the sea is very green overlay on brown.

White caps bringing children in on their body boards, little legs shaking with cold but faces laughing and screams echoing joy.

Mum and Dad never learnt to swim. But they made sure that I could. I took to it like a literal duck to water. They always called me a water baby and in the water I found my other home. My piscean element. At the beach on British summer holidays my Dad would stand at the shoreline watching over me as I swam up and down. Every so often he would wave frantically to me to come back in nearer to the shore. I loved the sea. I revelled in the sense of freedom and power I got from being out of reach. I could pretend to ignore my poor Dad for a while as I kept going just that bit further out, pushing the boundaries wave by little wave. I would get just that bit more out of my depth until his frantic waving and signalling to come back in towards the shore tipped me into compliance.

My youngest son was born in water at home. He was number four and his birth was more intense and quicker than the others had been. We hired a birthing pool through my family doctor and set it up in the living room. My midwife, Trish, had delivered Ben at home twenty months previously. When Joe was born I pushed him out into the water and she guided my hands down so that I could touch his head as he came out. I felt the hard hotness of it and the softness of baby hair and as I reached for him he swam up to the surface. It was beautiful and gives me goosebumps now. He was clean from the water and calm and he didn't take his first breath until he surfaced because that is what happens when you swim from one safe watery space inside your Mum into a world of warm water. The first sensations he had were of the water and my hands reaching for him. I held him to my bare skin with his cord still attached as we waited for the placenta to be delivered. He was an easy calm baby, laid back and contented. I knew he was going to be my last one and it felt like this was the birth that I finally got right.

Dear Julia

Baby girl in your ruched costume. I love you! Here you are in the sea, in our element. This is our place. Your mum Mary loved the sea too, you were both water babies. And your sisters too. You will have so many days of joy in the sea, by lakes and rivers. I want to pick you up and give you the biggest cuddle. Life is hard sometimes but you are strong and sensitive and water babies always swim. Waving not drowning my love. Love, Me xxxxx

CHAPTER 20 KALEIDOSCOPE

When my Insides Became my Outside

A kaleidoscope make magic of tiny pieces of coloured glass. They tumble together with a turn and fall into new patterns. This is my 'coming out' story. It was my kaleidoscope moment. The day that my world turned upside down and inside out was a culmination of many tiny pieces of the puzzle. I couldn't see the whole until I turned around and looked at it all another way. Suddenly it all made sense.

2002 on a plane to the USA. I was travelling alone to New Mexico for a week's stay. The whole experience felt immense and surreal. I was anxious, excited, guilty and joyful. I was going to a retreat for food addiction. My husband was at home looking after our four children. They had all waved me off that morning from Manchester. I felt bad for leaving them and free all at the same time. It was my first plane ride. I was feeling hopeful for the first time in many years about recovery from my sugar and food bingeing. I had discovered that I had an imbalance in my system which might be able to be healed. I was losing weight and feeling better than I had for years. So I was going to meet a hundred or so other recovering addicts in a hotel for a three-day retreat. It was my combined Christmas and birthday present for that year and it was about to change my life in more ways than one.

I had an amazing week. I loved the people and the place and I learnt a lot. Everyone was warm and friendly and loving. I felt understood. I found myself being quieter than usual, trying to cope with the change of culture and language. I made new friends and found ones that I had gotten to know online. Some were so different to their online personas. I met a woman there who intrigued me. We agreed to keep in touch. I just wanted to get to know her better. No touching except our eyes meeting. She was younger than me and single and a lesbian. She was beautiful and different from anyone I had known before. She lived in the USA and I in the UK. I had four children and was married with a house and a job and a whole life of commitments. We would just be friends.

When I got home I thought about her a lot. We emailed and messaged and talked about everything. She challenged my comfortable existence. I was waking up from my coma. At first I thought I'd just got a little crush, and I tried to believe it didn't mean anything for my marriage. I'd often thought my life would have been simpler if I was gay. I liked women. I loved women. But I had always assumed I was straight. I had been married twice to men. But sex was a problem for me. It was a problem we didn't talk about. But it was there and it was real. I had been pregnant three times with husband number two and once with husband number one. My mum said when I got pregnant the third or fourth time, 'You must be very fertile'. She said it with an air of distaste and slight disapproval. In fact I think she was right.

Something was happening and my feelings were stirring. I was in the middle of the biggest emotional upheaval of my life. I tried to carry on as normal. Going to work, being married, raising children, doing the school run and planning our family holiday that was coming up. We went to Northern Spain. Two weeks exploring the Costa Verde. We saw vultures fly over a ravine in the mountains. We ate tapas and paella. Our older two boys were teenagers, one brought his guitar on holiday and played outside the tent in the evenings. The rest of my sons, and me, were reading the latest Harry Potter book. We all had our own books. I remember being on a nearly empty beach with the family. The younger boys were running and playing with their Dad and we were walking slowly along the shore line. I dropped further and further behind. All I could think about was Her.

On that beach I recognised something in myself. I had fallen in love. Are you crazy? Oh don't be so ridiculous you can't possibly be in love, you barely know each other. This is infatuation. How old are, you anyway, sixteen? You are so selfish. How can you even think this way? What does it mean? It's just not possible, nothing can come of it. You need to just stop thinking about her and get on with your life. Forget about her. Be sensible.

We had agreed to not be in touch whilst I was away. I thought that would help me get everything back into perspective. But I couldn't stop thinking, and when I thought of her I was happy. I felt scared and trapped.

What can I do? Who can I talk to? What would I say? Surely I should know if I am gay or not? What if I'm not and this is all just a fantasy? Are you seriously thinking of breaking up this marriage and your family for something you don't even know is true? You must be insane. You can't get divorced. Can you? What about the kids? How can you do that to them? Where would you live? I don't know what to do. Please help me.

This went on and on. And I tried to behave like I was just the same whilst my world slowly and irrevocably shifted on its axis.

Somewhere on that beach I knew. I had bare feet in the waves as I slowly followed my family and I tried to look as if I was just immersed in the view. Inside I felt like I was breaking apart. I know I was crying. I was breaking wide open.

If you do this everything will change for ever. But I can't not know this any more. Everything that seems wrong with me before was part of this. I'm not wrong even though I feel horrible. I am in love. With a woman. And that explains everything. So now what? Can I just carry on as before? Can I shut the door on this? What happens if I don't? And what happens if I do? Who am I going to hurt? And if I pretend that I don't know this, then what? Can I choose not to accept this? You have a choice between 'yes' and 'no'. Life or slow death. Being real or not. Always being the chameleon.

I cannot tell you how hard it was and how terrified I was of the pain I would inflict. But I just couldn't live with knowing that the reason our marriage didn't work was that I was with a man when I should be with a woman. I tried to argue myself out of it, I imagined every conversation with everyone I could think of. I had no map for this, no guidance. No-one I knew had done it. I only knew a small handful of lesbians and I had never had an honest conversation about sexuality in my life. I still find it hard.

I had started to read more, novels that had women in relationships with other women. I kept checking myself to see if I identified with them or not. It was a mystery to me. I felt naive and ignorant and stupid and I felt on the edge of the biggest transformation of my life. On the beach I cried and breathed in the sea air and I looked at my kids and I thought, "I want them to know the real me". When I turned the kaleidoscope and saw myself through it as a woman who loved women then the world seemed to shift the right way up. Everything I had ever known about myself shifted in hundreds of coloured pieces of glass and came together in a new pattern. Suddenly my life fell into place. I couldn't imagine how I was going to get from that beach to my new life but I knew I would have to.

I look back and wonder how we survived that marriage where we just weren't communicating. Both of us were just too scared of the consequences of having the difficult conversations. When I told him that I had to leave he said, "Are you a lesbian?"

He knew. I'd always got a reason why sex wasn't ok. Tiredness and four kids, work stress or exhaustion, drinking too much, headaches, stomach aches, periods, stress, having to be up early, going to bed too late, and so on. We had tried a couple of tentative conversations but neither of us had the language for it. I had said 'It's not you, it's me' and meant it but I didn't know why. I loved him. He is a good man, and a great Dad. I still love him, and his wife, because we are family. We were meant to be friends, not partners. I am sorry.

I know now what happened to me was that I took a step out of my usual life when I made that journey across the Atlantic. I shook the kaleidoscope and although I didn't know it I was willing to let the pieces fall into a new pattern. I had the space to see myself and my life from the other end of the glass. Long before that journey I used to love the film 'Shirley Valentine'. It was my film. I was the carer, the fixer, the organiser. I had everyone's timetables in my head and I got lost somewhere. Bits of myself were everywhere. The real me was in scattered parts and they all lived and functioned in their separate boxes. The social worker, the mother, the wife, the friend, the writer, the seeker, the artist, the daughter, the adoptee. I didn't know how to be me. I was depressed and anxious and I ate addictively and binge drank to numb out. I shopped and spent to make myself feel better.

On that retreat my mind was clear because it was free from the addictive substance of sugar and I was high on the excitement. I went up in the mountains one evening in a cable car and walked along a trail at the top and then watched the sunset over the deep valley below, through which a river flowed. It was a moment of breathless peace and silence and it brought tears to my eyes. I carried that home with me.

Meanwhile, I knew this marriage couldn't go on like this. I wasn't clear what was happening to me. But I knew that I couldn't do it any more. I couldn't keep turning myself inside out and trying to make myself into somebody I wasn't. I couldn't keep pretending that my disinterest in sex was just a phase or due to tiredness or hormones. I recognised deep inside me, underneath the layers of trying so hard to be the woman I thought I should be, was a spirit saying 'No'. I couldn't do it to keep the peace, I couldn't do it to make him happy, I couldn't do it to save my life. My body said, "No" and it had been saying, "No" for a very long time.

Back home nothing changed and then everything.

I went to therapy. I saw a marriage counsellor. The first time I went by myself and didn't tell anyone. I sat there and in that room I told a woman I had never met what I was feeling and thinking. It was my first Coming Out. Once I had said it and nobody died I felt like I could breathe again. Everything shifted. I felt like the world had turned on its axis and now I was seeing it the right way up for the first time. But the hardest part was still to come. I had to have that conversation with my husband. I don't remember it all. It was traumatic and devastating and necessary and hard. We went to a session together with a different marriage counsellor. It was cold and wet and it all felt miserable. The session was awkward and uncomfortable and I felt judged. I didn't know how to be or what to say or how. Neither of us did. The counsellor seemed shocked and I felt like she took my husband's side but that might just have been my fear. I knew this was the end. Afterwards we sat in a cold cafe in the same building and our marriage was left behind with the cold coffee and empty sugar packets.

Dismantling a relationship of nearly twenty years takes time and some things happened almost overnight. I moved out into a rented house not far away. The kids divided their time between us. It was hard. I don't know how I did that year and survived. My parents were living nearby too by then and getting older and more frail, they had physical health problems and my mum was starting to show signs of what would turn out to be dementia and delusions. I was spending time trying to keep them safe and navigating trying to be a mum. Telling the children was the worst conversation I have ever had. I felt like I was the worst person in the world. I felt like I was abandoning them. The ultimate sin. But I couldn't live the lie. I didn't tell the kids why, not then. I thought it was too much for them to know why their Dad and I couldn't be married any more. That wasn't my best thinking. Sometimes I still hate myself for the pain I caused.

My relationship with that woman didn't last. It was never meant to. The purpose was to wake me up. She was a glittery fantasy and both of us wanted the same things but from different people and several thousand miles apart. We met again in the same time and space some time later and then the relationship floundered across the telephone wires and Atlantic.

I was scared of being a cliche. I was scared it wasn't real, that I was still searching for the answers to myself and my identity. Was I breaking hearts and lives apart because I was so messed up I didn't even know who I should be having sex with? Was I having another adolescence? But deep down I knew the truth. I just knew. I had woken up and recognised myself.

I talked to family and friends. I talked to my lesbian friends and my sisters. I sat with myself and I did a lot of crying, I couldn't read a book for a year. My heart felt broken but I knew I was free to be myself. I lost friends and family members. People I expected to be there for me just melted away. I felt their judgment burn through me like acid. Some people re-surfaced years later as if nothing had happened. I couldn't manage to reconnect, it was too much. The people who stuck by me were my parents, Mum and Dad, my birth mum and my sisters. My sister Jane was the first person I told that I was leaving. She rang me out of the blue one Sunday and asked me how I was. So I told her. And why. Jane just listened and accepted me. She said, "Mum will be alright with this you know". And she was.

Mum and Dad never flinched either. They were there for me on the phone, they gave me money when I had none to pay the rent. Their love didn't change. My children were aged eight, ten, fifteen and eighteen. My husband wanted us to stay together until the boys had all left home. I couldn't do it. It is never the right time to leave when you have children. It is never going to be easy. It was selfish and brave and the only thing I could do. I am sorry that I hurt people, it breaks my heart to have caused that pain. Everything that has happened since, every moment of struggle in my kids lives I have wondered, 'Is this my fault? " "Did I do this?" I still do. Sometimes I have let them get away with anything because I couldn't bear to say, 'No'. I felt like I'd done the worst thing in the world so anything they wanted that was mine to give they should have. That didn't work out too well. I had to work on my boundaries. I hope that I have been a real person with them. I hope that they know that I tried to be truthful and kind. With my wife and their father and his wife and kids we have formed our own extended family. We feel bound together and we love and support each other to be the best parents we can be. I am proud of that. And none of us did it alone. Our truest and deepest selves came through. Being adopted meant not feeling rooted. It was like I had no past. My book started with Chapter Two, no prologue, no first chapter. The pages had been ripped out and scattered to the winds. Coming out of the cocoon of my previous existence continued the process of discovering my true self.

CHAPTER 21 THE YELLOW SCARF

Connecting with a broken brain

When the people I love go away it feels as if they have gone for ever. If Teresa goes away for a weekend I know logically that I won't die. A part of me looks forward to the space and being alone. I can do whatever I want. I can read with the light on in bed. I can watch trashy TV without feeling like I'm being judged. I love being by myself. I am never bored. I can do yoga and write and read and I can go for walks or see a friend or knit. But people go away I detach. I find it hard to connect on the phone. I shut down a little bit and go inside my own safe weighted blanket space. I just want to be left alone.

When my children left home I was happy for them even whilst knowing I would miss them. I wanted them to go and fly free. But I didn't know what to do with my feelings. I felt lost. A tiny part of my brain said they didn't love me any more if they weren't in the room. I know that it isn't true. I know they are out there living their own sweet and painful lives. What I know in my head is not always what my heart believes. Sometimes my heart knows best. But not in this. I want my kids to be happy and free, to be safe and successful. I am proud of the men they have become. I want them to feel fulfilled and be in relationships with people who adore them and vice versa. I want all the things for them that you want for your kids and the people you love beyond words. I know my connection to them is indelible. But it can be hard for me to see it clearly. I just have to trust it.

When I left my second marriage it felt like a cataclysmic event in all our lives. I felt like the bad guy.

I rented a house ten minutes away from the family home and I moved in. The house was furnished and I took the bare essentials with me because I felt like that I couldn't take more. I bought bunk beds for the younger boys and put up pictures and used colourful throws and cushions to make the place cosy and homey. The day I turned the key in the front door and walked inside I breathed deep into my stomach. It felt like the first breath I had taken in a long time. Sanctuary. I felt safe and I had the feeling I would stay in that house for a long time. A few years later Teresa and I bought the house together and we have lived here ever since. Maybe we will live here for ever. It is home.

My ex-husband and I made an arrangement that the boys would spend half their time with each of us. One son stopped speaking to me for a while. He was blindsided by it all. The younger boys asked. "You're not a lesbian are you Mum?" They were ten and eight, and it wasn't the conversation any of us expected. They ran to phone their Dad and he told them that it was all right. He gave us all the gift of being kind. We both knew that tearing each other apart was not a way to live. All of us were hurt or frightened or angry. Our relationships took months, if not years, to heal. Some days I felt broken. I sank into despair and depression but I kept trying. I cried. Eventually I hit a point where I knew I just had to accept that this was how it was. I was scared that my son would never speak to me again. The pain was excruciating. And the worst part was seeing his pain

But I recognised a truth about myself. I saw that my love for my kids was indestructible. I learnt that I would love them till the seas froze over and the moon fell from the sky. I learnt that I would never ever leave them no matter what. I had already known it. But now I knew it deep in my bones and with every part of me. That umbilical cord that connected us might stretch but it could not break. They might stretch their side of it or even cut it through but mine would still be there. With every breath in my body. Until my breath left me and then for ever.

So I learnt that I wasn't really broken, the part that loved was real. I was real. I was fighting for the truth in my own way. The truth that is indestructible. The part that is brave and fearless and strong even when she is breaking. I learnt that by letting go it didn't mean I had lost. When my Dad died and then my Mum and then my second (first) mum I didn't lose them. I'm not sure they have gone anywhere other than the sky or the stars or the wide blue ocean or the sandy shore but I know they are carried within me. We are all stardust after all. Grieving meant finding a place for them to live. I wonder if I grieve differently to 'normal' people. I feel like I don't cry like other people.I think I ran out of tears. But I hurt. I feel. I have big feelings. My head separates from my body. My body breaks down and I fall. I trip. I break things and tear skin and ligaments. I bang my head. Twice in the last two years I have given myself concussion. My skin used to be a red raw explosion of eczema all over my hands and legs. I would scratch till it bled because the bleeding was better than the itching. I had to wrap my hands in bandages and gloves because they were so painful. I looked like I had third degree burns. I would leave skin behind me everywhere. I would visit someone and realise that where I had been sitting I had left a pile of flaked off skin from my legs where I had sat and scratched surreptitiously all through our visit. Under my trousers my legs would be bleeding.

After my adoptive parents died my skin cleared. Nothing else had helped. I had tried every treatment, lotion and cream. Doctors and well-meaning bystanders and relations would tell me not to scratch. I began to understand that it was a form of self harm. I listened to cutters who used razor blades or pieces of glass. The pain of cutting they said was easier to bear than the pain inside. The bleeding was a release. It was addictive. It made sense. I bled out my feelings and left my skin behind like a snake.

I have places to go that soothe me. Places my brain can be quiet. I resist those places too. I fight with myself about going there, about sinking into meditation, about laying out my yoga mat. It is easy to be miserable when it is familiar but it is not where I want to live. I am an optimist more than a pessimist. I seek out joy but I find it hard to let go. I have a craving for silence, for peace and quiet. And I want distraction and colour and sound.

I thought I had to find a way to save myself and that was the problem. My old beliefs meant that I had to do it by myself. But that wants working. To save myself from the wounds of being relinquished is not done in isolation. I had to ask for help and then follow through. Finding out the truth not about my parents or my birth family but about myself. I bled it out onto pages and in meetings and through sharing with other recovering adoptees, addicts and survivors of trauma. I stopped eating sugar and flour or drinking alcohol or smoking cigarettes or spending wildly to get by. Well, I mostly did. I am not perfect. I try to keep it real.

When I am old I reserve the right to deep dive into all my addictions. Tomorrow I might pick up that drink or that cake or that cigarette. But not today. I am aiming for never today. I know that numbing my feelings with a fix means lose my mind and my freedom. No-one who loves me wants me to go there again. I know because they've told me so.

Connection is my saving grace., but oh it's hard sometimes. The benefits are the solace of emotional, physical and spiritual touch. Connection brings a lightness to the dark days. Touch is such a basic need that we die without it. And yet opening up to that vulnerability is still a struggle for me. This time of a pandemic is tricky. We are forbidden the natural closeness that lubricates daily life. We are wearing masks and unable to hug. For someone like me who finds touch complicated it is both a relief and a loss. I have taught myself to hug. I want to hold my kids and their partners and my friends. My arms truly miss the shape of them. I loved holding my babies. They taught me how to touch. I have learnt to make connections and to keep them even sometimes when everything in me wants to run.

My own addictions taught me about connection because it took me deep into isolation. The irony is that the path out of addiction is relationship. Relationships confused me especially the one with myself. Other people have been the healing grace in my life, and that remains true even when I want to hide away in my turtle shell.

I go to online meetings and have virtual chats with strangers who share my crazy fucked-up relationship with sugar or alcohol. I have been to retreats and drunk endless cups of coffee or herbal tea. One day we will be able to do that again. All the connection made me feel seen. I stopped feeling invisible. I could take off the mask for a moment. I didn't have to perform all the time. I could wear my insides on my outsides and nobody died, not even me. There is laughter and acceptance as well as war stories and tragedy. Dark humour is healing. There is no judgement because we are all the same. It is humanity at its best and worst and knowing I am just one amongst many.

Being with other survivors has taught me how to be real at least some of the time. I use the term survivors for all of us. The addicts, the traumatised, abused and adopted. And being real means that once I have been there I want it again. It is peaceful and energetic. It is a lightness of being. It is wanting to dance. When I stopped fighting food addiction and came to understand that some foods are just poison to me then I found peace of mind. My body and my brain started to heal. And then the miracle happened because there was a space available to start to see what else was going on. I was used to being stalked by a feeling that I didn't name. It was heavy in my chest just behind my breastbone. There was a physical pain there, an ache that I would rub sometimes with my hand. The feeling was so familiar, it felt like home. I began to realise it was in the region of my heart. It made me feel tired and sad and frustrated that I couldn't make it go away. Now I call that feeling grief. This sadness is ancient and multi-layered. It comprises all the sadness, all the people, all the missing. I don't know if grief leaves or if it just mutates. I am not sure if it is a place we heal or if it is a place of transformation. Is grief perhaps the cocoon that we wrap our tenderness in whilst we grow inside? Emerging as the butterfly with wet, fragile wings to perch trembling on a leaf. Growth is painful but necessary for evolution. We wait for the sunlight to dry us. The quake and quiver that we feel runs through us as we breathe. A little movement shifts our energy.

I have friends that like and love me for being me. I have learnt that I have something to give. They see me. I can be funny and brave and loyal and kind and sensitive and creative. They see the things in me that I want to be, the things that are true and real and that mean I am being myself. My friends have mirrored back to me that I am good enough. And my friends are people who know what it is like to struggle. The people I love most in this world are the people who have been wounded too. We know each other. And I see their strength and bravery and fun and big loving hearts and I just want to have them all in a room where I can be surrounded for ever with their warmth and grace and humour. Of course in reality we would all run very fast the other way because most of us really love our own space and the quietness. And we know that about each other too so it is all okay.

My journey has been all about finding my way back home. Home doesn't have to be a place although it is good to have a place that is mine. But really home is a feeling, a sense of belonging, of being seen and heard and understood. Of being accepted as I am. As an adoptee that is difficult territory because I can spend so much time trying to find out what the people around me want me to be then morphing into that person. That was my survival strategy. Watch, Look, Learn. Observe, Imitate, Change. I knew instinctively that it was possible to lose everything and everybody that mattered. A baby needs its mother. Just anyone won't do, quite honestly. Babies need love and security and to have their needs met to be able to bond. Bonding gives us that sense of home. Our first home is in the womb. In that place of warmth we hear our mother's voice filtered through the layers of skin and bone and amniotic fluid, and we recognise her unique sound. We may recognise our father too if he is around and other people but primarily we will know the feel and sound of the person who has carried us inside them. The person we rely on for our survival.

We know now that babies' brains develop in the womb and that means that they respond to the mother's feelings and experiences. It is not just the impact of a few glasses of wine or a strong curry which may affect the babies comfort it is also the stress levels in her body. Fear and worry and stress cause her stress hormones to rise and the baby responds to this. Babies and mothers are the same organism until that umbilical cord is cut. When I had my babies I held them straight away. The bloody, slippery, sticky bodies wrapped in soft cotton cloth and I held them close as I touched their tiny hands and looked at their scrunched up little faces. I admired their soft baby hair and was in awe at the petal softness of their perfect skin. And I inhaled that new baby scent. That scent that stays for a few days even with their first baths, that scent of togetherness that comes from our mingled fluids. When you have sex with someone you love and there is that scent of them afterwards on your fingers or the taste of them in your mouth it is a connection of body and spirit. It says I belong to you and you to me. The phrase 'two become one' is not just for heterosexual sex. We become more than we are on our own.

Sex, babies, talking, hugging, these are all connections we make with others. If the connection is true and real we start to see ourselves. We see ourselves as other people see us first. As a mother I saw my sons' faces and I drank them in. I loved them and I absorbed them into my soul. I knew that they were beautiful and wonderful and that I would love them for ever. And I told them so. I sang to them and held them and fed them and I talked to them. I talked baby talk and nonsense and I named them and I knew that other people could love them too, like their fathers and grandparents and my friends. To them my parents were their grandparents, their Nana and Grandpa. I wanted them to know that I was adopted. I needed them to know that there was more to our family than what was on the surface. Nana and Grandpa never mentioned it. It was still a big secret to them, something shameful that we didn't talk about. They wanted it never to be mentioned because then they could pretend it wasn't true. Then they could pretend that the story they had created was the real one. They wanted me so much to be their 'real' daughter that it had to be so. If only they could have held the space for the paradox. I belonged to them and I was their daughter but I was also another mother's daughter and another father's child. I wasn't an orphan. They would say things to my children like, "Your great-grandfather" or "Your great-great-Grandma" and I would cringe inside. Back then I was still conforming. I was a nice girl, a well-behaved adopted person whose voice was too quiet. I didn't rock the boat about those things. I wanted to say, "But that's not actually true is it?" Because it didn't feel right to me. But I didn't know how to say it without hurting them so I never did. I colluded with the lie. And it made me sick.

I know that when I was growing up adopted it would have helped to know that other people felt like I did. It would have made a difference to be told that it was normal to want to know who I was and where I came from. I am sure that it would have made a difference to my Mum and Dad if they had been taught that I needed to know everything I could about my birth family, that it would give me a sense of my own special identity and it would mean I grew up with a sense of who I was. I know because they loved me, they would have wanted to do the right thing for me. The adoptions of my era were closed adoptions and both birth parents and adoptive parents were encouraged to get on with their 'new' lives with, or without, their new baby. I didn't just need information. I needed pictures and places and a way to connect. I needed to know where I got my brown eyes from and my love of books and reading and water. I needed to know that I was part of a pattern and then I could have shown my kids too that they were a part of this ongoing mosaic. I hope I can still do that now. I know that being adopted affected me. It stopped me knowing who I was, what I wanted and who I could or should love. It stopped me from being able to know my true authentic self and to be able to say, "Yes, I like that," or "No". It stopped me from saying,'No' at all.

I was an easy child on the surface. I was polite and good and I followed the rules. People told my mother what a nice girl I was and how polite. Being polite seemed to be the most important thing. Being polite is grown up code for 'don't upset anyone'.

And the rage and terror inside me stopped me from being able to love the people who raised me in the way I could have done. I never felt like I quite fitted in. So fitting in became essential for my security. Because we moved house and I moved schools several times I learnt how to fit into a new group. I can chat and smile and perform. Conflict makes me feel sick, my stomach hurts and my brain goes onto high alert. But fight or flight is my M.O. I will attack if you criticise me. I struggle to breathe. I stop hearing. I just hear, "You are wrong,"

Julia (L) and Teresa 2020

"I don't love you," and my terror tells me that the next phrase is "I am leaving you" or maybe you will just walk away from me.

On a Tuesday in our 'retirement life' Teresa and I have a day that is just for us. A date day. We go out walking or watch a film or do something creative together. One day not long ago we were going for a walk. I had been watching a talk on Addiction and Adoption by Paul Sunderland, a psychotherapist and addictions counsellor in the UK who has worked with many adoptees. Everything he said resonated with me. It confirmed my own experience and my own inner knowledge. I have a block of note paper on my desk and I kept having to pull another sheet to write as there were so many moments of recognition. I was telling Teresa about it as we were getting ready to go out.

As we were leaving the house I noticed she was wearing my yellow scarf. "That's my scarf" I said and she laughed gently. This voice came out of my mouth, sharp and whiny and vicious "It's not your scarf, it's mine. Not everything is 'ours'. Some things are just mine". Instantly I could see I'd gone too far. She had tears in her eyes.

We got in the car and I mumbled an apology. As she drove the fifteen or so minutes to our walk I stared out of the window. I didn't know what had happened but I knew I'd had reacted from somewhere that felt 'off'. We started walking. It was a crisp autumn day with sunshine. The leaves are changing colour and the beech trees glinting golden in the light. As we walked she said, "It makes sense what you were saying earlier about the trauma of relinquishment being there is no pre-trauma personality". And I started to lose it. I was crying and talking and I had to stop and hold her so that I could hang on to something and someone steady and safe. The processing of what I had heard and taken in that morning had begun to emerge.

Later that evening I talked with one of my my online support groups. We have been doing some of that 'inside' work together and we go deep. As I heard myself talk I recognised my wounded child part. She had come to the surface when she saw that yellow scarf, wanting to reclaim with a passion out of proportion to the moment. "Give that back, it's mine" she cried, feeling scared and angry and overwhelmed and later she felt sick. I felt too sick in my stomach to eat, the act of eating literally made me throw up. I had to get right down into self-nurture with some intensive care. I had a hot bath and snuggled down in bed for a couple of hours under my weighted blanket. I couldn't settle to sleep because my mind wouldn't let go of the feeling of dread. My brain and body responded to the feeling of threat with the need to shut down. My limbic system had gone on high alert and everything in me was wired. Later Teresa and I watched a film and I ate porridge for my dinner. Living with an adoptee can be complicated. Understanding trauma helps. So does a sense of humour and a healthy appreciation of personal space. It takes time to understand a person. When I am re-experiencing trauma then my stomach gets upset and my digestion gets compromised. I shake inside like a jelly pressed with a finger then released. Soft, 'carby' food like porridge is soothing and easy on the system. Baby food. No coincidences. Yesterday was a three breakfast day. Self-soothing is a skill that I try to practice in a healthy non-addictive way.

I can hear my own hollow laughter as I write. My addictive behaviours were rooted in the need to numb out, shut down and sleep it all away. Food is a primary addiction for me and feeding is a primal need.

I have found a system that works for me. It is called Bright Line Eating and I reference its creator Susan Pierce Thompson in the resources section at the end of this book

CHAPTER 22 LIFE IN-BETWEEN.

As I was writing this book I realised that the life in-between was one of my turning points. I always felt uncomfortable in that difficult space between yesterday and tomorrow. I would much rather live in the past or project myself into a different future. I found out that I was an 'in-betweener' when I was told that I was adopted. Some adoptees live their lives in-between being relinquished and the discovery of their adoption. It can come as a huge shock. Life changing, volcanic and often overwhelming.. We often know instinctively that we are in-between one world and the next. Our bodies know what our conscious knowing is yet to learn.

I was raised not to hurt other people's feelings. Conflict scared me. It is still a surefire way to make me cry. Maybe that is why crying feels too dangerous. Physical pain and being ill make me cry. It is much easier to cry at my physical vulnerability. I used to have a story that ran:

"Everyone leaves".

"If I upset you, you will leave me. If I make you angry you will stop loving me."

I have black and white pictures of little me on the wall of my study, and I didn't even know who she was. I have been reclaiming the past because I didn't know to live in the present. But really the present is all that we have. And the earth-shattering moment for me was the thought that the present is always in the in-between. I have been scared of the in-between my whole life but it is just where I am. I wanted to know the real me. And I wanted her to be known. The me that the people who loved me sort of knew and the me that they didn't.

I used to find criticism hard, I would get defensive and come back ready to attack. The terror of abandonment meant I wanted to make conflict go away. I am often a mediator and a referee or I am ready to run. If I thought someone I cared about was going to leave me I might tell them to go. That is my first response, the one that shoots from my wired-up hyper-vigilant brain to my mouth. Usually it involves bad language. I try to refrain from breaking stuff or people. In-between made me anxious, it unsettled me. In-between land didn't feel like a safe place. Unfortunately real life is in the in-between. I had to find a way to put down my roots in the in-between. An inability to tolerate the in-between made it hard for me to feel like I was real. I always wanted to run away. I dreamt of another life, one where I was the hero, the brave one, the adventurer. I pictured myself in a story not realising that in-between I was already creating a world of my own. My imagination was my magic carpet to another dimension because tolerating waiting for the next moment was insufferable. In spending my life waiting for this one to start I missed seeing the terrible beauty of being present.

I was only half real for the first half of my life. And that is no way to live. The hardest times of my life have been in the in-between and they have also been the most meaningful, the most rewarding, the most sacred. In-between was where I was when I sat beside my Dad's bed in the hospital waiting for him to leave this world. I had wrapped myself in his teddy-bear fleece jacket and we took each breath together, in and out until the breaths became further and further apart. I held his hand and said, "I love you Dad it's all right, you can go home'. I was with him as he left. My mum had gone home to sleep and my overwhelming first thought was, 'She will kill me when she finds out he's died and she wasn't here'. But I was wrong. She left because it was too much to bear and she had already let him go. She trusted me to be with him as he went. In the in-between there was the deepest silence possible, a ceaseless pause. I waited for the next intake of air through his dry lips. But the waiting was over. It was a holy place of transition.

In-between has been where we lived when we watched someone we love struggle with depression and anxiety. When the fear of the outside world was so great that he couldn't leave his room. When the sickly sweet smell of weed escaped under the door and when his mood changed from anxious to aggressive and he slept all day and prowled the house at night raiding the kitchen and eating sugar by the bucket-load. In-between was holding on to hope and praying for dawn. In-between was saying, 'Goodnight" and 'I love you" every night. In-between was struggling to find boundaries and ways to break through. In between was screaming and despair. It didn't feel like a holy place then but it was. It was the holding on.

In-between was how Mum Mary and I kept going. Twenty-two years of in-between and struggling to connect. In-between was realising that this is all we have. I accepted the in-between when I admitted that I wanted her to be someone she wasn't. I accepted my own failure and imperfection and hers and that this precious in-between was what we had created together. We had made a relationship and a connection out of threads. The fabric of us had been ripped apart leaving only torn and tattered ends and we carefully and lovingly and angrily and resentfully darned ourselves back together.

In-between was also the relationship I had with my adoptive Mum. Our fabric was frayed too but we had so much longer to do the darning. It took me far too long to see the value of what we had. Our life together was made up of the in-between moments. Collecting autumn leaves together and making a collage when I was five. Watching her with her first grandson and knowing he was the newest baby she had ever held. Painting her nails in the care home. Eating cake. Always asking her to finish off my knitting when I got stuck. Buying Christmas presents together. The later years are easier and harder to remember. We bumped up against each other constantly like a marriage where you want to leave but love them too much to go. We fought or I did. She tolerated my irritation with her far better than I do when my sons get exasperated with me.

In between was being pregnant and knowing my body for the first time. A starburst of light like a pin pricking a balloon as conception sparked. A knowing that I can't explain but was the realest and truest moment I had ever had. There was no surprise in the discovery weeks later, just confirmation. Coffee became impossible, the taste turning bitter and repulsive in my mouth. Learning to drink weak milk-less tea and munch on ginger biscuits to alleviate the nausea of the first trimester. Talking to the baby inside as he grew. Feeling more myself than at any other time in my life. Each wanted and longed for pregnancy brought me into my body, heart and mind and body aligned. I felt whole and complete, that this was my purpose. Motherhood became an unexpected vocation, a spiritual discovery, a place where each new discovery was precious. And in the in-between of pregnancy I learnt that being a mother was both easy and impossible. That the ease of conception was an accidental, maybe genetic chance and that the same was true of giving birth. But that motherhood was more than a choice, more than circumstance and luck and time and destiny. That motherhood was exhaustion and tears and blood and shit and the terror of watching a newborn breathe. That to hand over my heart to a small being the size of a couple of bags of sugar was to be forever in debt, a hostage to fortune. That the depth of feeling that motherhood aroused was incomparable to anything I had known before except maybe in infancy where overwhelming need translated into the fear of loss. I found that the only option for survival of such awesome belonging was acceptance.

I can write this now looking back on those times but in the moment I was often thrown from a state of being afraid to joy, from anger and exhaustion to a need for comfort and understanding. As my babies grew to toddlers and childhood and into boys becoming men the battle within me raged more. I wanted to be everything. To be the perfect mother, to belong. I wanted to work, to be useful and to be valued for my skill and my mind. I wanted to be wanted and needed and I wanted to be a free spirit, a rebel and an artist not bound by convention and expectations. I wanted to swim against the tide and also to be part of a shoal that swam together.

In-between has been the place I hated and feared. It was the place I felt most lost, the most fearful. In-between was somewhere I couldn't settle so I thought I had to change to make it easier. Moving house, changing jobs, a new relationship, another baby, have a drink, eat a bag of cookies or buy more clothes I don't need. In-between made me want to escape, to press the flight button. I was always living in a story in my head. The one where I was driving to Scotland to escape from war-torn Europe, the one where I was walking across mountains carrying a toddler like a modern Gladys Aylward, the one where I was walking across a university campus in the USA carrying my lecture notes and going to teach a class. Each story was more romantic and more colourful than my life and it meant I didn't have to live in-between.

In-between is sitting in a room in a church hall on a Friday night drinking instant coffee and listening to another story of rock bottom and recovery. Living in the in-between is knowing that there is something bigger than me and that fellowship is where I will find another place to call home. In-between is learning that I can tolerate waiting from one meal to the next, that I can live without the next drink, that I can breathe, pray and breathe again right here in-between.

Living in the in-between is where I try to live now. If I look out of my window on a winter's morning and I see the sun start to appear over the horizon I am in-between. If I am walking round the lake holding Teresa's hand and watching the heron swoop down to catch a fish I am in-between. If I am talking to a friend or one of my sons is sitting at the kitchen table drinking tea I am in between. In-between is right here, right now. It is the space between yesterday and tomorrow. It is this moment. Anything could happen tomorrow. The world can change on a pin head. But this moment, this sacred in-between space is now and I am here in it.

Life in-between is being able to write. In my in-between I am looking at the two spider plants on the window-sill that started as cuttings from a friend. There is a pink geranium that I have brought in from the garden for the winter and two cacti, one tall and phallic and one small and squat with multiple prickly eggs. There is a plate of scavenged stones and shells and pine cones and a small brass ornament of the three wise monkeys. There are two pieces of driftwood with interesting holes and an old candle jar filled with sea glass. These are the objects I see every day. They ground me. I hold the stones one at a time and I appreciate the cold smoothness and how they warm in my hand and I wash the dust off the sea glass so that it remembers where it came from. The memories are of places I love and walks we have been on together. The pine cones make me smile remembering family treks to the beach and getting lost on the way. I don't live in the memories but they keep me company. I collect things around me, pictures and objects of sentiment or beauty. I have notes of recipes and a new friend's contact details. There is a list of books to buy next month and another new pile of books as yet unread on the shelf. The candle is lit in my buddha who sits serenely beside me on the table where I write. He shines a light of being present in this in-between moment.

In-between is the place of un-knowing. It is a place of transition, a time to watch and wait. For many this is a sacred liminal space, a threshold between what was and what is next. Liminal space always made me uncomfortable and that looked like anxiety and being unable to settle. I believed that being in-between was too hard for me. I needed action and to make a decision because I couldn't tolerate the uncertainty. When I had to make a choice I couldn't wait. I appear impulsive and sometimes reckless. I spend money fast, it drains from my bank account like water from a leaky pail. I could never wait for someone to ask me to marry them, the tension of not knowing was too great. I always asked first then regretted my haste because I didn't know if they would have asked me anyway. I wanted children and got pregnant without consultation, I couldn't wait. I still make decisions based on impatience and the fear of staying still.

When my first romantic relationship with a woman ended I felt broken. I had apparently traded a secure and settled life for a fantasy. I was living in a rented house with no washing machine and I had very little money. My dad was paying my rent to help me out until I could get more work. I had lost some good friends and my kids were finding their parents break up distressing. I was living in in-between land. Between this relationship and another? Between the end of my marriage and the future. Between being able to pay the bills and wondering how I would manage. Between having my first relationship with a woman and coming out to my kids. Between living a lie and becoming authentic. Between being a Christian and believing in something wider and deeper and more universal and with less rules made by men or money.

I made a decision in that in-between space. One night I lit candles in my fireplace and I wrote. I wrote about what I wanted. I wrote about what I would let go. I had pages of lists. When I had finished I knew there was a choice I could make. It was the choice between. The choice to live in-between.

I wanted to live an authentic life

I wanted to make a home for my kids to live in

I wanted to be in relationship with other people

I wanted to travel, to learn and to teach

I wanted to be useful

I wanted to be well

I wanted to love

I wanted to be loved

I wanted to go for walks in the woods and hold hands and come home to a warm fire and making a meal together

I wanted ordinary companionship and I wanted extraordinary joy

I wanted to have space for creativity

I wanted to deepen my spiritual life

I wanted to grow

I was willing to trust that all would be well

I was willing to say yes

I was willing to keep going

I was willing to take the risk to love

I was willing to be brave

I was willing to put one foot in front of the other until I got wherever I was going next

I was willing to believe in next

I wanted to be all in. There was s a choice between 'Yes' and 'No', between living and dying. There are different ways to die. I realised that refusing to live in the in-between is one of them. The choice was simple. "Yes' or 'No".

I chose 'Yes.'

Staying Put, Growing Roots

I have had to learn to stay put. When I moved into the house we live in now I felt like I had found home. But fifteen years on and the kids have grown and moved on and I was ready to pack up and go somewhere new. We stayed because my wife said,"No, I don't want to do that". It took me by surprise. I am used to pushing until I get my own way. I can manipulate and wheedle and present all the arguments for my point of view. Usually I just wear people down. But this time it was different. She said, 'We have made a home together here and it is the first place I have felt like home. I don't want to move". I could have kept pushing, but I had to stop and think about it. It mattered to her. And it really didn't to me. I can make a home anywhere and my childhood pattern has left me with an anxiety that means I just get the urge to move on. It is like a ticking time bomb but never before have I been asked to just stay. When we talked to the kids about our plans they were all pleased. They liked the idea that we were staying here. It made them feel safe I think and also to feel happy for us. They can see the security we have together. I bought her a picture a couple of years ago, it has a map of the UK on it and it says, 'You'll always be my home". Cheesy. But true.

So much of my relationship with myself has been in relation to food. Both my mothers were feeders as well as eaters. When I think of them it is impossible not to remember meals and special foods. The kitchen table, the picnics, cafe and pub lunches and dinners and special meals for special occasions. Every event needed a meal to go with it. I do that now too. We have meals for holidays and birthdays and graduations, for weddings and funerals and to meet new additions to the family. Bringing a girlfriend or boyfriend to tea is a sign that they are getting serious. Coming for Christmas means they aren't going anywhere. Welsh cake ice cream for the last trip out with Mum Margaret before she died. Crab sandwiches with little Mum by the sea. Chocolates for both of them. Pub lunches where they would pay the bill and arguing was pointless. Chinese buffets for Mother's Day meals out with the family and turkey at Christmas.

I am nearly there. What will it take for me to be finished with this story? The wonderful Heather Small in M People sang 'Search for the Hero". That song keeps coming to me. I had to look up the lyrics and play it over and over. It's become my anthem of this journey. It is what I have done. I don't want to live in misery and grief, who does? Too many adoptees don't make it out. Suicides are much higher among those who are adopted. So is self harm and addiction and mental health struggles and eating disorders. I've got those too.

2020 has been the year the pandemic came, Covid 19 swept into the world and shut us all in our own spaces. Contact and connection with others has mostly been online. Family has felt more important than ever before. We have witnessed grief and loss on a global scale and we have also seen people find ways to live differently, more simply, wholeheartedly. We have grown our own vegetables, walked for miles round our own neighbourhoods and made yogurt and hummus and cooked beans. I started to write again, every day through lockdown. Charting the feelings and experiences of daily life. It made me step into a new identity as a writer. I started to think about what I wanted to say. I started tuning in to talk on the internet, blogs and books and people on Instagram and Twitter. Adoptees coming out of the woodwork and saying "we are here!" I found that other people might also want to tell the world about our experience of adoption. I knew I had to write my story.

To be able to write this book I needed to have something different. I didn't know it until I started and then I knew what it was. I needed space. The year I wrote book my last remaining chicken son left home for his own place. My wife and I live in a house by ourselves for the first time ever. I find myself spending time at home in a different way than ever before. I retired from working outside the home. It was a perfect storm.

I set myself up in my son's old bedroom at the back of our house looking over the garden. I stripped the walls, cleaned and painted and made it into my own creative space. I meditated on what colour to pain the walls. The rest of the house is Magnolia. I wanted lilac. Lilac meant creativity, serenity, hope and peace. I envisaged myself in that space and took myself off to the store. I found the perfect colour, it was called 'Lavender Cupcake'. I love my room. The walls are a soft and gentle colour that soothes my soul and holds my creative space. I can shut the door. No-one disturbs me. It is the first time since I was a kid that I have had a room of my own. Virginia Woolf eat your heart out. When I was telling my wonderful writing coach Anne Heffron about the room and showing her the colour of my walls via Zoom she said, "You have a Womb of Your Own". It made me laugh out loud.

I have found the hero inside myself. She is brave and persistent and creative and scared and funny and kind and beautiful. She tries to tell the truth as she sees it and to stand by it. She is trying not to be perfect or organised or to have to seek approval in every living moment. I like her, I even love her. She is able to love you too. She can say, "I love you" and mean it. She can even say, "No" sometimes.

She is the grown-up version of the kid on the beach who is sitting engrossed in her own task of just being herself. Little Fiona who had her name changed and then grew up and changed it right back to be the person she had always known she was inside. I love that about her, about me. I love that I just knew and that I was willing to stick my head out right over that parapet of disapproval and do it anyway. I love it that even though my voice shakes and my legs tremble and my stomach churns I will be me. I love my wife and my kids and my army of friends.

Quarantine

I am writing in self isolation because of Covid. I am in my writing room and the spare bedroom for nine more days by myself. I am lucky I have space and a spare bedroom and a garden I can go and be outside in for exercise. My wife is looking after me by cooking our meals and we catch up three times a day in person but from a social distance. I want to stay well and I want her to stay well so we are following the rules. But it is hard. Last night when I went to bed I snuggled under my weighted blanket and read for a few pages before I turned the light off. I lay there and thought, "I don't know if I can do this". Being separated is triggering for me. I think maybe she is angry with me when we are apart, it is hard to breathe properly. We are in the same house but it feels like we are detached from each other. It makes me edgy. The thoughts have already started creeping in and I tried to start an argument this morning whilst stating "I don't want to fight". I feel unsettled and anxious. I want a hug and to be held but I can't have that. I want to be able to be in the same bed and sit on the sofa together. I miss her. I know she has the same feelings. This morning I told her that I didn't know if I could do it. We agreed that if it is too hard we will just be together and both isolate. That makes it easier because I know I can say, 'This is too much for me'. I couldn't do that as a child.

With adoptees there is a feeling of homecoming. It feels safe.

The effect of trauma at birth or just after cannot be expressed with words because the feelings and experiences are pre-verbal. When I realised that it was a revelation. But pre-verbal doesn't mean we don't feel, it just means we have to find a way to use language to express the almost inexpressible. It matters how we use words to tell our stories. In recent years more and more adoptees are coming out of the woodwork and telling their stories. The common threads are there but each story is unique. We are learning that the way through is to start to share our experiences. Trauma is healed by connection, by talking, by re-experiencing in our bodies and letting the pain out. Trauma is always characterised by an experience of helplessness and powerlessness, a situation where we have no control over the awful thing that happens to us. To heal we need to discover a sense of safety and establishing a felling and place of safety is essential for us to be able to do the work needed to recover. When something traumatic happens to us our bodies and brains change in a primal way. Stress elicits responses in the body that are from our response to danger. Fight, flight or if all else fails, freeze. As babies we are completely powerless when we are taken from our mothers. It doesn't matter what the reasons are, the experience is a shock. Shock is stressful. A baby can't fight or run away so we freeze. The feelings of trauma become encoded in our brains and bodies and they stay there. Unfortunately our bodies can't tell the difference between a physical threat, the lion is going to eat me, or an emotional one, my mother is not here and I am not safe. So our physical bodies store trauma in what we call implicit memories. Implicit memory is what we feel, our emotional response to situations. The hard part of that for an adoptee is that growing up our bodies and emotional responses tell us that we are in danger. We are triggered because our nervous system responds to the threat of abandonment with all its stored up fear, rage and grief. But we have no idea what is happening to us or why and neither do the people who love us most, our parents and family. We have learned to survive by adapting to our environments, sometimes to multiple different environments and to do that we have to push those feelings down and fit in. So healing from trauma is complex fro an adoptee. The feelings that come from birth separation and trauma are deeply rooted, maybe the most deeply rooted. To access them we have to feel safe. For me that safety has come in relationships with the people I can lean on and into. Breathing is fundamental. Slow and steady, long breaths in and longer breaths out. Yogic breathing. Stillness. Silence and lying down. A weighted blanket has helped because it works by calming the parasympathetic nervous system. I bought a weighted blanket for my wife when she had been having trouble sleeping when work was extra stressful. She started sleeping. One weekend she went away and didn't take the blanket so I slept under it. Usually when she is away I struggle to sleep. I find it hard to relax and settle. That first night I slept 'like a baby'. I think I slept better than the baby I was. My anxiety went away. The feeling of the blanket wrapping me with its gentle steady weight soothed me in a way I hadn't imagined. Now I don't want to sleep without it. Talking and therapy helps but it has to be with the right person. Therapists who don't understand adoption trauma need to stop practicing on adoptees. We deserve better.

This is what I want to say :
I won't abandon myself any more when shit happens
I have a right to my life. I have a right to be OK.
Be Kind
Tell the truth even when it hurts
Connect, LOVE, hold on, let go

The other day I found a page from a journal that I wrote in 2002. It said 'In my next life, I would:
Travel more
Learn more languages
Live abroad
Become a writer
Be more spiritual
Be more confident
Laugh and love more
Not to be held back by fear
Follow my intuition
Not keep making nests and tying myself down only to have to cut free

Rely less on 'should' and 'ought to'.

Now I see this is a list for how to live THIS life. And I am living it, now.

Mum and Dad, Margaret and Stephen 1954

Birth parents Mary and David c. 1957.

Search for the Hero

Sometimes the river flows but nothing breathes.
A train arrives but never leaves.
It's a shame.
Oh life — like love that walks out of the door,
Of being rich or being poor.
Such a shame.
But it's then, then that faith arrives
To make you feel at least alive.
And that's why you should keep on aiming high,
Just seek yourself and you will shine.
You've got to search for the hero inside yourself,
Search for the secrets you hide.
Search for the hero inside yourself
Until you find the key to your life.
In this life, long and hard though it may seem,
Live it as you'd live a dream.
Aim so high.
Just keep the flame of truth burning bright.
The missing treasure you must find
because you and only you alone
can build a bridge across the stream.
Weave your spell in life's rich tapestry -
Your passport to a feeling supreme.
You've got to search for the hero inside yourself,
Search for the secrets you hide.
Search for the hero inside yourself
Until you find the key to your life.
Search inside yourself. (You've got to search)
Search inside yourself. (You've got to search)
Search inside yourself. (You've got to search)
You've got to search for the hero inside yourself,

Search for the secrets you hide.
Search for the hero inside yourself
Until you find the key to your life.
You've got to search for the hero inside yourself,
Search for the secrets you hide.
Search for the hero inside yourself
Until you find the key to your life.
You've got to.
(Search inside yourself)
You've got to.
(Search inside yourself)
You've got to.
(Search inside yourself)
Search.

— M People Track 2 on Bizarre Fruit (Pickering and Heard)

Resources that I have found helpful or interesting

Author's Note: This is by no means an exclusive list. This is a selection of resources I have found interesting, moving or useful. There are lots more. An internet search on 'adoption' will bring up a lot of stuff that you may find distasteful — I do. Some resources are heavily biased to one side of the 'adoption triangle' ie: adoptee, birth mothers or fathers and adoptive parents. In my opinion, many films should have a Health Warning for adult adoptees as they promote an evangelical saviour complex of rescuing orphans and 'neglected' children. This is usually a very one-sided picture. This can be particularly discriminatory and offensive in relation to the children of black mothers and transracial adoption. My experience of adoption is centred on the closed adoption system of Britain in the 1950's. I was a white baby raised by white middle class parents.

Generally useful

Brené Brown *Braving The Wilderness* 2017, *Rising Strong, Daring Greatly, The Gifts of Imperfection, I Thought It Was Just Me*

Gabor Mate *Scattered Minds: The Origins and Healing Of Attention Deficit Disorder* Penguin 1999, *In The Realm Of Hungry Ghosts:* Close *Encounters With Addiction; When The Body Says No: The Cost of Hidden Stress*

Byron Katie *Loving What Is* Rider 2002

Eckhart Tolle *The Power of Now* 20th Anniversary Ed. 2020   Yellow Kite

Glennon Doyle *Untamed* Vermilion 2020

Julia Cameron *The Artist's Way* Pan 1995 UK

Anne Lamott: *Some Instructions on Writing and Life*. (I love everything Anne has ever written) Canongate GB 20Bird by Bird20

Pema Chodron *Start Where You Are* Shambhala 1994

Jean Shinoda Bolen *MD Crones Don't Whine: Concentrated Wisdom For Juicy Women Conari Press 2003*

James Clear Atomic Habits- An Easy and Proven Way to Build Good Habits and Break Bad Ones Random House 2018

Dana Morningstar *Out of the Fog : Moving from Confusion to Clarity after Narcissistic Abuse* Morningstar Media 2017

HH Dalai Lama & Howard C. Cutler *The Art of Happiness: A handbook for Living* Coronet 1998

Anna Black *Living in The Moment* Cico Book 2012

Lindsay C. Gibson *Adult Children of Emotionally Immature Parents: How to Heal from Distant, Rejecting or Self-Involved Parents* New Harbinger 2015

Addiction and Recovery

Organisations - Food, Alcohol or drugs (substance misuse)

12 Step Programmes including; Overeaters Anonymous,(OA); Food Addicts Anonymous, (FAA); OA HOW, Food Addicts in Recovery Anonymous (FAR), Eating Disorders Anonymous (EDA) Anorexics and Bulimics Anonymous (ABA), Compulsive Eaters Anonymous HOW (CEA-HOW) - all usually have face to face meetings, online and phone meetings. The recovery programmes are international and free.

Alcoholics Anonymous (AA)

Narcotics Anonymous (NA)

Co-dependents Anonymous (CODA)

Books

Alcoholics Anonymous

Susan Pierce Thompson Ph.D Bright Line Eating ; The Science of Living Happy, Thin and Free Hay House 2017

brightlineeating.com (This is the programme that I follow and that has given me food freedom)

Kathleen DesMaisons Ph.D *Potatoes Not Prozac: A Natural Seven-Step Dietary Plan to Stabilize the Level of Sugar in Your Blood, Control Your Cravings and Lose Weight;* 1998 Simon & Schuster; *The Sugar Addict's Total Recovery Programme* 2000 Simon & Schuster

Kay Sheppard MA *From the First Bite; A Complete Guide to Recovery from Food Addiction* 2000; *Food Addiction: The Body Knows* 1989

Joel Furhman *MD Eat to Live*

Susie Orbach *Fat is a Feminist Issue* Arrow 2016

Toko-pa Turner *Belonging 2017*

Adoption

Betty Jean Lifton *Lost and Found: The Adoption Experience 1979; Twice Born: Memoirs of an Adopted Daughter 1975; Journey of the Adopted Self: A Quest for Wholeness 1994*

Nancy Newton Verrier *The Primal Wound* 1993 Gateway; *Coming Home To Self* Coram BAAF 2003

Coram BAAF 2003

Gabrielle Glaser *American Baby* Viking 2021

Jane Rowe *Yours By choice* Routledge 195

Websites

PAC-UK *for Adopted Adult support, counselling, searching help*

adoptees.on.com- *a brilliant website of podcasts with adult adoptees and a huge collection of resources by Hayley Radke*

Anne Heffron http://www.anneheffron.com *blog posts on adoption by Anne and many guests*

Amanda Woolston http://www.declassifiedadoptee.com

https://howtobeadopted.com London UK

http://www.thelostdaughters.com

http://kevingladish.blogspot.com late discovery adoptee

The GSA forum (Genetic Sexual Attraction) https://thegsaforum.com

https://dearadoption.com

Adoption
Kamila Zahno *Chasing Ghosts: not just an Adoption Memoir* Rahila

Gupta 201

Susan Devan Harness *Bitterroot: A Salish Memoir of Transracial Adoption (American Indian Lives)* Univ. Nebraska 2018

Anne Heffron *You Don't Look Adopted* 2016 3rd Ed. Amazon

Lauren J. Sharkey *Inconvenient Daughter;A Novel* A Kaylie Jones Book 2020

Zara H. Phillips *Somebody's Daughter* John Blake 2018 *Mother Me* BAAF 2008

Sue Elliot *Love Child* Vermillion 2005

Patricia Moffat *She Turned Her Head Away* Crowsnest 2020

James Mulholland *Special & Odd* BAAF 2017

Pam Cordano MFT *10 Foundations For A Meaningful Life (No Matter What's Happened)* Balboa Press 2020

Jeanette Winterson *Why Be Happy When You Could Be Normal?* Jonathan Cape 2011

Jacqueline Wilson *Tracy Beaker books and Children's TV series, Dustbin Baby* BBC.co.uk

Michelle Bell *Elfa and The Box of Memories* BAAF 2008

Lisa Wingate *Before We Were Yours* Quercus 2018*; Before and After* 2019

Nicole Chung *All You Can Ever Know* One 2020

Catherine Taylor *IlligitimatelyYours, Michael and Me: A Memoir of Secrets, Adoption and DNA* Amazon 2019

Briggita Baker and Jo Willis *Awoken: Surviving and Thriving Through the Adoption Journey* Amazon 2021

Poetry
Veronica Aaronson *Emily's Mothers* Dempsey and Windle 2020
Jackie Kay *The Adoption Papers* Bloodaxe Books 1991

Films and TV
Philomena
Secrets and Lies
Closure - documentary (Amazon prime)

The Queen's Gambit (Netflix)
Lion
Anne of Green Gables
Black, White and Us Amazon Prime
Children of Shame (About Tuam) Amazon Prime
Sisters Amazon Prime
The Magdalene Sisters
British TV
Long Lost Family ITV
Kiri Channel 4
DNA BBC I-Player 2021

Paul Sutherland 'Adoption and Addiction' full lecture on Youtube
Adoptees On Healing 'Is Adoption Trauma' with Lesli A Johnson MFT
The Adopted Life podcasts from Angela Tuckere to support transracial adoptees
April Dinwoodie 'Born in June, Raised in April' aprildinwoodie.com
Dr Gabor Mate Keynote speech ACEs to Assets 2019 Glasgow YouTube Trauma as Disconnection from Self
Gabor Mate 'How Childhood Trauma Leads to Addiction' illustrated video on YouTube
BBC Radio 4 *Tracing Your Roots.* https://www.bbc.co.uk/programmes/b00mw15r
BBC Radio 4 *The Untold* https://www.bbc.co.uk/programmes/m0001xpj
BBC Radio 4 *The Other Side of Adoption* https://www.bbc.co.uk/programmes/b0650jwh
WLM We Love Memoirs Groups on Facebook 'the friendliest group on Facebook' https://www.facebook.com/groups/welovememoirs

More from Julia
being60timetolive.wordpress.com Life In-Between Adopted. Recovered.

Connected

Facebook Page Julia Richardson Life In Between https://www.facebook.com/Juliafiona.richardson

Instagram @juliaf_richardson Life In Between

ABOUT THE AUTHOR

Julia is a writer and an artist. She is a dreamer. She is a woman, wife, mother, friend, daughter, sister, adoptee, adventurer, truth seeker, colour-loving, nature-worshipping, sun-loving English person who is genetically and spiritually connected to islands and mystery and sea and sky.

Julia lives with her wife, Teresa in Staffordshire, UK. She is a retired social worker, university lecturer and therapist who now loves to make friends with dogs, knit socks and travel anywhere with their caravan.

Mum and Dad, Margaret and Stephen with
Julia as a 'new to them' baby 1958

.Dear You
All is well. I see you.
You are loved
Follow your curiosity and trust yourself
I love you.
Me xxxx

Printed in Great Britain
by Amazon